'Once again, Harrington centers the student voice with extraordinary care. This wonderful book pushes us to learn directly from our students' experiences about which instructional strategies foster engagement (and why they do) in online teaching and learning environments. Educators across the disciplines, in diverse institution types, and with varied levels of online teaching experience will likely find encouragement to continue to refine their winning strategies and to implement some new approaches, too.'

**Jonathan Iuzzini**, *Associate Vice President of Faculty Development & Learning Innovation, Howard Community College, USA*

'*Keeping Us Engaged Online* offers a powerful exploration of online learning through the most critical lens possible—the students themselves. This book is a roadmap that transforms how we understand engagement, connection, and meaningful learning in the digital classroom. Prepare to be challenged, inspired, and completely reimagine what's possible in online education through the most powerful lens of all: the student voice.'

**Linda L. García**, *Executive Director, CCCSE, USA*

'Dr. Harrington's pairing of evidence-based teaching strategies with authentic stories from students is something you will not find anywhere else. This book not only brings forth the student voice but provides practical takeaways that can be used in any course. I will be sure to return to this text for ideas and insights again and again!'

**Bridget Arend**, *Associate Director of Teaching and Learning, Metropolitan State University of Denver, USA*

'Online education is a viable and flexible option for diverse college students to achieve their dreams. This text offers strategies to guide faculty in prioritizing pedagogical approaches that cultivate connection, promote reflection, and empower students in online learning experiences.'

**James K. Winfield**, *Associate Dean for FYE, General Education & Retention Strategies, Southern New Hampshire University, USA*

'In *Keeping Us Engaged Online*, Harrington and her 50+ student co-authors have done a magnificent job of sharing engagement strategies specific to online learners. With important topics such as mental health and relationship rich education, it is a must read for faculty who want to create a much more enriching educational environment for all students.'

**Chris Hakala**, *Director, Center for Excellence in Teaching, Learning, and Scholarship and Professor of Psychology, Springfield College, USA*

'Harrington has collected dozens of compelling, in-depth student reflections that reveal the significant, and often life-changing, role that instructors played in their success, serving to affirm the lasting impact of instructional choices, a compassionate mindset, and meaningful relationships.'

**Patty Payette**, *Executive Director, Quality Enhancement Plan, University of Louisville, USA*

'Through authentic student narratives, Keeping Us Engaged Online provides actionable insights into building connection, motivation, and meaningful interaction in digital classrooms.'

**Carlos Morales**, *Founding President of TCC Connect Campus, USA*

# Keeping Us Engaged Online

Building from the success of *Keeping Us Engaged* and dedicated fully to online teaching, this book centers student perspectives on instructional strategies to maximize engagement and increase virtual learning.

By pairing stories from 50+ students with the most up-to-date research on online instruction, readers will discover easy-to-implement strategies to help online students develop a sense of belonging, inclusion, and academic confidence. Ranging from topics such as welcome messages and assignment feedback to synchronous and asynchronous discussions, these firsthand student narratives validate and inform faculty practices while inspiring readers to adapt individual techniques to their own online realities. Each chapter is accompanied by insightful reflection prompts ideal for individual use or as discussion points for faculty book groups and professional development workshops.

Masterfully founded in student-centered active learning principles and endorsed by the learners themselves, this book is a springboard for all faculty looking to engage students online.

**Christine Harrington** is a professor in the Department of Advanced Studies, Leadership, and Policy at Morgan State University, USA, and a part-time lecturer at master's level in the Department of Learning and Teaching at Rutgers University, USA. As an expert in teaching, learning, and student success, she has authored numerous acclaimed books and is frequently invited to present at colleges and universities.

# Keeping Us Engaged Online

Student Perspectives (and Research-Based Strategies) on What Works and Why

## Christine Harrington

*with Over 50 College Students*

Routledge
Taylor & Francis Group
NEW YORK AND LONDON

Designed cover image: Getty Images

First published 2025
by Routledge
605 Third Avenue, New York, NY 10158

and by Routledge
4 Park Square, Milton Park, Abingdon, Oxon, OX14 4RN

*Routledge is an imprint of the Taylor & Francis Group, an informa business*

© 2025 Christine Harrington

The right of Christine Harrington to be identified as author of this work has been asserted in accordance with sections 77 and 78 of the Copyright, Designs and Patents Act 1988.

All rights reserved. No part of this book may be reprinted or reproduced or utilized in any form or by any electronic, mechanical, or other means, now known or hereafter invented, including photocopying and recording, or in any information storage or retrieval system, without permission in writing from the publishers.

*Trademark notice*: Product or corporate names may be trademarks or registered trademarks, and are used only for identification and explanation without intent to infringe.

ISBN: 978-1-032-78964-4 (hbk)
ISBN: 978-1-032-78936-1 (pbk)
ISBN: 978-1-003-49001-2 (ebk)

DOI: 10.4324/9781003490012

Typeset in Optima
by SPi Technologies India Pvt Ltd (Straive)

# Contents

FOREWORD — xiii
*Flower Darby*

ACKNOWLEDGMENTS — xvi
*Thank You to the Student Contributors*

INTRODUCTION — 1
   Defining Online Learners — 1
   A Brief Historical Overview of Online Learning — 2
   Online Learning Federal Regulations — 3
   Effectiveness of Online Learning — 4
   Why an Online Version of the Book? — 5
   Why Does Student Engagement Matter? — 6
   A Framework for Online Student Engagement — 6
   Focus on Student Voice — 8
   Suggested Approach to Using this Book — 8
   Overview of this Book — 9

1  EARLY ACTIONS — 14
   Helping Students Get to Know You — 15
      *Sharing Personal and Professional Information and Establishing a Respectful Learning Environment* — 15
         RJ Portella
      *Sharing an Inspiring Journey* — 17
         Marie Zephier

  Getting to Know Your Students    19
   *A Getting-to-Know-You Activity*    20
    Sean Connelly
   *Don't Forget the Quiet Ones: Get to Know Us*    21
    Madyson Poole
   *Accessible from Day One*    23
    Hunter Ramos
  Sharing Expectations, Resources, and Tips for Success    25
   *The Syllabus as a Roadmap to Success*    26
    Masoud Juya
   *Setting Expectations During the First Class*    29
    Raymond Matson Jr.
   *Sharing Helpful Resources*    30
    Adeoluwa O. Folami
   *Introductory Email and Flexible Due Dates*    32
    Abaynesh Berecha
  Sending Encouraging First-Day-of-Class Messages    34
   *Teaching us the Three P's: Patience, Practice, and Perseverance*    35
    Haruka Whitcroft
   *Easing My Fear*    36
    Devin Browne
   *Guided Meditation on Day One*    37
    Leah Josefowitz
  Faculty Reflection Questions    38

**2 RELATIONSHIPS**    43
  Being Accessible Outside of Class    44
   *A Quick Email Response and Emphasizing Growth over Perfection*    45
    Gabrielle Land
   *Clarifying Concepts During Office Hours*    46
    Jaymala Chavan
   *Learning Chemistry in an Asynchronous Course with a Supportive Professor*    47
    Monica Davish
   *Encouraging Words and Suggested Actions*    49
    Karen Mae Ebel
   *Making Time for an In-Person Meeting and Tour*    50
    Jennifer Malue Bartone
  Assisting Students Struggling with Personal and Financial Challenges    52

*Reaching Out and Investing in Me*    53
    Persephonie Cole
*Connecting Me to Resources*    54
    Brenda Santiago
*Putting Well-Being First*    56
    Madyson Poole
*Supporting Me in a Time of Need*    56
    Nicole Manta
*Helping Me Access a Scholarship and Plan for Success*    58
    Jeremy J. Walk
*Sharing Opportunities*    59
    Gretchen Thomas

Offering Career Mentoring and Supporting the Development of a Professional Identity    60
  *Inspiring Me to Trust My Instinct and Explore a Different Career Path*    60
    Stacey Fishler
  *Personalized Mentoring Aligned with My Career Goals*    62
    Damaris Sargent
  *An Affirming Relationship with my Professor*    63
    Keyshawn Moncrieffe
  *One-on-One Zoom Meetings*    65
    Jennifer Malue Bartone

Advising a Club    66
  *Zoom and Draw*    67
    Leah Josefowitz
  *An Unofficial Drawing Club*    68
    Nicholas Bashore

Faculty Reflection Questions    69

## 3   TEACHING STRATEGIES    73

Attending to Mental Health and Well-Being    73
  *The Mindful Minutes*    74
    Adeoluwa O. Folami
  *The 15-Minute Check-In*    75
    Adedoyin Soyele
  *Emotional Well-Being Checks*    76
    Patricia B. Ateboh-Briggs

Using Inclusive Teaching Practices    77
  *Inclusive Pedagogy with Active Cultural Humility*    77
    Daylan Moore

  *Weaving Feminist Perspectives into a Course*    79
   Annabelle Hicks
 Prioritizing Collaborative Learning Opportunities   81
  *Online Discussions*   82
   Steven Revelian
  *Yellowdig, Richard*   84
   A. Hilpert
  *Student-Directed Conversations*   88
   Madyson Poole
  *Virtual Verdicts: Mock Trial of Supreme Court Case Arguments via Zoom*   89
   Ashley Jaramillo
  *Breakout Rooms and Receiving Feedback*   91
   Lori Jean Bushey
  *Fishbowl Technique*   93
   RJ Portella
  *Peer Debriefing Groups*   94
   Krista Quinn
 Using Varied, Creative Teaching Approaches   96
  *Varied Teaching Strategies*   97
   Patricia B. Ateboh-Briggs
  *Learning about AI via Readings Discussions, and Reflective Writing Assignments*   98
   Annabelle Hicks
  *Using Technology Tools to Foster a Sense of Community*   100
   Bridgette Harris
  *Making Learning Fun through a Friendly Review Chat Competition*   101
   Victoria Bahary
  *The Power of a Picture*   103
   Katie Williver
  *A Creative Independent Study: Connecting Work with School*   105
   Chelsea Bock
 Faculty Reflection Questions   106

## 4   ASSIGNMENTS   111
 Developing Foundational Knowledge   112
  *Reading Guides and More*   113
   Casey Bond
  *Mind Maps*   115
   Mia Pepe

| | |
|---|---|
| *Building Blocks toward Mastery* | 117 |
| RJ Portella | |
| *Building Knowledge and Skills via Case Studies* | 118 |
| Karuna Taneja | |
| Fostering a Growth Mindset | 119 |
| *Learning about Growth Mindset and Course Content* | 120 |
| Megan Doyle | |
| Assigning Relevant and Meaningful Learning Tasks | 122 |
| *Emphasizing Practical Applications: Using Case Studies and Other Collaborative Learning Activities* | 123 |
| Kamel Johal | |
| *Reflective Journaling* | 125 |
| Annabelle Hicks | |
| *Meaningful Assignments* | 126 |
| Chelsea Bock | |
| Providing Opportunities for Collaboration on Projects | 128 |
| *A Collaborative Assignment: Developing a Business Plan* | 130 |
| Kamel Johal | |
| *Current Issues Group Project Assignment* | 131 |
| Bridgette Harris | |
| Giving Varied Assignments and Choice | 132 |
| *Diverse Assignments* | 133 |
| Wesley Russell | |
| *Choice, Creativity, and Challenge in Assignments* | 134 |
| Patricia B. Ateboh-Briggs | |
| Faculty Reflection Questions | 137 |

## 5  FEEDBACK — 142

| | |
|---|---|
| Motivational Feedback | 145 |
| *Feedback that Encouraged Me to Pursue My Goal* | 145 |
| Ashley McWilliams | |
| *A Little Encouragement Can Go a Long Way* | 147 |
| Tabatha Jones | |
| *Encouraging Feedback Even When I Got an 'A'* | 148 |
| Kellye Irvin | |
| Fostering a Productive Mindset about Feedback | 150 |
| *Using Analogies as a Motivational Feedback Technique* | 151 |
| Abaynesh Berecha | |
| Personalized, Specific, and Constructive Feedback | 152 |
| *Personalized, Detailed Feedback from a Trusted Professor* | 153 |
| Kamel Johal | |

| | |
|---|---|
| *Ongoing Specific Feedback with Reflection Assignments*<br>Chantel Moore | 154 |
| Fostering Critical Thinking | 156 |
| *The Power of Questioning*<br>Jennifer Scully | 157 |
| Discussion-Based Feedback | 158 |
| *Keeping Us on Track During Breakout Room Group Work*<br>Sean Connelly | 159 |
| *Feedback via Online Discussions*<br>Andy Sokolich | 161 |
| Using Video and Audio Tools | 164 |
| *Using Videos to Share Class-Level Feedback and Create a Sense of Community in an Asynchronous Class*<br>Charlenne Medina | 166 |
| *Faculty Reflection Questions* | 167 |
| **ABOUT THE AUTHOR** | 173 |
| **INDEX** | 175 |

# Foreword

Online education makes it more possible for more people to earn a college credential, degree, or an advanced degree. Each of these achievements enables people to make a better life for themselves and their families. Earning potential is increased, and multiple non-economic benefits are realized, such as increased health and longevity, more rewarding and fulfilling careers, and more time spent with family. College credentials do not simply confer a benefit on individuals and their families, however. Local communities are improved because graduates are more likely to be engaged in civic and volunteer activities. This strengthens the social fabric and improves the quality of life for everyone who lives in the area. Society, more broadly, also benefits when more people attain a post-secondary degree or credential: graduates earning higher incomes pay more taxes, meaning physical infrastructure, such as roads and social support infrastructure, such as public libraries and everything in between, are better maintained.

Most importantly, when more people attain a college degree, we are surrounded by thoughtful and engaged citizens who are more open to perspectives that differ from their own and who are better able to solve today's complex problems. In short, college provides a transformational individual experience that leads to increased well-being for all. But not everyone can attend physical classes on a physical campus. That is why it is so important to acknowledge the advantages of increased access and flexibility offered by online courses and programs. People who are constrained by work and family obligations or who do not have consistent work schedules from week to week are not held back from pursuing their goals. They, too, can make a better life when they are able to complete credentials and degrees online.

But online courses present unique challenges. Many faculty members do not feel adequately prepared to teach engaging, effective, and inclusive online classes.

Much of the existing professional development offered by colleges and universities is focused on creating well-organized courses that are intuitive to navigate and meet accessibility standards. These aims are important; after all, we do not wish to present online students with unnecessary barriers to their success. The structure of an online course is like the furnishings in a physical classroom. It is necessary, indeed important, to have functioning equipment so that students are set up to learn. But a well-designed physical or online classroom can still leave students feeling less than inspired, unmotivated—indeed, unengaged. And since we know that engagement is a necessary ingredient for learning to happen, it is critically important that we attend to this central question: what can we do to help students engage and remain engaged in our classes? Especially in online classes, which can feel lonely and isolating, engaging our students is a primary goal.

That is where this book comes in. It is one thing to analyze the empirical literature on what helps with this pursuit in online classes. It is another thing to hear from the students themselves about what their professors do that keeps them engaged. Students' authentic voices are powerful because we hear from them directly about what truly makes a difference in helping them to succeed. Author Christine Harrington admirably provides both: a comprehensive review of the teaching and learning literature related to inclusive student engagement online and the words of the students themselves: stories about dedicated instructors who empowered them to succeed despite the challenges of competing demands on their time and despite the psychological distance that can result from teaching and learning via screens. In these pages, you will find robust scholarly evidence paired with poignant accounts from students persisting despite health, work, or family challenges, gritty accounts from students who are determined to succeed, and grateful accounts from students whose lives were literally changed because of the support, availability, effective teaching, and mentoring of their online faculty.

These stories and evidence-based recommendations are organized into five chapters that reflect the main components of teaching a college course. Harrington provides practical ideas for what should happen at the very beginning of an online class, how to establish and sustain relationships online (and why it's important to do so), teaching strategies that help students learn and succeed, varied assignment options to scaffold student progress toward course learning goals, and feedback recommendations that are effective online. Every learner can benefit from a structured experience led by a caring educator who is approachable and who has provided opportunities to demonstrate new knowledge and skills, receive targeted feedback, and continue developing and refining new learning. This book provides a roadmap for how to do exactly that in virtual spaces. Whether you are new to teaching online or have years of experience under your online teaching belt, you will find affirmation of things you are already doing well, new ideas for next week or next semester, and, best of all, the voices of the students themselves.

Read the chapters in sequence or flip to a chapter or a story that provides new inspiration for an online teaching challenge you are experiencing today. However you choose to engage with this book and the student stories within it, both you and your online students will enjoy more engaging online teaching and learning experiences as a result of your time spent here.

**Flower Darby**

# Acknowledgments

It has been such an amazing process to work with over 50 student contributors on this book project. I am grateful to each of them for taking the time out of their busy lives to share their stories about how their online professors engaged them. I am confident that these stories will inspire readers to incorporate the many engagement strategies shared into their teaching practices. I am also grateful to my faculty colleagues who helped me find students willing to contribute to the book. This book would not have been possible if it were not for these educators and their students.

I am thankful to the skilled editorial team at Routledge. My editor, Alexandria Andrews, was extremely responsive and provided encouragement throughout the process, and Kyanna Nusom provided valuable support during the copyediting phase. I am grateful to have such an effective editorial team.

Most importantly, I would like to thank my family and friends for their ongoing support. I am incredibly grateful to my husband, Dan, my sons, Ryan and David, my father, my niece Ashley, her husband, Glen, and their children, Ariella and Isabella. I would also like to thank all my amazing friends and colleagues. I could not have completed this project without their encouragement and support.

## THANK YOU TO THE STUDENT CONTRIBUTORS

- Patricia B. Ateboh-Briggs, Morgan State University
- Victoria Bahary, Brookdale Community College
- Jennifer Malue Bartone, Marymount University
- Nicholas Bashore, Brookdale Community College

ACKNOWLEDGMENTS

- Abaynesh Berecha, Community College of Aurora, Colorado
- Chelsea Bock, University of Maryland, College Park
- Casey Bond, Johnson County Community College
- Devin Browne, Community College of Allegheny County
- Lori Jean Bushey, Rockhurst University
- Jaymala Chavan, University of Texas at Dallas
- Persephonie Cole, Texas Tech University
- Sean Connelly, Connecticut State Community College Norwalk
- Monica Davish, Rutgers University
- Megan Doyle, Gwynedd Mercy University
- Karen Mae Ebel, Lorain County Community College
- Stacey Fishler, Brooklyn College-CUNY
- Adeoluwa O. Folami, Morgan State University
- Bridgette Harris, Morgan State University
- Annabelle Hicks, University of Connecticut
- Richard A. Hilpert, Florida State University
- Kellye Irvin, Tarrant County College
- Ashley Jaramillo, Rutgers University
- Kamel Johal, Athabasca University
- Tabatha Jones, McLennan Community College
- Leah Josefowitz, Wesleyan University
- Masoud Juya, University of North Texas
- Gabrielle Land, Rutgers University
- Ashley McWilliams, Concordia University
- Nicole Manta, Nicolet College
- Raymond Matson Jr., Rutgers University
- Charlenne Medina, Rockhurst University
- Keyshawn Moncrieffe, Morgan State University
- Chantel Moore, University of Arkansas at Little Rock
- Daylan Moore, Regent University
- Mia Pepe, New Jersey City University
- Madyson Poole, Brescia University
- RJ Portella, Rutgers University
- Krista Quinn, Manhattanville University
- Hunter Ramos, Pensacola State College
- Steven Revelian, St. Louis University
- Wesley Russell, University of Oklahoma
- Brenda Santiago, Community College of Baltimore County
- Damaris Sargent, Morgan State University
- Jennifer Scully, Marymount University
- Andy Sokolich, Kent State University
- Adedoyin Soyele, Westfield State University

ACKNOWLEDGMENTS

- Karuna Taneja, Old Dominion University
- Gretchen Thomas, Arkansas State University-Newport
- Jeremy J. Walk, Paradise Valley Community College
- Haruka Whitcroft, Northwest Vista College, Alamo Colleges District
- Katie Wiliver, Georgian Court University
- Marie Zephier, University of North Dakota

# Introduction

Welcome to the online version of *Keeping us engaged: Student perspectives (and research-based strategies) on what works and why*. I am excited to share over 50 stories written by undergraduate and graduate students taking online courses. Student engagement can be particularly important in online courses. In the stories shared throughout this book, students describe the many ways in which their online professors have engaged them. I believe you will find the stories validating in many ways as students discuss strategies you are likely already using. In addition to being validated, I hope you will be inspired and motivated to modify, strengthen, or try new methods to engage students in online courses.

Although the student contributors for this book were enrolled in online classes, many of the stories they shared will have value for professors teaching in-person courses. In fact, the online student contributors for this book shared stories with themes similar to those submitted by students taking traditional in-person classes. As a result, this book has the same chapter headings as *Keeping Us Engaged: Student Perspectives (and research-based strategies) on What Works and Why, 2nd edition* (Harrington, 2025), which features stories about how professors engaged students enrolled in traditional, in-person courses. Additional stories from students taking online and in-person classes can be found in the first edition (Harrington, 2021).

## DEFINING ONLINE LEARNERS

For the purpose of this book, I have defined online learners as students taking a course that is taught in a synchronous, asynchronous, or hybrid format. Synchronous learning refers to online environments where students and the professor gather together in a virtual space at a specific time. In other words, the class has live sessions online instead of in a physical classroom. On the other hand, asynchronous learning refers to learning that does not require students and the professor to be together at a specified time. There is still substantial interaction in asynchronous learning environments but these interactions do not occur in real time. Hybrid learning environments combine online learning with face-to-face learning in a traditional classroom environment. Almost all the students who shared stories for this book indicated that they were writing about their experiences in courses using synchronous and asynchronous formats, and only a few indicated that the stories were based on their experience in a hybrid course.

## A BRIEF HISTORICAL OVERVIEW OF ONLINE LEARNING

There have long been alternatives to traditional in-person teaching options offered to students. Educators have used terms like online learning, distance education, and e-learning to refer to these alternative teaching and learning modalities. According to Oxford College (n.d.), distance learning began in 1728, with this term being first coined in 1892. The first online course was offered in 1984, and in 1986, the first fully online institution was established (Oxford College, n.d.).

Distance education began with correspondence learning, allowing students who did not live near in-person learning environments to benefit from education. Students learning via this correspondence approach would receive reading materials and assignments in the mail. Then, they would mail their completed assignments back to their professors and await feedback and grades (Kovanović et al., 2015). Despite the benefit of bringing access to education, many noted that this type of learning was not as productive because it did not allow students to interact with and learn from their peers, and the time delay caused by having to mail materials back and forth slowed learning progress (Kovanović et al., 2015).

With technological advances such as audio and video conferencing tools that have emerged, distance education has improved. Students opting for this type of learning experience can better connect with their professors and interact with their peers in a more efficient and effective way. Access to personal computers in the 1980s and the introduction of learning management platforms that gained popularity in the 1990s provided much-needed technology tools that substantially improved opportunities for professors and students to learn together in a virtual space (Bouchrika, 2024). Online learning environments have become more engaging with synchronous tools and gamification options (Bouchrika, 2024). Every day, new technologies provide innovative options for professors teaching online to increase student engagement and learning.

Online learning became the norm during the COVID-19 pandemic when it was unsafe for students and professors to gather together physically in classrooms. Bouchrika (2024) noted that the pandemic revealed the value of online learning options. Oxford College (n.d.) indicated that 'over 180 million people around the world use online courses to learn new skills' (para 2). Carlton (2024) reported that students of color, Black, Pacific Islander, and Native American students, are more likely to study online.

Current online learning tools have become even more accessible, with mobile learning options that allow students to learn using their phones. These advances enable students to learn from anywhere. Some students prefer to take synchronous online courses because they offer opportunities to engage with their professors and peers in a live learning environment while reducing transportation and time barriers that may make it difficult to attend courses in person. Asynchronous learning courses offer even more flexibility. Students taking asynchronous courses can engage in learning activities at whatever time of the day that works best for them. The flexibility provided by asynchronous learning can be especially important for students with work schedules that change regularly and those who have multiple family and work responsibilities that can make it challenging to commit to traveling to a college or logging into a virtual class on a certain day and time.

## ONLINE LEARNING FEDERAL REGULATIONS

The U.S. Department of Education differentiated between correspondence courses and online or distance education courses, with students only being able to access financial aid funding for the latter (Online Learning Consortium, 2019). Distance education required what was called regular and substantive interaction between the students and the instructor, either synchronously or asynchronously, and the use of at least two of these five activities: the Internet, one- and two-way transmissions, audio conferencing, or video tools such as DVDs (Online Learning Consortium, 2019, p. 2).

Regular and substantive interaction was not well-defined initially, but new regulations that became effective on July 1, 2021, brought much-needed further clarity (Kerensky, 2021). Regular was defined as

> providing the opportunity for substantive interactions with the student on a predictable and scheduled basis commensurate with the length of time and the amount of content in the course or competency; and monitoring the students' academic engagement and success and ensuring that an instructor is responsible for promptly and proactively engaging in

substantive interaction with the student when needed, on the basis of such monitoring, or upon request by the student.

(Kerensky, 2021, para 10)

Substantive interaction was defined as

> engaging students in teaching, learning, and assessment, consistent with the content under discussion, and also at least two of the following:
>
> 1. Providing direct instruction;
> 2. Assessing or providing feedback on a student's coursework;
> 3. Providing information or responding to questions about the content course or competency;
> 4. Facilitating a group discussion regarding the content of a course or competency; or
> 5. Other instructional activities approved by the institution's or program's accrediting agency.
>
> (Kerensky, 2021, para 9)

Institutions must comply with these updated regulations for students to gain access to federal financial aid. Although direct instruction was not explicitly defined and may imply a synchronous learning experience, Kerensky (2021) noted that asynchronous courses could meet this requirement through two of the other activities.

## EFFECTIVENESS OF ONLINE LEARNING

Ulum (2022) conducted a meta-analysis and found that online learning had a moderate impact on student achievement. Some researchers have reported that online learning does not yield the same benefits as participation in an in-person learning environment, noting that students who struggle will struggle even more when in an online learning environment (Loeb, 2020). However, many researchers have shown that learning gains are similar for students taking courses in person and online (Nguyen, 2015; Woldeab et al., 2020), and some have even found that students learn more in online learning environments. Based on a meta-analysis, for instance, Kovanović et al. (2015) concluded that 'distance education is more effective, or at least effective as traditional classroom instruction' (p. 34).

As with traditional teaching modalities, the effectiveness of the online teaching modality can vary based on the different strategies and approaches used. For example, Martin et al. (2021) found that cognitive outcomes were higher for students taking synchronous versus asynchronous coursework, suggesting that different course modalities within online learning can lead to different results. A study by Yu et al. (2024) revealed that students in online courses that used gamification learned more, indicating that the activities within the course can also impact learning. Woldeab et al. (2020) reminded professors that the intentionality behind how courses are designed and delivered matters more than the modality of the course.

## WHY AN ONLINE VERSION OF THE BOOK?

Despite the evidence demonstrating the potential and value of online learning, professors have reported that they often struggle to engage online learners. During COVID-19 and even now after the pandemic, professors frequently find that students do not fully engage in online coursework, with many not even putting their cameras on during synchronous meetings. It is difficult for professors who are staring at black boxes on the screen to assess whether students are engaged. In a traditional classroom setting, professors benefit from seeing nonverbal communication cues that provide valuable information about student engagement. Professors can and do use this nonverbal feedback to adjust their teaching strategies and approach when needed. Not surprisingly, professors teaching in-person or virtual classes with students who are present, visible, and participating can be motivated by these student actions and, as a result, be more engaged themselves.

On the other hand, professors may find themselves less engaged in online classes, especially if students are not turning their cameras on or there are no opportunities to connect in real time. Professors often share that it is most challenging to engage students in asynchronous learning environments. Because there is no designated day and time to connect, and there is typically a delay in communication, there is no visible surge of energy or excitement that often emerges through live discussions online and in person.

Although many effective teaching practices are relevant in traditional in-person and online learning environments, professors desire engagement suggestions specifically for online classrooms. Participants at keynote addresses I have given at conferences, universities, and colleges on this topic frequently ask for engagement strategies that can be used in online synchronous and asynchronous courses. Based on these frequent inquiries, I decided that in addition to an updated second edition of the original book, *Keeping us engaged: Student perspectives (and research-based strategies) evidence on what works and why* (Harrington, 2021), an online version would also be of value to faculty. I therefore sought out stories from online students.

This book highlights stories about how professors engaged students taking online courses. Stories about how professors engaged students taking traditional in-person classes can be found in *Keeping us engaged: Student stories (and research-based strategies) on what works and why, 2nd edition* (2025). You will see that stories in both versions of the books come from a diverse set of students. I hope you find value in hearing about what engaged students in online courses that took place during and after the pandemic.

## WHY DOES STUDENT ENGAGEMENT MATTER?

Students are more likely to be successful when they are engaged through positive relationships with their professors and meaningful learning experiences (Bowden et al., 2021; Delfino, 2019; Kuh et al., 2007; Li and Xue, 2023; Xu et al., 2023). Students who reported positive relationships with their professors and believed their professors cared about them were more likely to be engaged, contributing to their success (Loots et al., 2023; Owusu-Agyeman & Moroeroe, 2023). Owusu-Agyeman and Moroeroe (2023) found that engagement was highest when professors used interactive teaching approaches. Researchers have found positive correlations between student learning and academic achievement, as well as their behavioral, emotional, and cognitive engagement (Lei et al., 2018).

Researchers have specifically explored the role of student engagement in the success of online students. For example, Doo and Kim (2024) conducted a meta-analysis evaluating data from 34 studies focused on student engagement in online courses. The studies in this analysis were published between 2010 and 2022. These researchers found a positive relationship between student engagement and learning in online classes, with the largest effect size found for graduate students (Doo & Kim, 2024). Martin et al. (2021) also conducted a systematic literature review on online teaching and learning. They found that student engagement was one of the most studied variables, with numerous studies showing connections between engagement and student success outcomes (Martin et al., 2021).

## A FRAMEWORK FOR ONLINE STUDENT ENGAGEMENT

Garrison et al.'s (2000) community of inquiry framework is one of the most widely used for understanding and promoting student engagement in online learning environments, especially asynchronous ones that are text-based in nature. According to the community of inquiry framework, students will be most engaged when they experience cognitive, teaching, and social presence in the online environment, and this engagement will lead to learning and academic achievement. A description of each of the three elements of the framework follows.

*Cognitive Presence.* In courses with a high level of cognitive presence, students can construct meaning through communication with their professors and peers. Garrison et al. (2000) shared that cognitive presence is needed for cognitively complex skills such as critical thinking. They noted that the social-emotional nature of the learning environment can support or hinder the development of critical thinking skills.

Garrison et al. (2000) explained that a triggering event or some type of communication is first needed for critical inquiry. Next, students need to engage in exploration, finding information that can help them understand the initial event or topic. The third step is for students to summarize what they have learned, integrating key concepts learned. Finally, students need to come to a resolution, which is typically their thoughts or ideas on the subject.

*Social Presence.* Students who share their perspectives and personalities in a learning community comprised of their professors and peers will experience high levels of social presence. This part of the framework emphasizes the social nature of learning and the importance of feeling a sense of belonging and connection to others in the learning community. Garrison et al. (2000) noted that a high degree of social presence can contribute to higher degrees of cognitive presence because when students are in an environment where they trust and collaborate with others, they are more likely to take intellectual risks and push themselves beyond their comfort zone.

Garrison et al. (2000) described three aspects of social presence. The first was expressing emotions. Higher social presence will be experienced when students have ample opportunities to express their feelings and learn how others feel. These opportunities help develop social connections in an environment where there is no or limited access to nonverbal communication. Open communication is also critical. Online courses that invite students to share thoughts and feelings in a respectful way promote connections between the members of the learning community. Garrison et al. (2000) noted that online learners may need more explicit recognition and validation because nonverbal indicators such as smiles and head nods are not available in text-based learning environments. Finally, group cohesion is important. For students to experience social presence, they will need to feel like they are a part of a group, having a sense of belonging and shared purpose.

*Teaching Presence.* Garrison et al. (2000) shared that the role of the educator is critically important in all learning environments but is particularly essential in an online learning environment. Professors demonstrate teaching presence through the design and delivery of the course. Students will experience higher levels of teaching presence when they see and understand the connection between the course goals, activities, and assessments. When professors are actively engaged in discussions and other learning activities, this too contributes to students' experiencing a high teaching presence in an online course. Teaching presence can be more challenging to establish in asynchronous learning environments. When students see their professors providing input and guidance during discussion forums and when they receive detailed and helpful feedback, this can contribute to their perception of teaching presence.

Garrison et al. (2000) explained how instructional management, building understanding, and direct instruction all contributed to teaching presence. Instructional management refers to intentional course design that conveys to students clear expectations about the learning experience and helps them see the connections between the different learning tasks. To build understanding, professors will need to reinforce on-target contributions, intervene when incorrect information is being shared, and ensure that all students are engaged and achieving the identified goals. Finally, direct instruction refers to the teaching strategies professors use in an online learning environment. Some examples of how professors can instruct in an online setting include facilitating and summarizing discussions, giving explanations, and providing feedback.

## FOCUS ON STUDENT VOICE

Like the original version and second edition of *Keeping us engaged: Student perspectives (and research-based strategies) evidence on what works and why* (Harrington, 2021; Harrington, 2025), I wanted student voice to be the central focus of this book. However, I also wanted to share theory and research related to the engagement strategies the students discussed. In the stories, students share specific actions their professors took to engage them in their online courses, both synchronous and asynchronous, and explain why these actions were so engaging. Students also give advice to professors who may want to use the described strategy with their students in their online courses.

## SUGGESTED APPROACH TO USING THIS BOOK

Before the semester, professors can read the stories and identify actions they can take to increase student engagement. Using the end of the chapter reflection questions, professors can reflect on their practices, consider how well they use the strategies, and determine if modifications to incorporating them into practice are needed. Professors can discuss the identified strategies and how they plan to incorporate them into current teaching practices with colleagues. During the semester, professors are encouraged to celebrate when student engagement and learning improve and problem-solve when challenges occur.

As a result of reading this book, I hope professors will:

- *Find validation in their current actions.* Stories in this book can remind professors of the importance of their actions and provide an inspirational boost. These stories offer a great reminder that the work professors do every day really does matter and can have a long-lasting impact on their students. Professors who see themselves in these stories will find validation for their teaching actions.
- *Revisit strategies used previously.* Professors sometimes let go of strategies they once used. Reading the stories and related research can remind professors of the value of these strategies and prompt them to revisit strategies they may have used previously but are not currently using.
- *Incorporate new strategies into current teaching practices.* Professors can be inspired by how their colleagues have engaged students and aim to modify their current teaching approaches. Incorporating new teaching methods into their current practices can improve student engagement (Harrington, 2025, p. 4).

## OVERVIEW OF THIS BOOK

This book features almost 70 stories shared by over 50 students from diverse backgrounds. Stories come from students attending 43 different institutions in 19 states and Canada, including 12 community colleges, 22 public universities, and nine private universities. The stories come from undergraduate and graduate students representing a variety of disciplines and lived experiences. Many of the students who shared stories, for example, are adult learners juggling many roles.

Similar to the first and second editions of *Keeping us engaged: Student perspectives (and research-based strategies) evidence on what works and why* (Harrington, 2021, 2025), there are five chapters: early actions, the power of relationships, teaching strategies, assignments, and feedback. In each chapter, students share stories that highlight the various ways that online professors have engaged them and provide recommendations to professors who want to find ways to use the strategies shared. I also review the theoretical and research support for the engagement strategies shared by students in each chapter.

At the end of each chapter, readers will find faculty reflection questions that can help them think through ways to apply what was learned to their classrooms. Although professors can use these questions for independent reflection, they are encouraged to connect with other professors and discuss them. A great way to do this is through a campus-wide book group, where professors from different disciplines come together to discuss student engagement strategies. Reflecting with colleagues will likely lead to creative and innovative applications of the student engagement strategies shared by students.

Chapter 1 focuses on the early actions that professors can take to engage students. Students share why it is so important for them to get to know their online professors and for their professors to get to know them. Student stories also emphasize how students are more engaged when their professors share their expectations, resources for success, and encouraging first-day-of-class messages. Several students shared that they were new to online learning and that these early actions alleviated their anxiety and helped them feel connected to and supported by their professors. Readers will learn how seemingly simple, early actions such as sending an introductory email, sharing their professional journey, and communicating expectations clearly via the syllabus can engage students at the start of the semester.

Chapter 2 highlights the role of relationships in student engagement. Student stories illuminate the power of relationships in engagement and learning. Student contributors share how important professor accessibility outside of class is to them as online learners and provide examples of how their professors made themselves available to them. Several of the students who shared stories discussed encountering financial and personal stressors that made it difficult for them to focus on and prioritize school and how their professors helped connect them to much-needed resources. They shared that they often did not know about the resources and that when their professors shared information about these resources, this enabled them to persist in school and continue to pursue their educational goals. Online students also appreciated it when their professors took on the role of mentor. For example, students shared that being able to talk with professors about career issues engaged them. Students also valued opportunities to work with professors outside of class. Some examples of how students engaged with professors outside of class included research projects and clubs or organization meetings.

Chapter 3 focuses on various teaching strategies and approaches. For starters, students appreciated it when their online professors showed they cared about their well-being. Several stories illustrated how professors dedicated a few minutes of synchronous class time for check-ins or to encourage students to practice self-care. Students also provide examples of how professors used inclusive teaching practices to help them feel a sense of belonging in the virtual classroom. Student stories also highlight the importance of collaborative teaching approaches, enabling them to learn from and connect with their peers in the online learning environment. Finally, students share how varied teaching approaches and the use of technology keep them engaged, emphasizing how much they appreciate being able to engage in different or new tasks.

Chapter 4 focuses on how professors can use assignments to engage online students. Students explain they find assignments that help them develop foundational knowledge and skills engaging because these tasks help them build confidence in their ability to complete academic tasks. Readers will find stories that illustrate examples of how professors have helped students develop a growth mindset and how relevant assignments were used to engage students. Online students also share how working with peers on collaborative assignments engaged them. Student contributors also emphasized the importance of having choices related to assignments.

Chapter 5 emphasizes the important role of feedback in student engagement and how professors have provided personalized and meaningful feedback in the online learning environment. In this chapter, students share examples of how their professors helped them develop a positive mindset about feedback so they could see feedback as a way to help them grow and develop their skills. Student contributors share that feedback that is personalized, specific, and constructive is most engaging, and they give examples of how their professors provided this type of feedback. Stories also highlight how online professors have provided meaningful feedback in synchronous and asynchronous discussions. Finally, students have shared how they were engaged when their online professors used video and audio tools when giving feedback. They shared that the use of video and audio tools humanized the feedback process and that their professors often provided more substantial and helpful feedback when they used these tools.

## REFERENCES

Bouchrika, I. (2024, June 11). *History of eLearning: Evolution from stenography to modern 2024 LMS platforms.* Research.com. https://research.com/education/history-of-elearning

Bowden, J. L.-H., Tickle, L., & Naumann, K. (2021). The four pillars of tertiary student engagement and success: A holistic measurement approach. *Studies in Higher Education, 46*(6),1207–1224. https://doi.org/10.1080/03075079.2019.1672647

Carlton, G. (2024). 2024 online learning statistics. *Forbes advisor.* https://www.forbes.com/advisor/education/online-colleges/online-learning-stats/

Delfino, A. P. (2019). Student engagement and academic performance of students of Partido State University. *Asian Journal of University Education, 15*(1), 1–16. https://doi.org/10.24191/ajue.v15i3.05

Doo, M. Y., & Kim, J. (2024). The relationship between learning engagement and learning outcomes in online learning in higher education: A meta-analysis study. *Distance Education, 45*(1), 60–82. https://doi.org/10.1080/01587919.2024.2303484

Garrison, D. R., Anderson, T., & Archer, W. (2000). Critical inquiry in a text-based environment: Computing conferencing in higher education. *The Internet and Higher Education, 2*(2–3), 87–105. https://doi.org/10.1016/S1096-7516(00)00016-6

Harrington, C. (2021). *Keeping us engaged: Student perspectives (and research-based strategies) on what works and why*. Routledge.

Harrington, C. (2025). *Keeping us engaged: Student perspectives (and research-based strategies) on what works and why* (2nd ed.). Routledge.

Kerensky, K. (2021, August 26). *Regular and substantive interaction refresh: Reviewing and sharing our best interpretation of current guidance and requirements*. WCET. https://wcet.wiche.edu/frontiers/2021/08/26/rsi-refresh-sharing-our-best-interpretation-guidance-requirements/

Kovanović, V., Joksimović, S., Skrypnky, O., Gašević, D., Dawson, S., & Siemens, G. (2015). The history and state of distance education. In G. Siemens, D. Gaševićs, & S. Dawson (Eds.), *Preparing for the digital university: A review of the history and current state of distance, blended, and online learning* (pp. 9–54). https://research.monash.edu/files/256525723/256524746_oa.pdf

Kuh, G. D., Kinzie, J., Cruce, T., Shoup, R., & Gonyea, R. M. (2007). Connecting the dots: Multi-faceted analyses of the relationships between student engagement. Results from the NSSE, and the institutional practices and conditions that foster success. *Center for Postsecondary Research, Indiana University* Bloomington. https://scholarworks.iu.edu/iuswrrest/api/core/bitstreams/9c7b7c33-4fb5-4991-88b5-397785f93aee/content

Lei, H., Cui, Y., & Zhou, W. (2018). Relationships between student engagement and academic achievement: A meta-analysis. *Social Behavior & Personality: An International Journal, 46*(3), 517–528. https://doi.org/10.2224/sbp.7054

Li, J., & Xue, E. (2023). Dynamic interaction between student learning behaviour and learning environment: Meta-analysis of student engagement and its influencing factors. *Behavioral Sciences, 13*(1), 59. https://doi.org/10.3390/bs13010059

Loeb, S. (2020, March 20). How effective is online learning? What the research does and doesn't tell us. *Education Week*. https://www.edweek.org/technology/opinion-how-effective-is-online-learning-what-the-research-does-and-doesnt-tell-us/2020/03

Loots, S., Strydom, F., & Posthumus, H. (2023). Learning from students: Factors that support student engagement in blended learning environments within and beyond classrooms. *Journal of Student Affairs in Africa, 11*(2), 73–88. https://doi.org/10.24085/jsaa.v11i2.4897

Martin, F., Sun, T., Turk, M., & Ritzhaupt, A. D. (2021). A meta-analysis on the effects of synchronous online learning on cognitive and affective educational outcomes. *International Review of Research in Open and Distributed Learning, 22*(3), 205–242. https://doi.org/10.19173/irrodl.v22i3.5263

Online Learning Consortium, UPCEA, and WCET. (2019). *Regular and substantive interaction: Background, concerns, and guiding principles*. https://files.eric.ed.gov/fulltext/ED593878.pdf

Owusu-Agyeman, Y., & Moroeroe, E. M. (2023). Relationality and student engagement in higher education: Towards enhanced students' learning experiences. *International Journal of Emotional Education, 15*(2), 37–53. https://doi.org/10.56300/ZANL1419

Oxford College. (n.d.). The history of distance learning. https://www.oxfordcollege.ac/news/history-of-distance-learning

Ulum, H. (2022). The effects of online education on academic success: A meta-analysis study. *Education and Information Technologies, 27*(1), 429–450. https://doi.org/10.1007/s10639-021-10740-8

Woldeab, D., Yawson, R. M., & Osafo, E. (2020). A systematic meta-analytic review of thinking beyond the comparison of online versus traditional learning. *E-Journal of Business Education and Scholarship of Teaching, 14*(1), 1–24. https://papers.ssrn.com/sol3/papers.cfm?abstract_id=3642032

Xu, X., Shi, Z., Bos, N. A., & Wu, H. (2023). Student engagement and learning outcomes: An empirical study applying a four-dimensional framework. *Medical Education Online, 28*(1), 1–13. https://doi.org/10.1080/10872981.2023.2268347

Yu, Q., Yu, K., & Li, B. (2024). Can gamification enhance online learning? Evidence from a meta-analysis. *Education and Information Technologies, 29*(4), 4055–4083. https://doi.org/10.1007/s10639-023-11977-1

CHAPTER 1

# Early Actions

The early actions that professors take can make a big difference in terms of student engagement and learning. For example, students appreciate it when professors send welcoming messages before classes begin or during the first week (Strickland-Davis & McMican, 2024). Carrell and Kurlaender (2020) found that when students received welcoming emails, they viewed their professors more positively. They also found that Black and Latine first-generation college students earned higher grades in the courses where welcoming emails were sent (Carrell & Kurlaender, 2020). One likely reason that welcoming emails made such a difference is that this action conveys that the professor cares about their students, and the perception of professor care has been linked to student success (Buskirk-Cohen & Plants, 2019).

Intentional actions to create a welcoming environment can be especially important in an online classroom. Online learners sometimes feel alone and may not have a strong sense of belonging (van Heerden & Bharuthram, 2023). DiGiacomo et al. (2023) found that some online students did not feel included. Fortunately, researchers have found that professor actions can contribute to higher levels of inclusion and belonging. For instance, community college students reported increased satisfaction with online courses where their professors conveyed their enthusiasm and created learning environments where students feel comfortable asking questions (Jackson et al., 2010). Students have also shared that having opportunities to interact with their professors and classmates fosters a sense of inclusion and belonging in online courses (DiGiacomo et al., 2023; Morrison, 2021). According to Addy et al. (2023), intentional welcoming activities at the start of the semester can help students see that they are valued and belong.

## HELPING STUDENTS GET TO KNOW YOU

Early actions taken by professors, such as sharing information about themselves and encouraging students to share information about themselves, can help students develop relationships with their professors. Even sharing a photo can be helpful. Shane-Simpson et al. (2024) found that having professor photos in course materials led to students perceiving the learning environment to be inclusive. Photos can also serve to promote teaching presence (Garrison et al., 2000; Shane-Simpson et al., 2024).

Students want to get to know their professors, but this can be more difficult for them to do in online classes. In traditional in-person classes, students often learn about professors through informal conversations that take place before, during, and after class, but online students do not have these opportunities to get to know their professors. It is, therefore, important for professors to find ways for their students to get to know them. For instance, it can be very helpful for professors teaching online courses to share information about themselves in synchronous class meetings or via a video if their classes are asynchronous. Darby and Lang (2019) encouraged professors to share personal and professional information in videos to help students get to know and connect with them. In the following story, RJ shares how learning personal and professional information about his professor in an online course, along with other strategies such as clearly conveying expectations, was engaging.

ഌഌഌഝഝഝ

### Sharing Personal and Professional Information and Establishing a Respectful Learning Environment, RJ Portella, Rutgers University

At the height of the pandemic quarantine, I had an online class called Social Contexts. There were about 30 doctoral students in the class. I had the good fortune to have a professor who immediately humanized the course and issued clear expectations at every turn in our path together. My professor did so with a level of seamless dispatch that still astounds me to this day.

In the first class, she took time to introduce herself through a PowerPoint she had created, showing us personal pictures of her professional evolution, her classmates and their time studying together, and most notably, her dissertation journey. She also established professional credibility by telling us how she became a professor and how she arrived at teaching our class.

As doctoral students in our first semester, we often felt that this process of earning a degree was daunting. She took time to connect with us by sharing the fears she had at the time and how she worked through them. She then gave us space to share what we were feeling. Not only did I immediately feel trust in her, but I also felt a closer kinship with my cohort, who has become like family to me. That introductory session set a positive tone for the rest of our class; it was a wise investment of our time.

This professor also discussed trigger warnings for topics that can be sensitive and might be uncomfortable to talk about. Those issues included privilege, racial discrimination, socioeconomic class divisions, disparate student access to resources, gender inequalities in society, and various other civil rights topics with which our diverse class grappled. Conversations were consistently respectful and insightful as we learned about our shared and unique lived experiences.

Because of the trusting environment she created, my classmates and I shared brave stories of our personal and professional lives. The professor made sure to acknowledge elements of our courage and resilience while celebrating victories we achieved and talking through struggles. In addition, she made sure to connect ways that we could use our personal narratives in our classwork and later for our research studies, fostering a feeling that we were valued and seen.

For professors wondering how to set a successful tone for the class, I encourage them to share their journeys even before the first day. Syllabus language can be a powerful guiding tool. Professors can introduce themselves and establish expectations while humanizing themselves to the class. On that first day, I was fearful of how to navigate tough topics while I managed my own impostor syndrome. Intuitively feeling that I had a trusted mentor guiding me diffused stress and cleared mental space so I could succeed. Because the professor took time to share her experiences and expectations, I was relieved that I did not have to spend time trying to figure out who this professor was and what they wanted.

ಐಐಐఴఴఴ

RJ's story highlights the importance of professors sharing their journey with students. As RJ explained, hearing about a professor's struggles and fears created an environment where all members of the class were encouraged to share their feelings and experiences. When RJ and his peers shared their own struggles, experiences, and accomplishments, this helped them feel more connected to each other. In the next student story, Marie provides another example of how students are engaged when they get to hear about a professor's inspiring journey.

## Sharing an Inspiring Journey, Marie Zephier, University of North Dakota

As an Oglala Lakota woman, I found it engaging to learn about my professor's journey from humble beginnings to being a renowned physician and public health advocate. Professor Donald Warne shared his story with us at the start of the semester, and it deeply resonated with me. It ignited a sense of pride and empowerment. His remarkable achievements and unwavering dedication to Indigenous health illuminated the path forward and served as a beacon of hope for future generations. Born and raised on the Oglala Sioux Tribe reservation, Professor Warne embodies the resilience and strength of our people. He shared how he seamlessly integrated traditional Indigenous healing practices with modern medicine, addressing pressing health disparities within our communities while revitalizing ancestral healing traditions.

Professor Warne's leadership and mentorship underscore the importance of uplifting the next generation of Indigenous leaders. His willingness to share his story, knowledge, and expertise with aspiring scholars like myself embodies the spirit of reciprocity and community that defines our cultural values. As I navigate my own path in academia and public health, Professor Warne's journey serves as a guiding light, reminding me of the importance of embracing my cultural heritage and leveraging it to create positive change. His legacy inspires me to strive for greatness and honor his teachings through my own contributions to Indigenous health and well-being.

In Professor Warne, I see not only a mentor but also a role model – a living testament to the limitless potential that lies within each of us. His example reminds me that no dream is too big and no obstacle too daunting when fueled by passion, resilience, and a deep connection to one's roots. As I continue my journey, I carry Professor Warne's teachings and spirit with me, drawing strength from his example and striving to honor his legacy through my actions. In doing so, I hope to pay homage to the generations before us and pave the way for a brighter, healthier future for Indigenous peoples everywhere.

As Marie shared, professors' stories can serve as a source of inspiration. Students are more likely to connect with their professors when they know something about them and their journey. Students can find it particularly engaging to hear about how they overcame challenges. Establishing relationships with professors is important in all courses, but it is particularly important for students taking online courses because researchers have found that having positive relationships with professors predicts their success (Lammers & Gillaspy, 2013).

It can take time for professor–student relationships to develop, but early actions such as sharing personal and professional experiences with online students can help build connections at the start of the semester. Professors can help their students get to know them in an online course by creating an introductory video and providing some basic background information about themselves (Wengier, 2022). Students will be more engaged when they learn about their professors and perceive them to be warm and caring (Buskirk-Cohen & Plants, 2019; DiGiacomo et al., 2023).

Researchers have also found that when students see what they have in common with their professors, this can positively impact their academic performance (Gehlbach et al., 2016). It can, therefore, be helpful for professors to share parts of their identity, such as being a first-generation student, that their students would not know otherwise if they are comfortable doing so. In a series of research studies, Hansen-Brown et al. (2023) found that students had positive reactions, including liking their professor more and having higher levels of perceived warmth of their professor when their professor disclosed their first-generation status.

In asynchronous online courses, professors can share information about themselves through pushed-out communication, such as via an announcement message or email, or it can be housed on a page in the learning management system so students can easily refer back to it. Video introductions are ideal as they are a more personalized approach that closely resembles face-to-face conversations. Griffiths and Graham (2020) found that end-of-the-semester student evaluations were higher in all categories for an asynchronous class where recorded videos were used than in traditional in-person courses. After sending out an introductory video where the professor introduced themselves and shared course expectations, students had to create their own video, introducing themselves and responding to a question posed. The professor then recorded a personalized video for each student with encouraging words and feedback on their response to the question (Griffiths & Graham, 2020).

Students find that introductory messages their professors send help them get to know them and better understand how the online course is set up. Students have indicated a preference for introductory messages being sent via video rather than written statements (Harrington, 2024). Introductory videos do not need to be made professionally. Students appreciate authentic videos, so there is no need to record numerous times in an attempt to be perfect (Darby & Lang, 2019).

## GETTING TO KNOW YOUR STUDENTS

Professors who want to engage their online students will also want to get to know them. Spending time welcoming and getting to know students helps students know they matter, and this helps create an inclusive learning environment. Addy et al. (2023) recommended that professors use getting-to-know-you activities to learn their students' names and some important information about them. Pronouncing names correctly and using appropriate pronouns is important (Goering et al., 2022). During these getting-to-know-you activities, professors who want to help students feel like they belong can acknowledge and celebrate the varied lived experiences they bring to class (Addy et al., 2023). Professors can ask students about their interests, needs, emotions, and aspirations.

There are a variety of ways that online professors can use to get to know their students. One strategy professors can use is to survey their students. Students can be asked to answer survey questions about their experiences, goals, and interests before the semester even begins or during the first week of class (Mowreader, 2023; Strickland-Davis & McMican, 2024). Another often-used strategy is a getting-to-know-you activity. Researchers have found that icebreakers or getting-to-know-you activities have helped students become more comfortable and develop a sense of belonging (Baker, 2012; Sasan et al., 2023). Students taking online courses have indicated that introducing themselves via icebreakers is the most important way professors could engage them (Martin & Bolliger, 2018).

Professors teaching in-person classes have long recognized the value of icebreaker activities and, in many cases, have spent time on the first day of class engaging students in getting-to-know-you activities. However, it can be more challenging for online professors to identify icebreaker activities that work well online. Some professors have adapted in-person icebreaker activities to the online environment. For example, Kirby (2020) adapted a bingo card activity into one called the share-out grid. In a share-out grid, students are provided with a table or matrix containing prompts for students to type out responses to questions about themselves. These responses are visible to all students. Students can then be asked to read their peers' responses and respond with an emoji (Kirby, 2020).

Others have leveraged technology tools and created new icebreakers for online learning platforms. Sat et al. (2022), for example, shared that professors could ask students to share information about themselves, such as a favorite quote or song, on various technology platforms. They provided a list of technology tools that professors can use for getting-to-know-you activities in an online course (Sat et al., 2022). Roberto (2021) recommended recording and storing student responses so that professors can refer back to these documents throughout the semester and even later when students ask for letters of recommendation.

In the following story, Sean shares an example of a simple yet powerful getting-to-know-you activity that was used in an online course. In this example, the professor used the information learned from the getting-to-know-you activity to help students connect and personalize the learning experience throughout the semester.

ಶಿಶಿಶಿಲ್ಲೆಲ್ಲೆಲ್ಲೆ

### A Getting-to-Know-You Activity, Sean Connelly, Connecticut State Community College Norwalk

My professor employed a number of effective strategies throughout the semester to engage me and the other students. The first assignment that she tasked us with was to write a short self-introduction about ourselves. Each student was given a set of predetermined questions, such as our name, where we were from, what kind of aspects of Japanese culture we found interesting, and what our hobbies were. Once the questionnaire was completed, we were asked to send their answers virtually via email to the professor. Although we could not see the answers of our classmates, we all benefitted from this activity because my professor used this information to help us connect with each other. She invited students with shared interests to talk to one another. These conversations served as a very effective way for us to get to know one another because she told us we had something in common.

My professor also used our responses in class. She would talk about our interests throughout the semester. If we were going over a lesson that involved playing music, for example, my professor would point out which students were musicians and relate the lesson back to this interest. These personalized connections helped to keep us engaged with the course because we could easily see how the course related to activities we did in our daily lives. I found this to be extremely effective in engagement for several reasons. The task was relatively simple, yet the implication was grand in that she used the provided information to create a personal bond between herself and each student. It served as a way to make us feel more comfortable in the classroom and around the professor. I felt more comfortable in this class because the professor actually noted something about me that was indicative of my identity. It made me feel more connected, knowing that she cared enough to note some things about me that were unique to me as a student and a person. I appreciated the effort she put forth to get to know her students. It showed me that she cared.

My advice for professors who wish to engage their students more would be to employ this tactic because it makes students feel like their professor truly cares about them. Many of my peers have told me that they sometimes feel like they are just a number in the eyes of their professors and do not feel a personal connection with them. Taking action on the very first day of class can show your students that you want to get to know them, and they will appreciate this. To do this, you can ask students:

- What interests you about the course?
- Why are you taking this course?
- What kind of interests do you have outside of the course?
- Who are your favorite authors, artists, or musicians?
- What books or movies do you like?
- What are your career goals?
- What kind of help might you need with assignments?

൸൸൸ ౘౘౘ

Sean's example illustrates how simple strategies that are designed to help professors get to know them can have a big impact. Students do not need their professors to use super creative activities; it is the intent and spirit of the action that seems to matter most to students. In the example shared by Sean, one of the simplest communication tools, emails, was used. In the next student story, Madyson shares another simple getting-to-know-you activity used in an online class, emphasizing that the genuine interest in getting to know students is what matters most.

൸൸൸ ౘౘౘ

### Don't Forget the Quiet Ones: Get to Know Us, Madyson Poole, Brescia University

All my life, I have struggled with social anxiety, especially when it came to school. This anxiety is part of the reason why I opted for online classes throughout my undergraduate experience. In my college courses, I was a student in class who did not speak unless I was absolutely required to. I dreaded it. I did not know any of the people in my class, and they did not know me. My anxiousness made me believe that if I were to speak up, my peers and professors would think I was not smart enough for the class. However, I am pleased to say this is no longer the case for me. In fact, more often than not, I wonder if I am speaking up too much!

Todd Palmer was my Social Work Field Practicum professor and the director of the social work program. His dedication to providing a welcoming classroom environment, even through Zoom sessions, helped me overcome the anxiety I was so used to experiencing in school. I had him for two classes: Field Practice I and Field Practice II.

Of course, like most classes, we did the classic 'get to know you' segment at the beginning of the semester. In my experience, I felt like some professors did this as more of a formality rather than out of genuine interest for their students. Professor Palmer, though, did express interest. He did not use an extravagant icebreaker activity. He simply asked us to each share who we were, where we were from, where we were placed for the internship, and a fun fact about us.

What made this different from other icebreaker experiences I have had before was that Professor Palmer retained what we told him so he could truly get to know us. I found it impressive that he often recalled what we said about our personal lives and internships on this first day and mentioned these in future classes. These mentions throughout the semester made the activity meaningful.

Because it was an online class, we had students from many different states who were doing their internships at several different places. Professor Palmer remembered where we were all located, as well as our placements. You may be wondering why this mattered to me. For me, his efforts to retain facts about me made me feel more comfortable in each and every class. It was evident that he cared and wanted to get to know me and my classmates as people. He continued to ask us questions and remembered what we told him throughout the entire class.

I would not have shared information if not asked to do so. Through these questions that stemmed from a genuine interest in us, I became more comfortable participating in class. Professor Palmer cares about each of his students and wants us to be successful.

Professor Palmer is one of the most encouraging and relatable professors I have ever had. Because he was so passionate about seeing his students succeed, he connected with us and conveyed genuine care for our well-being. As a result, I opened up more in this class. I felt comfortable enough to participate in conversations. I no longer allowed my anxiousness to cause me to doubt my intellectual abilities. My willingness to share even transferred over to other classes!

My recommendation for professors is simple. There may be students who are very extroverted and willing to participate without force, but do not forget about the shy and quiet ones. Just because they do not say anything does not mean they do not want to. Please get to know the quiet students and make it known to them that they are in a safe space where their thoughts and ideas are welcomed. When you do your 'get to know you' activities, make a mental note or jot down some things about your students to remember. I know this may seem like a simple or obvious thing to do, but recalling what you learned about your students can go a long way, especially in a virtual class where connections are not so easily established. The effort you put into getting to know your students shows them that you do pay attention to them, even through a screen.

In addition to getting-to-know-you activities, professors can also convey their interest in and care for students by being available outside of class. Students have responded positively to invitations made by their professors to talk with them (Hansen-Brown et al., 2023). Morrison (2021) also noted that students appreciated being invited to meet and having their professors inquire about their well-being.

It can be especially important for online students to know that their professors are accessible should they have questions or need guidance because they will not be able to ask clarifying questions in the same way that students taking traditional classes in a physical classroom can. Being accessible during online office hours and encouraging students to set up appointments are great ways for professors to get to know their students and find out how they can support them. In the next student story, Hunter describes how the accessibility of a professor and being able to converse with a professor outside of class increased engagement and learning.

### Accessible from Day One, Hunter Ramos, Pensacola State College

As a high school dropout, I was not sure what to expect entering higher education. Adding to that fog, I am a first-generation student, so I could not gain insight into the college experience from my family. At least half a dozen professors at Pensacola State College have left an imprint on my journey, including the professor I will talk about in this story.

From the classroom to office hours, my professor has informed me, helped me discover myself, and prepared me for my future. On the first day, it was clear that my professor was passionate and genuinely wanted his students to understand the material. I came into his ethics class with a surface-level understanding of the material, but he made exploring ethics seem easy.

My professor was excited to have us engage with the material and invited us to visit him during office hours during the first week of class. I took him up on this offer and visited his office that first week to discuss ethics and philosophy. I continued to meet with him throughout the semester. Often, these conversations would last over an hour. My professor noticed a trend in my worldview that I did not know existed, which was the trend of existentialism. He recommended I read 'Existentialism is a Humanism' by Sartre. After many reads, it has helped me understand my perspective of the world. My professor's willingness to sacrifice his time so his students understand the subject beyond the scope of his class has been a true gift. I am beyond grateful for his time and effort.

During these meetings, my professor has gone out of his way to help me understand what the world of academia looks like after college. The differences between research institutions, liberal arts colleges, and universities were vague to me, but my professor spent quite some time helping me understand their differences, what to expect in each type of institution, and their pros and cons. With this advice in mind, I structured my transfer list.

Thanks to my professor's tutelage, I am more informed and better understand the course concepts. Because of professors like this one, college means more than a degree. These conversations have expanded my thinking. I encourage professors to make themselves available outside of class right from the start of the semester so students can use these opportunities to learn more about themselves and the class.

༄༅༄༅༄༅

Hunter's story reminds us of the importance that one-on-one conversations with students outside of class can have. Some students may be reluctant to attend office hours, though. Lowenthal et al. (2017) engaged students in an iterative design process to revise virtual office hours to make them more meaningful and engaging for students. Students were more likely to attend the revised virtual office hours, which were renamed happy hours. The researchers reported that while only 10% of their students attended office hours previously, 50% attended the revised happy hours. Students reported attending virtual office hours to get to know their professors better, understand course material and expectations better, and get their questions answered. In addition to renaming the office hours, some of the other changes included offering the hours at various dates and times indicated on the syllabus, inviting students using a calendar invite, inviting students who could not attend to ask questions in a different way, and enabling students to earn points for attending the happy hours. Attending office hours has been associated with increased engagement and linked to improved performance in the course (Lavooy & Newlin, 2008).

## SHARING EXPECTATIONS, RESOURCES, AND TIPS FOR SUCCESS

Clearly communicating expectations is important in all courses but is particularly critical in online classes. In online asynchronous courses, professors must convey expectations via written words or videos. In this course modality, students do not benefit from explanations in real time and must wait to have their questions answered. Written and video-based explanations can be challenging because professors do not have access to student nonverbal cues that indicate student understanding or confusion. When professors share expectations in a traditional class setting, they can immediately clarify when students look confused or when questions are posed. In online courses, discovering points of confusion can be more difficult and delayed. Students also do not have opportunities to gain clarity through informal in-person interactions that take place in traditional classrooms.

Although there are challenges with conveying expectations in online courses, there are also some benefits to how expectations are communicated in an online environment. First, professors are more likely to describe their expectations more explicitly in online courses. Students will appreciate not having to guess what is expected when details about expectations are shared. It can also be helpful for students to have resources they can refer back to when completing the assignment. In online courses, students can revisit the written or video-based explanations when needed. In an in-person class where assignments are shared verbally, students may not recall the specifics when it is time to complete the assignment and will not be able to listen to the initial explanation again later.

Jackson et al. (2010) found that community college students had higher satisfaction levels in online courses when their professors clearly communicated course and assignment expectations. Winkelmes (2023) developed a transparency framework for assignment expectations. Transparent assignments include the following three components:

1. Purpose. Share the why behind the assignment, articulating what knowledge and skills students will gain from the learning task and the value of this knowledge and skills.
2. Tasks. Explain the task that needs to be completed, including the steps students can take to successfully complete the assignment.
3. Criteria. Provide grading criteria so students know how their work will be assessed. Consider sharing examples of model work.

The first component, purpose, is especially important in student motivation and engagement. When students understand the why behind the learning activities and their value, they become more motivated and put forth increased effort, which can improve achievement. Roberto (2021) encouraged professors to answer the So What? question for all their actions and to share these explanations because students will be more engaged when they know why what they are learning and doing matters. What is obvious to the professor may not be obvious to the student, so it is important to convey the why behind learning activities and tasks clearly. The details about the tasks are also important because this provides a roadmap for students, helping them figure out what to do to meet the goals of the task. Finally, knowing how they will be assessed can decrease anxiety related to being evaluated.

Transparency in expectations can be particularly useful to first-generation students and students of color (Wasserman & Ayeni, 2024). However, Winkelmes (2023) cautioned professors that expectations can become overwhelming when provided in too much detail and that different students will need different levels of transparency and clarity. When too many details are provided, the student may have difficulty discerning what is most important. One potential way professors can provide varying levels of transparency is by including links in course documents to more detailed expectations. This way, students will not be overwhelmed by what is included in the main document but have access to further details via links embedded in the document. Students have reported appreciating having all course information in one document, even if it is longer, because this way, they know where to go to learn about course expectations and assignments (Harrington & Gabert-Quillen, 2015).

The syllabus is an excellent communication tool that can be used to transparently share expectations about the course and get students motivated and engaged (Harrington & Thomas, 2018). Some professors have questioned the value of a stand-alone syllabus, given that professors can convey all the information that would be contained in the syllabus in modules within a learning management system. However, research has found that both professors and students at a community college and a university preferred that the syllabus be a separate document, even if the content was also provided in a learning management system (Harrington, 2023). Interestingly, graduate students were more likely than undergraduate students to want a separate syllabus. In the following student story, Masoud, a graduate student, shares why a syllabus with clearly communicated expectations and varied learning tasks was engaging.

### The Syllabus as a Roadmap to Success, Masoud Juya, University of North Texas

In the digital corridors of online learning, I encountered a meticulously crafted syllabus that helped transform the virtual classroom into a dynamic learning environment in my graduate course. My professor believed that a well-structured syllabus served as the course's backbone, and I could not agree more. In the syllabus, he included a course outline sharing the steps we would take each week to accomplish the course goals. He clearly shared the specific objectives for each week and how the tasks and assignments were designed to meet these goals. This clarity in structure and purpose made the course exceptionally engaging. I found the goal-oriented structure to be very motivational. The syllabus was not just a document; it was a roadmap to success.

The course began with a clear set of objectives for the first week, setting a tone of precision and focus. For example, in week one, the objective was to explore the foundational principles of higher education administration, and the assignment involved analyzing contemporary administrative challenges and proposing viable solutions. This alignment ensured that every activity was purposeful and contributed to our overall understanding.

My professor's syllabus went beyond mere scheduling. It was a narrative that connected each week's objectives to a larger educational journey. The second week's objective, for instance, delved into the organizational structures of universities with assignments that had us explore different administrative models. This progressive deepening of topics, week by week, maintained a sense of continuity and progression.

The beauty of this approach lies in its interactive nature. Each assignment was crafted to not only meet the week's objective but also to encourage critical thinking and peer interaction. For example, in a module on governance in higher education, we were tasked with creating a collaborative presentation, fostering teamwork and deep analysis. The synergy between the syllabus and the assignments cultivated an active and participatory learning atmosphere.

Moreover, my professor ensured that the assignments were diverse and catered to different learning styles. Visual projects, written essays, and interactive discussions were all part of the mix, appealing to a broad range of preferences and strengths among the students. This variety kept the course fresh and engaging, encouraging consistent participation.

The course's success was also due to the transparent and frequent communication facilitated by my professor. He provided regular feedback, ensuring that we were not just completing tasks but truly understanding and engaging with the material. This feedback loop was crucial in an online setting, where the physical distance can often lead to a sense of disconnection.

This syllabus was a testament to the power of thoughtful course design. It was not just a list of topics and deadlines but a carefully plotted journey through the complexities of higher education administration. This class showed me that a well-planned syllabus could transform an online course into an immersive and intellectually stimulating experience.

For educators looking to replicate this success in their online courses, I recommend focusing on three key elements: Clear objectives for each module, assignments that directly align with these objectives, and a variety of tasks to cater to different learning styles. Additionally, maintaining active communication and providing regular feedback are essential in keeping students engaged and connected.

In conclusion, this online course was a masterclass in effective syllabus design. It showed that with the right approach, an online course could be just as engaging, if not more, than traditional classroom settings. This experience has profoundly impacted my perspective on online education, highlighting the potential for deep, meaningful learning in a virtual environment.

※※※※※※

Masoud's story illustrates the importance of course documents such as the syllabus. Despite a preference for a stand-alone syllabus, professors will also want to convey expectations via the learning management system. According to Quality Matters (2023), who developed widely used standards for online courses, high-quality online courses include a course overview that contains information about how to get started, the purpose and structure of the course, guidelines about communication, policy information, technological requirements and skills needed, and opportunities to learn about the professor and share information about themselves.

A Start Here module is an excellent way to help online students learn how to navigate the course and about course expectations. Wengier (2022) encouraged professors to include essential course information in the Start Here module. Specifically, Wengier (2022) recommended that professors share information about themselves, provide students with an opportunity to get to know each other, and give an overview of how the course is set up, technology requirements, and other essential course expectations and requirements in an introductory module.

In addition to sharing expectations via the syllabus and learning management system, professors can also share expectations during a first online class if it is a synchronous one. Students who are new to online learning will especially appreciate the guidance provided by professors at the start of the semester. This was the case for Raymond. In the following student story, Raymond explains that learning about how the online course would work and what was expected reduced anxiety and was engaging.

ಶಿಶಿಶಿಚುಚುಚು

## Setting Expectations During the First Class, Raymond Matson Jr., Rutgers University

After an absence of over 30 years, I entered graduate school as a returning student. My prior learning experiences were traditional, taking place in a physical classroom. I was, therefore, quite nervous about how my learning experience in an online course would play out. I asked myself: How would I express my thoughts? How could I remain engaged? Would I be able to use technology correctly? I had so many fears.

Within the first five minutes of class, I knew I was fortunate. My professor explained how the course would work and laid out the steps we would need to take in this online classroom. During this overview, my professor mentioned that this was a work in progress, and if changes needed to be made, we would do so on the fly. I learned what to expect from this new learning format. Right from the start of this class, I was hooked on online learning. I am engaged when I have direction, and this first class gave me the direction I needed. Knowing what to do helps me feel confident, and because my professor explained what I needed to do, I was confident that this new learning experience would work for me.

My professor insisted we have the technology needed. The class was to be held in the early evening to accommodate our schedules as working adults. He told us that we should focus on connecting the best we could. If we were stuck in traffic, he said we could use our phones to log in. He preferred that we participate in a good place but told us to participate as best we could.

My professor used the breakroom function within Zoom, and this approach helped me engage in critical thinking and discussions. Once the groups were brought back together, groups would discuss their findings with the entire class. These breakout rooms created working relationships between students and allowed for complete engagement in the topic covered. I found that the online class allowed more voices to be heard than a traditional class might have allowed. Students are always more engaged when they are invited to participate and are heard. Within a class or two, I no longer had many questions about how online learning would work. My uncertainty and anxiety about taking online courses lessened.

My recommendation to professors teaching online is simple. First, never assume that the students have experience in an online classroom setting. Then, set clear and understandable guidelines on how the class will operate. Speak about the technology being used and how they can expect to learn. I also encourage professors to 'read' the classroom as they would in a traditional classroom and then adjust their teaching based on how students respond. The goal is to engage students as much as possible. I actually found that this learning experience was better than what I would have gotten if the class was an in-person one. My experience, due to my professor and fellow classmates, was more than I could have ever expected.

The importance of helping students understand course expectations was emphasized in the story by Raymond. In addition to providing an overview of the course, it can also be helpful for professors to share resources or tips for success. Researchers have found that sharing success strategies has led to improved academic achievement (Carrell & Kurlaender, 2020). In the following student story, Adeoluwa explains why helpful resources shared via a pre-class announcement and throughout the semester were engaging. Adeoluwa also shares how peers were viewed as a resource and how the professor helped students get to know one another through group activities.

### Sharing Helpful Resources, Adeoluwa O. Folami, Morgan State University

Students often have no information (aside from what is on the blurb of the registration portal) of what the course they registered for entails. My professor sent those who registered for their online research course a pre-class announcement a few weeks before the start of the course. In the announcement, my professor shared tips on how to be successful in the course and what we would need (texts, computer, and internet requirements) to have a successful start. My professor also provided links to mental health resources that could be helpful if we experienced stress. As an international student, these initial messages and resources were particularly helpful; they conveyed that my professor was concerned about our well-being and wanted us to be successful in the class.

My professor continued to provide helpful resources throughout the semester. They started every class by sharing the agenda for the day on a virtual whiteboard. The agenda document, which was available to us in a Google folder, made it easy for me to stay focused and on track. I also used the resource to reconcile my notes, check my knowledge, and anticipate the next class. We were regularly encouraged, guided, and reassured that we could succeed in the course, and more importantly, we were provided with the information and resources to help us achieve that success. Varied resources such as books, articles, videos, and websites helped us further our knowledge and see the application of the content being learned. I still use many of the resources from this class in my other courses.

Recognizing that our peers are also an important resource, my professor helped us get to know one another through group activities. We engaged in group discussions and assignments during every class. Group members and numbers varied, and we would usually be paired with different students so that we could all get to know each other. These small group activities made getting to know my classmates easier and helped us develop a good rapport with one another. The group activities also allowed us to share what we knew, and as a result, we learned from each other and improved our knowledge capital. Later in the semester, we were required to share our writings with classmates. If we had not known each other, I would not have been comfortable being vulnerable and sharing my writing with them, but because we knew each other and established a support system within the class, this became a valuable experience instead of a threatening one.

My recommendation to professors is for them to use a shared online space such as a Google Drive for the class. In this drive or folder, they can share resources that will be helpful to students in their class. Additionally, students could be asked to upload materials they found useful in connecting what was taught with viable examples or with resources they created. Students will appreciate having these resources to seek out as needed, and it is a great way for everyone to collaborate and support one another.

౭౦౭౦౭౦౦౩౦౩౦౩

In the story shared by Adeoluwa, the benefit of early communications about the course and resources was discussed. One of the early communications that Adeoluwa shared was the email that the professor sent. Chang et al. (2015) found that undergraduate and graduate students taking online courses preferred for their professors to communicate via email, with announcements being the second most preferred type of communication. Researchers have found that an email from their professor a week before the semester started led to higher student motivation levels and positively impacted student persistence (Legg & Wilson, 2009).

Email communication can contribute to the development of positive professor–student relationships, especially when email content is perceived as helpful and characterized as having a social-relational focus (Sheer & Fung, 2007). Dickinson (2017) found that the tone of the email was important in online courses, noting a 17% increase in success rates after intentionally writing emails with a warmer and encouraging tone. In the next student story, Abaynesh explains the value of a welcoming and informative email that describes expectations and provides resources that would be useful in the course.

ಔಔಔಚಚಚ

### Introductory Email and Flexible Due Dates, Abaynesh Berecha, Community College of Aurora, Colorado

I took English Composition II online with Professor Patrick Munnelly. Professor Munnelly sent out an email to his students a few days before the start of the semester. In this email, he introduced himself, explained what we should expect on the first day of class, sent the syllabus and the link for our Zoom classes, and informed us about our course materials and how to best communicate with him. I appreciated this communication because it always bothered me when I went to the first day of class with no clue about the professor or what the class would be like.

Because he sent this communication before the first day of the semester, I was able to learn about my professor and his expectations of us. Knowing this information helped me to prepare for the course. Reaching out to students before class even started showed me that he cared about his students. This simple outreach made me feel comfortable and welcomed to his classroom. A brief email like this can open the door for students to be engaged and build trust between students and professors.

I also found his approach to due dates unique and engaging. At the start of the semester, Professor Munnelly shared that the assignment due dates in his class were very flexible. He told us that he wanted to reduce our stress and create an inclusive learning environment for all of us. Professor Munley acknowledged that we were adult learners who were navigating through the education system with a lot of responsibilities on our shoulders. He listed due dates but said they were not rigid or formal but rather there for guidance purposes and for people who need a due date to keep them on track. We could simply reach out if we needed to adjust these in any way. The only requirement was that Professor Munnelly expected us to communicate with him about our due date needs. We were also encouraged to share why we fell behind with our assignments if that happened and to let him know how he could help us get back on track. He was always willing to provide support.

I have a lot of responsibilities in life, so many may not think I should even be in school. However, having professors who are very understanding, caring, and flexible, especially with due dates, means I can be a student. This flexibility took the deadline stress away and allowed me to focus on the work instead. Without this flexibility, I may have gotten sick from the stress of being overloaded and unable to submit work by rigid due dates. His mission was to ensure we got the work done and gained the knowledge and skills needed. By having such flexibility, I felt I belonged and was comfortable in the classroom. Also, this respect motivated me to do even better in the course.

My advice to professors is to remember that there are a lot of adult learners in their classes. Most adult learners want to do well and are managing a lot. They will want to complete assignments by the due dates, but having rigid due dates may cause them stress. I hope that you will allow students to have flexibility on due dates and that you will work with students who may need your grace due to their many responsibilities. By sending a welcoming email and recognizing their busy lives, you can gain their trust and help students be very comfortable in class. Your actions can be the reason why a student does not drop out of school when life struggles happen. You can make a difference in a student's academic journey.

৪০৪০৪০৫০৪০৫০

In addition to sharing the power of a welcoming email to learn about course expectations, Abaynesh also discussed how flexible deadlines reduced stress and were motivating. Wanner et al. (2024) suggested that giving students flexibility with assignment due dates and other choices empowers students and enables them to take ownership of their learning journey. Students in courses with flexible assignment deadlines report having lower stress levels (Hills & Peacock, 2022).

Kruger (2023) argued that flexible late policies are an equitable practice. When professors shared late work policies that involved point reductions, students taking an online course believed that their professors would rigidly follow the policy even though professors indicated they would be flexible to accommodate students (Santelli et al., 2020). If professors are going to be flexible, conveying this in the syllabus can foster a more inclusive learning environment where the policies are more transparent. Students with privilege may be more likely than those from historically marginalized communities to ask for exceptions to rigid policies, which could contribute to inequitable outcomes for students (Harrington & Thomas, 2018).

Professors may be concerned that giving too much flexibility might be overwhelming for them and could negatively impact their schedule and workload.

However, Kruger (2023) found that most students submitted their work on time and did not need to ask for an extension. When students did request to use the flexible policy, they typically submitted their work within one week. Hills and Peacock (2022) reported that most students did not ask for an extension in a class with a flexible policy (35%) or only asked for one extension (35%) on formative assessments. However, most students did ask for an extension on the high-stakes assignment.

Recognizing the potential challenges flexible deadlines could pose for professors and how different approaches would work better in different courses, Boswell (2023) suggested giving parameters around flexible due date policies, such as limiting the number of times students could ask for an extension or the number of days an assignment could be turned in late. Professors are encouraged to consider balancing the needs of their students with their well-being when determining late work policies for their classrooms.

## SENDING ENCOURAGING FIRST-DAY-OF-CLASS MESSAGES

The first day of class has long been viewed as important by educators. The messages professors send on this first day can have a positive and long-lasting impact. Many students have emphasized the importance of smiling, having a positive attitude on the first day, sharing words of encouragement (Harrington, 2021), and these actions can easily take place in a synchronous course.

In an interesting study by Meaders et al. (2021), STEM student perceptions of messages sent by professors on the first day were explored. Based on classroom observational data, these researchers discovered that professors varied in how much time they spent sharing non-content messages on the first day of class. The non-content messages included discussing instructional practices, building professor–student relationships, and sharing strategies for success. They found that students were more likely to detect and receive messages when professors spent more time communicating the message, suggesting that it is important for professors to spend more time on important messages during the first class (Meaders et al., 2021).

Although synchronous online courses have a first day of class, the virtual environment differs from the in-person classroom. Thus, professors may need to adjust how they develop an inclusive and welcoming learning environment on day one. For instance, Roberto (2021) described how a shared Google document could be used to collect information about students instead of using index cards, which can work well in a traditional in-person classroom.

It can be more challenging to convey first-day-of-class messages in an asynchronous course because there is no live gathering. However, announcements and Start Here modules can be used for this purpose. Griffiths and Graham (2020) found that recorded introductory videos can effectively convey encouraging messages and engage students. Students have indicated a preference for video-based introductions (Harrington, 2024).

One of the most important messages for students to receive is that their professors care about them (Roberto, 2021). Buskirk-Cohen and Plants (2019) reported that when students believed their professors cared, they performed better. In the following three stories, Haruka, Devin, and Leah share examples of how their professors shared positive and encouraging messages conveying their care and explain how much these small actions meant to them.

ಠಠಠಯಯಯ

### Teaching us the Three P's: Patience, Practice, and Perseverance, Haruka Whitcroft, Northwest Vista College, Alamo Colleges District

In the very first lecture of my precalculus course, Professor Patterson showed a video of herself receiving her doctoral degree at commencement. Seeing this video left me feeling inspired and filled with respect for my professor. Watching her proudest moment motivated me and other students to strive for excellence in our own academic pursuits.

During our first precalculus lecture, Professor Patterson emphasized the three Ps – patience, practice, and perseverance. She explained that patience was crucial in achieving academic success, building strong relationships with others, and even functioning as a member of society. She shared that it was important to be patient and willing to take the time to understand things thoroughly rather than rush to learn or make immediate judgments. It is easy to decide to quit, saying, 'I cannot do this,' when we face a bunch of Greek symbols in math problems or daunting tasks to do in our other classes, like memorizing the 206 bones in our bodies in an anatomy class.

Professor Patterson explained that practice was the only way to truly make sense of what we were learning. She reminded us often that there are no shortcuts to success and that developing good habits of practice will lead to success. Recognizing that having access to resources can help us establish these habits; she always offered out-of-class time to have math conferences with us. She also connected us with on-campus resources such as tutoring. Finally, Professor Patterson emphasized perseverance or the importance of finishing what we started. She regularly reminded us that it might be tempting to give up when facing challenges, complex math problems, or life situations in general, but that it is crucial to remain committed and never give up.

Many students may feel that college is like an endless tunnel with no clear end in sight. It is powerful for professors to share their success stories as this can motivate and inspire students to keep striving toward success. Creating a supportive environment where students can develop positive thinking habits and seek help when they encounter challenges is also important. I encourage professors to inform their students of the importance of their mindset and actions. Sharing inspiring and impactful expressions or mottos can remind students to practice good habits and work hard.

༄༄༄༅༅༅

༄༄༄༅༅༅

**Easing My Fear, Devin Browne, Community College of Allegheny County**

As a single mom at the age of 36, finding myself on the front steps of a college campus was nerve-wracking, to say the least. I believed, based on my previous experiences and what others had told me, that I was not 'book smart.' This was a big reason I pursued a career as a cosmetologist for the last 15 years instead of seeking a college education. As life changed, so did my educational and career goals, and I found myself in college.

I had known for years that I had some type of disability that made learning certain ways a challenge, but I had never had an official diagnosis. I just knew I learned differently and needed support to succeed. Because I did not have a diagnosis yet, I could not access disability services when I started college. I was afraid I would not be successful because I had to wait for support.

One of my professors eased my fears. I recall this professor telling us on the first day of class that we would be successful if we showed up and did the work. My professors said they were rooting for us and would support us in whatever way we needed. They made it clear that if we actively participated in our education, we would do well and pass the class.

I spoke openly with my professor about my struggles and how I was on a waitlist for a diagnostic evaluation. Not only did this professor not judge me, but they also helped me figure out a game plan while I was waiting to access official services. For example, I was told about programs such as Grammarly to help me identify and fix grammatical errors. My professor also asked me questions to better understand where I specifically struggled and then gave me pointers. I also learned about how the professors provided tutoring. I was relieved that this professor was on my side and did not expect me to learn like everyone else.

I can say with confidence that if I had not had professors like this one who were invested in their students and viewed us as individuals rather than a number, I would not have been as successful in my college journey as I have been thus far. When professors like this one share their belief in students, it helps us know we can do well and eases our fears. I am proud to share that I have a 4.0 GPA and was accepted into the honors program. I encourage all professors to ease the fears of their students on the first day by sharing positive messages, trying to get to know students, and then providing them with the individualized help they need.

ಬಿಬಿಬಿ ಅಅಅ

ಬಿಬಿಬಿ ಅಅಅ

## Guided Meditation on Day One, Leah Josefowitz, Wesleyan University

My English professor introduced a brief yet impactful practice on the first day of class, and then we started the beginning of each class with this activity. The activity was a three-minute guided meditation from YouTube. A module on Canvas titled 'Before We Begin: Meditation for Personal Wellness' provided an introduction to the purpose of meditation, along with YouTube videos featuring three-minute guided meditations.

On the first day of class, our professor directed us to this module and discussed the concept and benefits of meditation. She told us she would incorporate a guided meditation session before each class, emphasizing that participation was optional yet strongly encouraged. This simple ritual served as a powerful tool for grounding and centering our minds, leaving behind the daily stresses. With closed eyes and deep breaths, we collectively let go of distractions and anxieties, fully immersing ourselves in the present moment. By the end of the meditation, there was a noticeable sense of calm and focus in the classroom, setting us up for a productive learning experience.

While I had tried meditation previously and was familiar with research demonstrating its amazing benefits, including stress reduction and enhanced focus, I struggled to find time for it and maintain consistency. By incorporating meditation into our class routine, our professor introduced us to a valuable tool for self-care and helped us form positive habits. To this day, I try to integrate meditation into my routine whenever I feel stressed or have trouble focusing. This three-minute activity had a great impact on me and my approach to both academics and personal well-being.

By starting each class with meditation, I was able to let go of distractions and anxieties, allowing me to absorb information with a clearer and more focused mind. I was then more present during lectures and discussions. It also helped me manage stress levels, which in turn improved my overall academic performance.

I hope other professors will send their students a message that they care about their well-being on the first day of class. For professors who want to use meditation to do this, I recommend starting with brief guided sessions, similar to what my professor did. Introduce the practice gradually and explain its benefits to students. Provide resources, such as guided meditation recordings or apps, to make it accessible for those new to meditation. Be consistent in implementing the practice; routine is key to forming habits. Creating a supportive and open environment for meditation can greatly enhance students' well-being and academic success.

These student stories highlighted the importance of professors showing that they care and believe in them. As Haruka, Devin, and Leah shared, these positive messages on the first day of their online courses, though shared in different ways, motivated and engaged them. When professors take just a few minutes of class or create recorded videos to communicate words of encouragement explicitly, students will carry these messages with them.

## FACULTY REFLECTION QUESTIONS

1. How do you help students get to know you? How can you use videos and synchronous class sessions to help students connect to you? What might you share about yourself and your journey that could inspire and motivate students?
2. How do you get to know your online students? How can you leverage technology to create icebreaker activities in online courses?
3. In what ways are you accessible to online students? How can you encourage students to reach out for support and attend your virtual office hours?
4. How do you communicate course expectations and the why behind learning tasks on your syllabus and in the learning management system?
5. What resources do you share with students? How do you encourage students to use these resources?
6. How do you create a welcoming, inclusive learning environment during the first day or week of class?
7. How do you convey that you care about your students?

# REFERENCES

Addy, T. M., Dube, D., Mitchell, K. A., & SoRelle, M. E. (2023). *What inclusive instructors do: Principles and practices for excellence in college teaching*. Routledge.

Baker, S. (2012). Classroom karaoke. *Youth Studies Australia, 31*(1), 25–33 https://search.informit.org/doi/abs/10.3316/ielapa.024026142156830

Boswell, S. (2023). Students' use and perceptions of a due date extension policy. *Journal of Effective Teaching in Higher Education, 6*(2), 1–16. https://doi.org/10.36021/jethe.v6i2.379

Buskirk-Cohen, A. A., & Plants, A. (2019). Caring about success: Students' perceptions of professors' caring matters more than grit. *International Journal of Teaching and Learning in Higher Education, 31*(1), 108–114. https://files.eric.ed.gov/fulltext/EJ1206948.pdf

Carrell, S. E., & Kurlaender, M. (2020). My professor cares: Experimental evidence on the role of faculty engagement. *National Bureau of Economic Research, Working Paper 27312*, 1–53. http://www.nber.org/papers/w27312

Chang, C., Hurst, B., & McLean, A. (2015). You've got mail: Student preferences of instructor communication in online courses in an age of advancing technologies. *Journal of Educational Technology Development and Exchange, 8*(1), 16–24. https://bearworks.missouristate.edu/articles-coe/7/

Darby, F., & Lang, J. M. (2019). *Small teaching online: Applying learning science in online classes*. Jossey Bass.

Dickinson, A. (2017). Communicating with the online student: The impact of email tone on student performance and teacher evaluations. *Journal of Educators Online, 14*(2), 1–11 https://www.thejeo.com/archive/2017_14_2/dickinson

DiGiacomo, D. K., Usher, E. L., Han, J., Abney, J. M., Cole, A. E., & Patterson, J. T. (2023). The benefits of belonging: Students' perceptions of their online learning experiences. *Distance Education, 44*(1), 24–39. https://doi.org/10.1080/01587919.2022.2155615

Garrison, D. R., Anderson, T., & Archer, W. (2000). Critical inquiry in a text-based environment: Computing conferencing in higher education. *The Internet and Higher Education, 2* (2–3), 87–105. https://doi.org/10.1016/S1096-7516(00)00016-6

Gehlbach, H., Brinkworth, M. E., King, A. M., Hsu, L. M., McIntyre, J., & Rogers, T. (2016). Creating birds of similar feathers: Leveraging similarity to improve teacher-student relationships and academic achievement. *Journal of Educational Psychology, 108*(3), 342–352. https://doi.org/10.1037/edu0000042

Goering, A. E., Resnick, C. E., Bradford, K. D., & Othus, G. S. M. (2022). Diversity by design: Broadening participation through inclusive teaching. *New Directions for Community Colleges, 199*, 77–91. https://doi.org/10.1002/cc.20525

Griffiths, M. E., & Graham, C. R. (2020). The potential of asynchronous video in online education. *Distance Learning, 17*(4), 93–102. https://eric.ed.gov/?id=EJ1292003

Hansen-Brown, A. A., Lavigne, C., & Frade, K. (2023). "I'm proud to say I was the first in my family to go to college": How students perceive professor self-disclosure of first-generation status. *Social Psychology of Education, 26*(6), 1499–1526. http://doi.org/10.1007/s11218-023-09791-1

Harrington, C. (2021). *Keeping us engaged: Student perspectives (and research-based strategies) on what works and why.* Routledge.

Harrington, C. (2023). Is the syllabus passé? Student and faculty perceptions. *Journal of Scholarship of Teaching and Learning, 23*(4), 19–32. https://doi.org/10.14434/josotl.v23i4.34371

Harrington, C. (2024). Instructor and student perceptions of online welcome messages. *Journal of Educators Online, 21*(4), 1–12. https://www.thejeo.com/archive/2024_21_4/harrington

Harrington, C., & Gabert-Quillen, C. (2015). Syllabus length and use of images: An empirical investigation of student perceptions. *Scholarship of Teaching and Learning in Psychology, 1*(3), 235–243. https://doi.org/10.1037/stl0000040

Harrington, C., & Thomas, M. (2018). *Designing a motivational syllabus: Creating a learning path for student engagement.* Routledge.

Hills, M., & Peacock, K. (2022). Replacing power with flexible structure: Implementing flexible deadlines to improve student learning experiences. *Teaching & Learning Inquiry, 10*, 1–25. https://journalhosting.ucalgary.ca/index.php/TLI/article/view/73960

Jackson, L. C., Jones, S. J., & Rodriguez, R. C. (2010). Faculty actions that result in student satisfaction in online courses. *Journal of Asynchronous Learning Networks JALN, 14*(4), 78. https://doi.org/10.24059/olj.v14i4.129

Kirby, C. S. (2020). Using share-out grids in the online classroom: From icebreakers to amplifiers. *Biochemistry and Molecular Biology Education, 48*(5), 538–541. https://doi.org/10.1002/bmb.21451

Kruger, J. S. (2023). Rethinking penalties for late work: The case for flexibility, equity, and support. *Pedagogy in Health Promotion, 9*(4), 234–236. https://doi.org/10.1177/23733799231198778

Lammers, W. J., & Gillaspy, J. A. (2013). Brief measure of student-instructor rapport predicts student success in online courses. *International Journal for the Scholarship of Teaching and Learning, 7*(2), 1–15. https://digitalcommons.georgiasouthern.edu/ij-sotl/vol7/iss2/16/

Lavooy, M., & Newlin, M. (2008). Online chats and cyber-office hours: Everything but the office. *International Journal on E-Learning, 7*(1), 107–116. https://eric.ed.gov/?id=EJ780477

Legg, A. M., & Wilson, J. H. (2009). Email from professor enhances student motivation and attitudes. *Teaching of Psychology, 36*(3), 205–211. https://psycnet.apa.org/doi/10.1080/00986280902960034

Lowenthal, P. R., Snelson, C., & Dunlap, J. C. (2017). Live synchronous web meetings in asynchronous online courses: Reconceptualizing virtual office hours. *Online Learning, 21*(4), 177–194. https://doi.org/10.24059/olj.v21i4.1285

Martin, F., & Bolliger, D. U. (2018). Engagement matters: Student perceptions on the importance of engagement strategies in the online learning environment. *Online Learning, 22*(1), 205–222. https://doi.org/10.24059/olj.v22i1.1092

Meaders, C. L., Senn, L. G., Couch, B. A., Lane, A. K., Stains, M., Stetzer, M. R., Vinson, E., & Smith, M. K. (2021). Am I getting through? Surveying students on what messages they recall from the first day of STEM classes. *International Journal of STEM Education, 8*(1), 1–16. https://stemeducationjournal.springeropen.com/articles/10.1186/s40594-021-00306-y

Morrison, J. S. (2021). Getting to know you: Student-faculty interaction and student engagement in online courses. *Journal of Higher Education Theory & Practice, 21*(12), 38–44. https://doi.org/10.4995/HEAd21.2021.13160

Mowreader, A. (2023, July 25). Engagement tip: Create a first-day survey. *Inside Higher Ed.* https://www.insidehighered.com/news/student-success/academic-life/2023/07/25/how-professors-can-use-first-day-class-survey

Quality Matters. (2023). *Specific review standards from the QM higher education rubric* (7th ed.). Author. https://qualitymatters.org/qa-resources/rubric-standards/higher-ed-rubric

Roberto, M. (2021, April 9). *Engaging students on the first day and every day: Seven strategies for connecting in the classroom.* Harvard Business Publishing Education. https://hbsp.harvard.edu/inspiring-minds/engaging-students-on-the-first-day-and-every-day

Santelli, B., Robertson, S. N., Larson, E. K., & Humphrey, S. (2020). Procrastination and delayed assignment submissions: Student and faculty perceptions of late point policy and grace within an online learning environment. *Online Learning, 24*(3), 35–49. https://doi.org/10.24059/olj.v24i3.2302

Sasan, J. M. V., Tugbong, G. M., & Alistre, K. L. C. (2023). An exploration of icebreakers and their impact on student engagement in the classroom. *International Journal of Social Service & Research (IJSSR), 3*(11), 2921–2930. https://doi.org/10.46799/ijssr.v3i11.566

Sat, M., Ilhan, F., & Yükseltürk, E. (2022). Web tools as e-icebreakers in online education. *Journal of Educational Technology and Online Learning, 5*(3), 721–737. https://doi.org/10.31681/jetol.1084512

Shane-Simpson, C., Obeid, R., & Prescher, M. (2024). Multimedia characteristics, student relationships, and teaching behaviors predict perceptions of an inclusive classroom across course delivery format. *Teaching of Psychology, 51*(3), 298–308. https://doi.org/10.1177/00986283221117621

Sheer, V. C., & Fung, T. K. (2007). Can email communication enhance professor-student relationship and student evaluation of professor?: Some empirical evidence. *Journal of Educational Computing Research, 37*(3), 289–306. https://doi.org/10.2190/EC.37.3.d

Strickland-Davis, S., & McMican, J. (2024) Getting to know your students: A first step in creating culturally affirming and meaningful assignments. In C. Harrington (Ed.), *Creating culturally affirming and meaning assignments: A practical resource for higher education faculty* (pp. 54–70). Routledge. https://doi.org/10.4324/978/003443797-5

van Heerden, M., & Bharuthram, S. (2023). "It does not feel like I am a university student": Considering the impact of online learning on students' sense of belonging in a "post pandemic" academic literacy module. *Perspectives in Education, 41*(3), 95–106. https://doi.org/10.38140/pie.v41i3.6780

Wanner, T., Palmer, E., & Palmer, D. (2024). Flexible assessment and student empowerment: Advantages and disadvantages – Research from an Australian university. *Teaching in Higher Education, 29*(2), 349–365. https://doi.org/10.1080/13562517.2021.1989578

Wasserman, E., & Ayeni, T. (2024). Being transparent about assignment expectations. In C. Harrington (Ed.), *Creating culturally affirming and meaning assignments: A practical resource for higher education faculty* (pp. 101–113). Routledge. https://doi.org/10.4324/978/003443797-8

Wengier, S. (2022). The Start Here module: Creating a first day impression in an online language class. *Dimension*, 35–56. https://eric.ed.gov/?id=EJ1346021

Winkelmes, M. (2023). Introduction to transparency in learning and teaching. *Perspectives In Learning, 20*(1). https://csuepress.columbusstate.edu/pil/vol20/iss1/2

# CHAPTER 2

# Relationships

Over 50 years of research studies have demonstrated the important role of professor–student relationships on student success, particularly for first-generation students and students of color (Kezar & Maxey, 2014). Guzzardo et al. (2021) reported that student interactions with their professors help them "feel like they belong in the class, their perspective is valued, and/or they have the ability to succeed" (p. 49). Students who have positive professor–student relationships are more likely to participate in class, exert more time and effort on tasks, and achieve at higher levels (Afzal et al., 2023; Dickinson & Kreitmair, 2021). Darby and Lang (2019) emphasized that relationships in online courses are even more important because it can be isolating to work independently on a computer. Researchers have found that professor–student relationships in online learning environments play a critical role in student motivation and achievement (Akram & Li, 2024).

Professor–student relationships are critically important in both traditional and virtual classroom settings (Felten & Lambert, 2020). In a study with students from 23 online courses at a community college, Jaggars and Xu (2016) found that 'interpersonal interaction predicted student grades in the course' (p. 280) and noted that professor–student interactions were the most important type of relationship. Student responses on a survey focused on how well their professor understood them, encouraged them, cared about them, treated them fairly, communicated with them, respected them, and the extent to which their professors earned their respect and were approachable were related to their success in an online course (Lammers & Gillaspy, 2013). A relationship with an online professor can help students develop a sense of connection and belonging (Kember et al., 2023) and feel a sense of inclusion (Shane-Simpson et al., 2024).

DOI: 10.4324/9781003490012-3

Although building relationships with online students can be challenging, especially in large classes, researchers have found that professors can use group activities to foster these important relationships. In a study with over 3,000 participants, Gay and Betts (2020) compared two versions of a large online class. One class was traditional in nature, and the other focused on building relationships between professors and students through group discussions. In the relationship-focused version, students were assigned to small asynchronous groups where they engaged in activities similar to business meetings, with the professor playing the role of facilitator. Findings revealed that students in this relationship-focused version of the course were more engaged and achieved at higher levels on the final exam than their peers who were in the traditional version of the course (Gay & Betts, 2020).

Another important strategy to foster positive professor–student relationships is demonstrating care. Barnett and Cho (2023) reported that students who believed their professors cared about them were likelier to stay in school. Jaggars and Xu (2016) found that online students could easily differentiate which professors cared and which did not. When they felt cared for, they were more engaged and committed, leading to higher academic performance (Jaggars & Xu, 2016). Students have reported that professors have demonstrated care by listening and being understanding (Guzzardo et al., 2021).

In this chapter, student stories illustrating the importance of professor–student relationships in online courses are shared. Several students explained that it was motivating when their professors reached out to them and when they were accessible to them outside of class. Students also shared that their engagement increased when their professors connected them to resources, were understanding in times of need, provided opportunities to build their skills, and offered career mentoring and support.

## BEING ACCESSIBLE OUTSIDE OF CLASS

Connecting with professors outside of class benefits students (Addy et al., 2023; Felten & Lambert, 2020). It is important for professors to share their preferred way for students to ask questions, such as via email or in a question discussion forum, and how to set up individual meetings with them (Quality Matters, 2023). Martin and Bolliger (2018) found that students indicated that it was important, as indicated by an average score of 4.36 on a 5-point Likert scale, with 5 being very important, for professors to create a forum students can use to reach professors with questions as needed. In addition to helping students connect with their professors, a discussion forum is also a great way for students to support each other. Question discussion forums can be especially helpful when students have a question during a time when the professor is not available. Students can help one another by responding to questions posed. Still, professors will want to review responses and provide guidance because there is no guarantee that student responses will be completely accurate.

It is also helpful for professors to share the expected turnaround time for responding to questions. Researchers have found that 42% of students expect a response to an email within 8 hours, and another 28% of students indicated they expected a response within 24 hours, meaning 70% of students believe professors should respond to emails within one day (Wilkie & Rosendale, 2021). Over 93% of students expected responses to emails on the weekend. Although Wilkie and Rosendale (2021) found that the majority of students reported their professors met or exceeded their expectations in terms of responding to emails, online students (63%) were less likely to report this being the case than students taking traditional courses (75%). Getting quick responses to questions via email can be very helpful to students, particularly online students who may need additional clarity on assignment expectations.

Professors, however, also have to balance work and life and cannot be expected to answer emails 24 hours a day, seven days a week. Professors are therefore encouraged to set and communicate boundaries around how quickly they will respond to emails sent during the work day, evening, and weekend so students know what to expect. In the next student story, Gabrielle shares how getting quick and encouraging email responses from the professor was engaging.

## A Quick Email Response and Emphasizing Growth over Perfection, Gabrielle Land, Rutgers University

I was sitting at my computer, trying to get VoiceThread to work. No matter what I did, refreshing the page and restarting my computer, nothing seemed to fix the issue. As the assignment deadline approached, I started to feel very anxious. It had been years since I had taken a class, and now I was dealing with a technical problem I could not solve on my own. I thought, am I going to miss the deadline?

Frustrated, I decided to email my professor. I was not sure what kind of response I would get. To my surprise, the reply came back quickly and was a positive one. My professor wrote, 'I will not allow stress in this class.' That simple line immediately eased my worries. Knowing that my professor was focused on my well-being and the learning process rather than the deadline made me feel supported. With that reassurance and a little extra time, I was able to resolve the technical issue and submit the assignment without any penalty.

Throughout the course, my professor emphasized learning over perfection in several ways. Instead of highlighting what was wrong, she framed feedback around improvement. She also gave us low-stake assignments to reflect on our progress and track our growth. An important lesson I learned was that I did not have to be perfect; I just had to learn.

I found this course to be engaging. The professor's quick and positive response helped me see that I was not alone in facing challenges. I became more comfortable asking questions and seeking help when needed, knowing that the emphasis was on growth, not perfection. I also became more confident in participating in discussions and working with others. My professor's actions kept me motivated and encouraged me to stay engaged, even when things did not go as planned. I encourage professors to respond to emails as soon as possible, within reason (like 24–48 hours), because a response can alleviate the stress that a student may be experiencing when working on an assignment. I also encourage professors to help students see that the goal is learning, not perfection.

ಐಐಐಐಐಐಐ

As Gabrielle explained, getting the support of a professor through a quick email response can be very helpful and engaging; it can also alleviate stress. Snijders et al. (2022) found that students indicated that timely responses to emails contributed to positive professor–student relationships. Email communication is a key component of the professor–student relationship.

To build strong relationships, one-on-one communication opportunities with professors are also critically important (Kember et al., 2023). Being accessible outside of class for one-on-one conversations can help online students stay engaged. Individual meetings with students can help them better grasp the course material, gain confidence, and encourage them to pursue additional learning opportunities outside of class. In the next three student stories, Jaymala, Monica, and Karen explain how meeting with their professors during virtual office hours improved their understanding of the concepts being learned, increased their confidence, and engaged them as learners.

ಐಐಐಐಐಐಐ

### Clarifying Concepts During Office Hours, Jaymala Chavan, University of Texas at Dallas

My professor was truly a great educator. I had the privilege of taking her advanced statistics course, a challenging subject made even more difficult by the shift to online learning during the pandemic. Despite the obstacles, my professor went above and beyond to ensure her students succeeded. One of the things that stood out to me the most about my professor was her willingness to make herself available to her students. Knowing that online learning could be isolating and challenging, she encouraged us to reach out to her with any questions or concerns. I took advantage of this offer and booked several online meetings with her to help me better understand the course material.

Each time we met, my professor showed patience, kindness, and a genuine desire to help me succeed. During our meetings, she took the time to clarify difficult concepts and explain them in various ways until I fully understood them. She was always willing to go the extra mile. Because she was so supportive, I stopped doubting myself and started to build my confidence in being able to learn statistics. If I needed more help or time to grasp a concept, she was always willing to provide additional resources to support my learning and extend deadlines.

My professor's dedication to her students, even in the face of personal struggles, truly amazed me. During the semester, she and her family contracted COVID-19, a frightening experience for all of us during the pandemic. Despite her illness, she continued to teach our course and support us in our learning journey. Her dedication and resilience in the face of adversity were truly inspiring. My professor was not just a great teacher but a mentor and a role model. Her commitment to her students' success, even in the midst of a global pandemic and personal challenges, is a testament to her passion for teaching and genuine care for them. I am grateful to have had the opportunity to learn from her and will always value the lessons she taught me in statistics and life. My professor was truly great, and I am thankful for her impact on my education.

For professors who want to make a difference in their student's lives, I suggest they make themselves available outside of class to meet with students. Please encourage students to attend office hours and when they show up, share new examples to help them understand the concepts they are struggling to learn. Students will appreciate having a professor who cares and is willing to spend time supporting them.

ཀྵཀྵཀྵཀྵཀྵཀྵ

ཀྵཀྵཀྵཀྵཀྵཀྵ

### Learning Chemistry in an Asynchronous Course with a Supportive Professor, Monica Davish, Bucks County Community College

I am a 39-year-old college student and a single mother. I have been taking almost all my courses at a community college online and have had positive experiences in these courses. One course in particular stands out. I took a chemistry class online, having to conduct all the experiments at home.

This chemistry course was a completely asynchronous online course with no Zoom classes involved, and it was by far the most difficult course I had taken online. It was very lecture and homework-heavy, and discussion boards were required twice a week. We had to interact with other students in our discussion boards, which was typical, but the engagement and feedback from this professor in discussion boards far exceeded what I was used to. My professor made many extremely helpful and insightful comments to further our understanding of that week's content.

My professor recorded lectures to help students taking a difficult class at home. The teaching approach was well thought out and designed to be helpful to her students. It was evident that she wanted her students to succeed and learn the content she was teaching. It was a very well-structured class.

Although the workload was very demanding, she set us up to learn time management skills and discipline needed to be successful in an online course. The weekly activities helped prepare us for our exams efficiently and effectively. The recordings, readings, and discussions gave us a deeper comprehension of the knowledge we needed to master the subject. Despite the intensity, the assignments helped us achieve our goals.

What I most appreciated was the responsiveness and compassion of my professor. There was never a time that she was not there to help. She cared about all her students. Her response time for answering emails was always the same day (even on weekends). She demonstrated compassion and genuine concern for her students' well-being. She was very understanding about life situations and circumstances and always worked with me and helped me through those times. She did not fault me for things out of my control and allowed me time to make work up. She even allowed me to reschedule exams, which had to be taken in person at the college.

Perhaps most importantly, she was always available for whatever we needed. She made ample time for students to do Zoom calls with her. I must have done seven Zoom calls with her over that semester. She worked with my schedule to accommodate me and made sure I got the help I needed. She carefully reviewed the work I sent her and gave me super helpful feedback. She pushed me to push myself and to believe in my abilities. I really appreciated the time she gave me. I know it was a key to my success.

I learned not only chemistry in her class but many ways to be successful as a college student. I also learned what a caring and compassionate professor looked like. I will never forget this professor and my time with her. I hope that other professors create structured courses that help students learn complex concepts and provide them with personalized support to help them succeed.

## Encouraging Words and Suggested Actions, Karen Mae Ebel, Lorain County Community College

When I started my journey taking online courses, I was excited to learn new things. I was also pretty confident because orientation went fine, and I had previous experiences in higher education. I knew that I would be able to make it through despite the overwhelming responsibilities I had at work and in my personal life. Even though I started with a high level of confidence, I slowly began to worry about not doing well in my online courses. I was also worried about having to juggle several different responsibilities.

My perception of college changed from easy to difficult so fast that I was beginning to have anxiety that I had never experienced before. During my first few online class meetings, I tried to be present, but I felt cringing embarrassment because what I thought was going to be easy to handle was now getting too difficult for me to manage. Eventually, I emailed my professor to see if there was any way he could spare some time to help me understand the content before I decided to give up. I fully expected a cold response and being encouraged to withdraw, but thankfully, this is not what happened.

I informed my professor that I learned best in an in-person class with interaction and was missing that in this module-based learning environment. I also shared that visual and audio supports helped me learn. I was ready to hear something like, 'Karen, this is not for you; you better withdraw and consider other courses.' Instead, my professor gently said, 'Karen, I think you are too hard on yourself. It is too soon for you to give up, and I believe you can do this.'

It was the first time that I experienced a professor believing I was able to rise above my worries and difficulties. My professor started itemizing the ways in which I could improve, such as focusing on the specific modules that apply to upcoming quizzes, utilizing the study guide to do the step-by-step process of learning, listening carefully for key points that he emphasizes during classes, and taking advantage of incentives offered. Moreover, he offered to tutor me on topics that I struggled to comprehend.

Because of his positive encouragement, I was motivated to fight the good fight and use the strategies he suggested. Consequently, I am proud to say that I was able to finish the class. I hope that other professors can encourage their students by telling them they believe in them and giving them suggestions on what they can do to succeed in the course.

ಙಙಙಲಲಲ

The stories shared by Jaymala, Monica, and Karen illustrate the importance of professors being available to students for virtual office hours. They describe how these one-on-one opportunities to learn from their professors contributed to their success. As Karen explained, encouraging words provided by professors can motivate students to persevere even if they find the coursework challenging or overwhelming.

Although most one-on-one meetings will take place virtually in online courses, professors may also want to offer in-person meeting options when possible. Online students often appreciate the opportunity to meet their professors in person if they live locally or are in the area. In the next student story, Jennifer shares her appreciation for an online professor who made time to meet in person.

ಙಙಙಲಲಲ

### Making Time for an In-Person Meeting and Tour, Jennifer Malue Bartone, Marymount University

In my online course in program evaluation and decision-making, Professor Jessica Marotta helped me learn how to analyze and evaluate my dissertation interview questions. She made time for us outside of class and encouraged us to offer ideas, brainstorm possibilities, and ask questions during office hours. I recall her sending an email after one of our sessions thanking the students who were on the call for sharing their work and giving authentic and caring feedback in an online environment.

During our last office hours session, I mentioned to Professor Marotta that I would be visiting friends, including a student I met in this online program who lived in the area. Even though it was the end of the semester, which is a busy time for professors, she quickly offered to meet with us in person and offered to give us a tour of the campus.

When I saw all the professors' names on their doors, it was thrilling. I had completed five semesters of the program and had not had the chance to meet any of the professors in person before this visit. Professor Marotta was thrilled to see us! Her presence was welcoming and inviting. She introduced us to the professor who helped to create our Ed.D. program. We enjoyed sharing how we have grown as leaders and asked the administrative assistant to take a photo of us with Professor Marotta. I was excited to share this experience on LinkedIn.

One of the highlights of the tour was the opportunity to stand on the field where the graduation will take place next year. We also visited the bookstore and tried on graduation robes. I honestly started to cry tears of joy. This visit was exactly what I needed to finish my dissertation on schedule.

I felt a true sense of belonging when Professor Marotta ensured that I had a Marymount student ID. Seeing my photo on the ID badge made the whole doctoral experience real. All the work that I was doing in the upstairs bedroom of my house in Erie, Pennsylvania was through a university that truly cared about me as a person and truly wanted to see me succeed. If it is possible, I would highly recommend that students who are learning in a fully online setting visit campus at least once before graduation. I encourage professors who teach online students to offer students the opportunity to come to campus. Welcome them to campus with a tour and lunch like Professor Marotta did for us. I am a proud Marymount Ed.D. student, and I now feel ready to take on this final year of the doctoral program.

෴෴෴෴෴෴

As Jennifer described, it can be very motivational for online students to visit campus and meet their professors in person. For this reason, many online programs have in-person requirements in the form of orientation, summer institutes, or weekend classes. As professors consider ways for students to benefit from in-person experiences, they do need to keep equity in mind. It can be a financial and time burden for some students to come to campus, so it may be important to have departmental conversations about the pros and cons of required in-person meetings. Offering optional in-person meetings may privilege students who live near the university and can take advantage of these opportunities. In contrast, students who live in a different state may find this to be a financial and time burden and, therefore, may not be able to take advantage of this opportunity.

## ASSISTING STUDENTS STRUGGLING WITH PERSONAL AND FINANCIAL CHALLENGES

Students often face many challenges while pursuing their education. Students appreciate it when their professors show they care about their well-being as a person, not just as a student. Although students appreciate it when their professors help them understand course concepts and skills, they also find it engaging when professors ask how they are doing. Oakton Community College illustrated the power of individualized, professor–student meetings. Professors were invited to participate in the Persistence Project, which required them to meet with each student in their class for 15 minutes (Supiano, 2020). These meetings started with a simple question, 'How are you?' Supiano (2020) reported that the persistence rates were higher for students who had at least one professor who met with them individually (66%) than for the overall student population (51%). The persistence differences were even more noticeable between Black students who participated in one-on-one meetings with their professors (61%) and the overall Black student population (42%) at the community college (Supiano, 2020). Although it can be more challenging for professors teaching large numbers of students to connect with all of them individually, Griswold (2024) found that students in a large class responded positively to very brief, six-minute meetings with professors outside of class. To further maximize professor time, Griswold (2024) recommended that professors meet with small groups of students together.

Students in online classes sometimes face more challenges than students attending classes in person. One of the reasons that students may opt into online courses, particularly asynchronous courses, might be that their personal situation makes it challenging to attend classes on a consistent basis (Gay & Barth, 2024). Legay-Jones (2023) found that Black women indicated that they would not have been able to enroll in a traditional face-to-face graduate program because of numerous work and family responsibilities and noted that the flexibility of an online degree gave them access to advancing their education.

Students can face an array of challenges, such as dealing with psychological distress and disorders (Abrams, 2022; Cleveland Clinic, 2023), food and housing insecurities (Broton & Goldrick-Rab, 2018), health issues, and caring for family members. Research has shown that the need for mental health services for online students has increased in recent years (Gay & Barth, 2024). Online students can also face increased loneliness and lack of belonging (Gay & Barth, 2024).

Students appreciate it when their professors notice that they may need support and reach out to them (Guzzardo et al., 2021). Professors can often be the first to notice if students are struggling with issues such as mental health (Abrams, 2022). Because of their regular interactions with students, professors can often spot changes in behaviors and mood, which can be indicators of psychological distress or disorders. Sarraf (2021) suggested that although professors should not take on the role of counselor, they can be a part of the student's support system.

Although it can sometimes be more difficult to spot concerns in an online learning environment, there are several indicators a professor can look for. For example, students may miss synchronous classes, not hand in assignments, or submit assignments late. Students who are facing challenges may also be less engaged in asynchronous discussions or participate in different ways, perhaps even expressing more negative feelings. In the next two student stories, Persephonie and Brenda explain how much they appreciated it when their professors noticed they needed help and reached out.

### Reaching Out and Investing in Me, Persephonie Cole, Texas Tech University

Domestic abuse is quiet. It is insidious. It is held behind closed doors where victims are left to feel powerless. I found solace in my studies. When the blue light of my laptop illuminated my face, I felt like my own person again. College was the thing I had control over. I was a 4.0 student when, about halfway through a semester, the cracks began to show. I had finally decided to leave my spouse. I did so quietly, relocating to a new city and beginning divorce proceedings. It was the hardest thing I have ever done.

After missing a few assignment deadlines and two lectures, my professor emailed to check in on me. I was at the point where the work and lectures I had missed meant I was failing. I debated how forthcoming I wanted to be. I did not want my professor to think I was a quitter or irresponsible if I failed. Would I be pity-seeking if I told my story?

I decided on a bare-bones explanation: I had just left a domestic violence situation. I am safe. I am trying to get reoriented. I apologize for missing class and my assignments. I hope you will consider admitting me to future classes.

Miraculously, my professor wrote back within the hour. She expressed concern and empathy for my situation and said she wanted to help. Together, we came up with a new set of deadlines for my work, and she offered me one-on-one tutoring for any classes I may need to miss. She told me about the Title IX program and how it might help give me some grace during this period of upheaval in my other classes as well. She walked me through the process of submitting my case and wrote a letter on my behalf to accompany it. Truly, it was the most profound kindness I had experienced in my academic career (which had spanned nearly 4 years already as a part-time student).

I imagine it is difficult for professors who see so many students every semester to be actively involved in their education, but in moments like this, it can be truly life-changing. If my professor had not reached out to me, I would have failed that semester without saying a word to anyone. Perhaps I would have even dropped out of college altogether.

I sincerely encourage professors to notice when a student may be in need and to reach out. Most importantly, do not give up on your students. If you expand your knowledge not just to the subjects you teach but also to the resources at your university that are there to help your students, this can be incredibly helpful to students in need. This is my story, but there are so many students like me who face their own challenges. We are trying to enrich our lives through education.

As a domestic abuse survivor, there are many things I thought I might lose when I left my spouse. Thank you to all the professors that semester who showed me empathy and ensured I would not lose my education. I am grateful to professors who invest in their students. Many of the battles we fight are in silence. Engaging through empathy may save someone's life.

## Connecting Me to Resources, Brenda Santiago, Community College of Baltimore County

I am 38 years old. I work full-time as a medical assistant and have a family to care for. I have a husband with a demanding job and two children, one in daycare and one in middle school. They have different schedules and needs. Attending college is a turmoil of emotions and experiences, both positive and negative.

I had a very positive experience in Professor Azimi's Composition and Academic Literacy class, which was taught fully online. Professor Azimi did so many things that were helpful to me. She took the time to get to know her students, gave personalized and direct feedback on assignments, and made herself available. When a big project was assigned, Professor Azimi would request that we meet with her to discuss the project. She would share a document where we could sign up for a time, and she told us that we could meet more than once if needed. The meeting was not mandatory but highly encouraged, and you could earn extra credit if you attended.

During the semester, I was struggling, feeling lost and down. I missed our meeting and was falling behind on my assignments. Although I did not reach out for help, Professor Azimi noticed that my torch was burning out and shared her light. She emailed me asking if I was okay or needed help, such as tutoring. This email showed me that she cared. I was so overwhelmed by life. Aside from everyday life struggles, kids being sick, work, and finances, I was having postsurgical health issues, mental and physical. It was like they say, 'When it rains, it pours.' Unfortunately, my relatives are in different countries, and our friends are not very close by, so I do not have much of a support system.

She reminded me that there is fuel (resources) available to keep my torch bright enough to see my path again and keep going without getting lost in this dark tunnel. In addition to Professor Azimi offering me encouragement and support, she also connected me with a success navigator, a person who helps students access outside resources to help with their needs, even if they are nonacademic ones. Her light is what I needed to be able to see my path again and keep going.

As an adult learner, the type of support I need might be different. The encouragement, flexibility, patience, and access to additional resources were very helpful to me. I hope that other professors will remember that many of their adult learners wear a lot of different hats and would appreciate some kindness and support. Reaching out to see what type of help may be needed can mean a lot to students and may make the difference between them staying in school or dropping out. Without Professor Azimi's interventions, I probably would have dropped out of classes and may have even given up on my college dream, but now I am on the Dean's List and am pursuing my dream. Remember the impact you can make on students. Let your students know you care and help them connect to the resources they need so they can pursue their dreams.

ಬಿಬಿಬಿ ಲಲಲ

The stories by Persephonie and Brenda illustrate the importance of professors noticing when students are struggling and reaching out to offer support. Given the high number of students facing mental health challenges (Abrams, 2022), it is not surprising that most professors (80%) have reported having conversations with students about their stressors (EAB, 2021). In addition to mental health challenges, students may also struggle with physical health issues. In the following student stories, Madyson and Nicole share why their professor's support during a difficult time was so important to them.

༄༅༄༅༄༅

### Putting Well-Being First, Madyson Poole, Brescia University

My professor was very observant of his students' well-being. Professor Palmer, who taught my practicum courses, regularly reminded us to practice self-care. I remember that on one occasion, he expressed concern about me not making enough time for myself. My professor told me that he would be checking in on me each class and that if he became concerned, he would make the time to reach out to me about it. This conversation had a great effect on me as I was dealing with a lot of stress personally. It was clear that Professor Palmer wanted to ensure I was doing well and did not burn out before finishing school and even beginning my career.

Professor Palmer did not know what my stressors were but was there for me. At one point during this class, I had felt comfortable enough to confide in him and my peers that I had recently found out I miscarried, and due to further complications with that, I was going to be doing chemotherapy treatments. His reaction was one of support. He wanted to make sure I was taking care of myself during this stressful time. He acknowledged that I had been going through a lot and told me that overworking myself at my placement would not help at all. I appreciated the support that he and my classmates provided me.

Later, during my midterm evaluation for Field Practice II, he acknowledged the fact that I had slowed down on getting my practicum hours in and stated that he was very proud of me for doing so. These words were so validating; it was nice to have a professor who cared more about me than the practicum hours.

I recommend that professors remind their students that self-care is important. Create a safe space for them to share what is going on in their lives and encourage them to take care of themselves when faced with significant stresses in their lives. These words can mean a lot to a student.

༄༅༄༅༄༅

༄༅༄༅༄༅

### Supporting Me in a Time of Need, Nicole Manta, Nicolet College

I am currently earning my associate's degree in psychology. One of my professors has played an integral role in my success as a student. I was going to drop out of all my classes, but she encouraged me to stay in school.

This fall, I had to get unplanned gastric bypass surgery. I wanted to have it done in the summer, but I could not wait. I had to have surgery right in the middle of the semester. I am a high honors student and strive to go above and beyond. I worked ridiculously hard to stay ahead in my classes, but still, I had to miss class for about two weeks. When I came back, I was so far behind I wanted to drop out because I did not want my performance to impact my GPA negatively, but my professor kept telling me not to give up and that I could catch up and do well.

I am a pessimist. I just say, 'I can't,' or 'This is too hard.' But my professor was optimistic. Her optimistic attitude helped me get into a positive mental state. I have bipolar and depression, and the little voice in my head has played a significant role in my performance. She would not let me focus on the negative vibes and told me to stop them in their tracks. Her encouragement was refreshing and helped me out of a rut and back on a positive track. She would say, 'You've got this,' and 'Don't say can't because you can.' She would always then add, 'How can I help?' She broke the larger assignments into easier and smaller chunks so I would not get overwhelmed. Although classes are not officially over, I can confidently say that I will earn an A in all my classes.

Without my professor's encouragement and patience, I would have dropped out. Even though each student has different struggles and obstacles, I believe professors can be positive and encouraging. When students seem overwhelmed, professors can help them break down tasks into smaller, more manageable ones. Sometimes, students can get so overwhelmed by the big picture and get discouraged. Your encouraging words and help can make a difference. I am grateful that my professor encouraged me to stay in school because now I am still on track to achieve my goal.

☙☙☙❧❧❧

The stories by Madsyon and Nicole are a good reminder of how encouraging words and supportive actions by professors can have such a positive impact on students, especially when they are facing health or other challenges. When students share their struggles with professors and their response is one of care and concern, this can give them the motivation they need to be resilient and stay on track with their goals. In some cases, positive professor responses during these challenging times can be the reason students remain in school. Demetriou et al. (2024) found that microaffirmations from professors and small actions that convey care contributed to student persistence and success.

Finances are often another significant stressor for students. A recent survey indicated that approximately 75% of students reported experiencing financial challenges, and about half of these students indicated that it negatively impacted their academic performance (Mowreader, 2023). Professors can help students connect to resources and encourage them to apply for scholarships. Based on a meta-analysis of data from 86 studies, LaSota et al. (2022) reported that providing financial support in the form of grants was linked to positive outcomes, including increased persistence and graduation rates for students. In the following stories, Jeremy and Gretchen share how helpful it was for a professor to share information about a scholarship, as well as provide support in many other ways, such as serving as a source of inspiration when determining what path to travel and helping them build their network.

ಬಿಬಿಬಿಛಛಛ

### Helping Me Access a Scholarship and Plan for Success, Jeremy J. Walk, Paradise Valley Community College

My first course with Professor Stacy Moreno focused on social work systems. Early on, I was trying to find direction in my field of interest. I was applying for scholarships and trying to figure out the transfer pathways. I asked for an offline conversation, where I disclosed some details from my background and how these prior experiences informed my motivations for choosing social work as a major, most of which were rather heavy on the heart. Professor Moreno encouraged me to take a shot at a particular scholarship and helped me understand the road map to get to the university.

She acknowledged my raw talents and passion for learning. I suspect that Professor Moreno also supported me from behind the curtain, drawing attention to me from stakeholders who could support me in my goals. Professor Moreno has continued to uplift me by encouraging me to come out of my shell. She regularly shared events and activities that were what I might call outside my comfort zone and encouraged me to get involved. She also offered varying insights into social issues that are relevant to the field.

I am not a social creature by nature, and she knows this quite well. As a part-time online student, it is difficult for me to engage with the campus outside my work schedule, but she finds ways to get me involved anyway. Her resourcefulness never ceases to amaze, and she serves as an excellent role model for anybody under her tutelage. Professor Moreno wears so many hats; she is a parent and professor, works another job, is in a doctoral program, and who knows what else. Despite all these roles and responsibilities, she still took the time to get to know me, recognize my talent, and encourage me. I describe her as the Wizard of Oz; she is very much like that voice behind the curtain, guiding people down their own paths. For me, I did not know where I was and felt like my house had been lifted off and dropped into an alien realm.

Her leadership has inspired me to not only pursue graduate school, but now I am very seriously considering following the path to my own Emerald City, aiming toward a doctoral degree. I do not know what lies before me on the path, but I do know if I have a good pair of shoes and keep on the path, I will find my way home. Much of my college experience has been so surreal that it is beyond description. Doors keep opening for me that I never imagined possible, and I owe that pretty much to Professor Moreno and her colleagues. For the first time in my life, I am excited about my future. There are so many possibilities. I encourage other professors to be the voice of hope and inspiration for their students. Draw attention to their talents and encourage them to take advantage of opportunities that they would not likely do otherwise.

ಬಬಬಚಚಚ

ಬಬಬಚಚಚ

## Sharing Opportunities, Gretchen Thomas, Arkansas State University-Newport

Although my program is online, we have monthly on-campus meetings. Whenever I am on campus, I meet with Professor John Twyford, who is my advisor. He always welcomes me, and we chat about where I am in life and how my classes are going. He has been very helpful with getting my transfer credits accepted, shifting from a certificate to a degree program, and choosing courses that I need to graduate.

I also appreciate how much he has done to help me learn about and take advantage of different types of opportunities. He has agreed to be one of my professional references, helps me network, and lets me know about possible scholarships or work opportunities. He helped me get a work–study position in the library. Professor Twyford also forwarded job opportunities, such as a teller position at a local bank, to me.

Another example of him helping me was that he informed me of a $500 scholarship that I was eligible for. I applied for and won the scholarship, which was a great help with my tuition bill. He also recommended me for the first-ever honors seminar at the university and told me about this opportunity to share my story.

He also helped me to make connections. He told me about the Career and Transfer Services department and introduced me to the director, who helped me figure out my career interests. He also introduced me to academic leaders on campus who became a part of my network.

I am grateful for everything Professor Twyford has done for me. I recommend that other professors do as he did and listen to their students. Then, based on their needs, interests, and goals, they can forward their students information about different opportunities or connect them to individuals who can become a part of their network.

ಬಿಬಿಬಿ ೞೞೞ

## OFFERING CAREER MENTORING AND SUPPORTING THE DEVELOPMENT OF A PROFESSIONAL IDENTITY

Another key way professors can support their students is by offering career mentoring and support. Not surprisingly, students often reach out to their professors for career guidance (Flaherty, 2024). According to Martin et al. (2019), award-winning online professors 'viewed themselves as a mentor or a coach who not only taught a course but also advised students about their academic and professional development' (p. 192).

Although colleges and universities typically offer career counseling and other services that can help students determine career paths, students are often most interested in learning about career information from experts in the field (Flaherty, 2024). Students will usually feel more comfortable discussing career issues with someone they know and who has expertise in their field of interest. In the next two student stories, Stacey and Damaris share how much they appreciated it when a professor got to know them and helped them determine their career goals. Their professors also encouraged them to pursue opportunities that would help them succeed in their careers, such as attending and participating in conferences, and they found this to be engaging.

ಬಿಬಿಬಿ ೞೞೞ

### Inspiring Me to Trust My Instinct and Explore a Different Career Path, Stacey Fishler, Brooklyn College-CUNY

I love learning and was studying secondary education. I was already in the habit of letting my professors get to know me and vice versa. But for some reason, this course, which was co-taught by two professors, was a little different. I would get to class early to talk with one professor, spend part of our break talking to both, and sometimes stick around after class, despite it being past 9:00 p.m., to continue chatting. Before long, they really got to know me. They knew that I was an engaged learner but that something was nagging at me. They must have picked up on this before the semester was halfway through, though they did not tell me. Instead, they encouraged me to really pay attention to how I was feeling as the course went on. I was encouraged to trust my instinct and that it would guide me.

The relationships that I formed with these two professors made me feel supported, and somehow, I knew that whatever was to unfold, I did not have to figure it out on my own. It was not hard to see what my gut already knew – that I did not want to be a teacher. The idea of student teaching completely overwhelmed me. I was under the belief, though, that teaching was the quickest, if not only, way that I could break my way into the field. If anything, I at least had to get through student teaching.

Toward the very end of the semester, the two professors asked me to attend a meeting with them via Zoom. Of course, I was scared. What was this about? What were they going to say to me? What had I done? My mind raced. When we met, they recommended I not student teach. At first, my heart dropped. Now what was I going to do with my life? Where was I supposed to go from there? Despite my tears, I was relieved. I told them what I had been holding in for quite a while, that I knew teaching was not for me. In hindsight, having that out in the open was probably a relief for all of us!

What scared me was not knowing where to go from there. I had been in and out of school for over two decades. It took nearly all those years to find something I was interested in and passionate about, and I was so close to graduating. When I said this to them, the response I received shocked me. They made several career suggestions that aligned with my strengths and interests. They made great suggestions because they knew quite a bit about my background and interests. They shared career paths that I would never have considered if they did not suggest them. In fact, I did not even know much about most of the career ideas they shared. These two professors offered their continued support as I explored different paths forward, and I have taken them up on that offer. More than anything, by encouraging me to go inward, I learned to trust my instincts.

For professors who want to be there for their students in this way, I think it is important to encourage students to first engage in self-reflection. Consider what questions you can pose to students and how these questions may need to vary based on where the student is currently at. Students need to trust that their professors are providing them with a safe, judgment-free space. Professors can reassure their students that they are there for them and encourage them to reach out if something comes up that they would like to discuss. These actions will help students to trust their instincts and make good decisions.

ಬಾಬಾಬಾಂಞಂಞಂಞ

ಬಾಬಾಬಾಂಞಂಞಂಞ

## Personalized Mentoring Aligned with My Career Goals, Damaris Sargent, Morgan State University

Throughout my academic journey, I have been fortunate to receive support from many dedicated professors. During my studies, I was given opportunities that made a real difference in my success. These professors provided me with essential academic accommodations, such as extended time on exams and alternative assignment formats, which not only allowed me to perform at my best but also significantly boosted my confidence and capability. Their willingness to adapt and offer support in the classroom was a powerful catalyst in shaping my educational experience.

One experience really stands out to me. While pursuing my degree, I participated in the Pipelines 2 Possibilities (P2P) fellowship program, which connected me with invaluable mentorship and professional development opportunities. During this time, I had the privilege of working with a mentor who supported and engaged me.

My mentor guided me, supporting my academic and professional growth in a unique way. He encouraged me to align my personal passions with my research and academic work, making my studies feel more meaningful and relevant to my long-term goals. He often helped me see the connection between what I was learning and how it could make an impact in the world. This level of personalized engagement made all the difference, shaping my academic and professional journey in a profound way.

Our conversations went beyond academic advice. He supported me on a personal level. This relationship gave me the confidence to take on challenges I might have otherwise avoided. For example, he encouraged me to present at conferences and to take on leadership roles. These experiences helped me gain skills and connect with other professionals, which will help me as I pursue my career goals in education.

I am grateful for the support I received from many professors. Their care and guidance have been instrumental to my success. These experiences have taught me the importance of creating an inclusive and engaging environment for students, one where they feel heard, supported, and empowered to reach their full potential. I encourage other professors to listen to students, provide accommodations when needed, and build their confidence so they can also take on challenges that will help them as they pursue their career goals.

෩෩෩෬෬෬

The stories shared by Stacey and Damaris serve as a reminder about the importance of career mentorship. Stacey shared how much she appreciated being encouraged by a professor to engage in self-reflection and explore a different career path. Many students, like Stacey, may not be fully aware of all the possible career options, so it can be very helpful for professors to expand students' knowledge of career paths within a discipline. Damaris described how it was engaging to be heard, supported, and challenged to pursue opportunities such as conferences.

By encouraging students to participate in professional events such as conferences, professors can help students develop their professional identity. When students attend conferences, they can build and expand their professional network. Professors can introduce students to professionals working in their field of interest through e-introductions or face-to-face conversations at conferences or other professional events. In the following stories, Keyshawn and Jennifer explain how their professors helped them develop their professional identity. In both cases, their professors supported the development of their research skills and encouraged them to present at conferences. These activities helped Keyshawn and Jennifer see themselves as experts and recognize how they could add value to the field.

෩෩෩෬෬෬

### An Affirming Relationship with my Professor, Keyshawn Moncrieffe, Morgan State University

Going through the doctoral process teaches you the importance of building and maintaining positive, affirming relationships. I was fortunate to have developed a very supportive relationship with Professor Virginia Byrne. I initially met Professor Byrne virtually in the Spring of 2020 at the beginning of the COVID-19 pandemic. During this time, most universities were completely shut down, and all courses were held online. She invited me to work with her on various Emergency Remote Teaching (ERT) research projects. On one of the research projects, Professor Byrne served as my supervisor and coach, and she consistently encouraged me to present at local and national conferences. I gained new experiences by presenting research posters with the research team at national conferences in Baltimore and Chicago. Collectively, we were able to produce over five research manuscripts.

Professor Byrne also served as a member of my dissertation committee. She was a hands-on committee member who helped me structure the various elements of my dissertation. Throughout the process, she spent a lot of time reviewing my work and provided clear, detailed, and constructive feedback. Her attention and support were especially helpful to me because I was going through a stressful time in my life. Her feedback kept me on track. Professor Byrne remained attentive to my needs as a novice researcher during the entire dissertation writing process. Whenever I needed her, she always answered my emails and, frequently, was able to jump into a spontaneous video conference meeting if needed.

The positive and affirming relationship I developed with Professor Byrne was very important for a number of reasons. First, she helped me develop an identity as a researcher; she was a very strong supporter of my independent research projects. Second, she helped me become a better writer through her consistent and helpful feedback. Third, she encouraged me to pursue research and other scholarly opportunities. Since my first introduction to her, she has always shown genuine interest in my professional growth and development and has used her skills and talents to guide me.

As a recent doctoral graduate, Professor Byrne understood the importance of preparing her students to be ready for the next chapter. She maintained open and honest communication with her students, which helped build positive, affirming relationships with them. I personally benefited from Professor Byrne's introduction to experts in my field of interest who became a part of my network. Perhaps one of the most important ways Professor Byrne supported my success was by helping me navigate professional conferences. She prepared me well for the presentation and networking. She has had a profound impact on my confidence and ability to pursue research opportunities.

For professors who want to develop affirming relationships with their students, I suggest asking students about their career objectives and having discussions with them about steps they can take to achieve their goals. Provide tips and feedback on their writing and research skills to help them build confidence. Push students beyond their comfort zone and invite them to co-present at conferences or co-author publications so that they, too, can develop their professional and researcher identity.

ഇഇഇഌഌഌ

**One-on-One Zoom Meetings, Jennifer Malue Bartone, Marymount University**

Professor Anna Macedonia taught my research methods class, which was a part of Marymount University's Educational Leadership and Organizational Innovation online doctoral program. As a secondary mathematics teacher for the past 15 years, I came to this class with limited educational research experience. The goal of this research methods class was to choose our topic for our dissertation in practice and write a draft of our literature review.

In my first year of the program, I was experiencing feelings of imposter syndrome. I expressed these feelings to Professor Macedonia in an email during the first week of the semester, and she suggested we set up an individual Zoom meeting to discuss further. During the meeting, Professor Macedonia actively listened to my concerns and validated my feelings. She shared her own experiences during her doctoral program. We set up a schedule to meet every Friday for the remainder of the semester. I looked forward to these weekly meetings because Professor Macedonia helped me to feel heard, seen, and valued. She affirmed the importance of my research topic and continued to remind me of the value that my research will bring to the field of teacher education.

During one of our meetings, I shared that I reached out to my cohort members because I felt disconnected from them. I recall Professor Macedonia telling me that I was brave to do so. I never considered myself to be brave before, so this compliment was a major turning point for me regarding my confidence in the program. I stopped overanalyzing every assignment I posted and how others in the program perceived me. I felt a new sense of belonging in this doctoral program, and I continued to remind myself that my research was of value to the educational leadership community.

Professor Macedonia goes above and beyond to help her students succeed. When students expressed the need for more time to collaborate, she added extra office hours on Mondays for the remainder of the semester. At the end of the semester, Professor Macedonia invited me to a Zoom meeting with the next cohort who would be taking the course. I was excited to share advice, provide encouragement, and suggest they meet with Professor Macedonia for weekly one-on-one Zoom check-ins.

During our weekly Zoom meetings, she provided me with so much more than academic support. Professor Macedonia also helped me create a CV, submit proposals for national conferences, and even invited me to be a guest speaker in one of her other online classes. She made me feel like an expert in my field for the first time. Through her guidance, I am proud to say that I am presenting at the National Council of Supervisors of Mathematics and the National Council of Teachers of Mathematics annual conference. I hope that she knows how many students' lives she has positively affected through student engagement and collaboration.

I recommend that professors use one-on-one Zoom meetings to connect with students, especially those in an online program, proactively. The one-on-one meetings kept me motivated to finish my work on time and to be ready with questions to ask during the next meeting. It was motivating to have this time carved out just for me. I am sure that other students would also find these meetings helpful.

ഌഌഌളളള

Keyshawn and Jennifer shared that meetings with their professors gave them the confidence needed to pursue scholarly activities such as presenting at a conference and publishing. These outside-of-class opportunities to connect can make a huge difference for students in terms of engagement, persistence, and the development of their professional identity. For example, Emma, a first-generation student, shared, 'These out-of-class experiences where you get to meet and connect with people, with faculty, with projects, that's what really keeps you here.' (Hopkins et al., 2021, p. 50).

## ADVISING A CLUB

Professors can also engage with students outside of class in ways that are not directly related to the course. For instance, professors often advise clubs. Students benefit from meeting with their professors and other students with shared interests outside of class (Griswold, 2024).

Researchers have found that participating in campus activities has been associated with an increased sense of belonging and lower levels of anxiety and loneliness (Knifsend, 2020). First-generation students reported that out-of-class opportunities to engage with their professors and peers contributed to their persistence and success (Hopkins et al., 2021). In the next student stories, Leah and Nicholas explain how meeting with a professor virtually with other students fostered personal growth beyond the course. Interestingly, both their stories center on drawing activities.

## Zoom and Draw, Leah Josefowitz, Wesleyan University

During the COVID-19 pandemic, as traditional classrooms transitioned to Zoom, one of my professors, who taught College Success Seminar, a course recommended for students in their first semester, introduced an innovative and optional weekly activity called Zoom and Draw outside of class. This hour-long session provided a laid-back atmosphere where we brought our drawing materials and sketched while engaging in casual conversation. The sense of community and creativity fostered during these sessions was incredibly meaningful and helpful.

This initiative communicated to us that the professor cared about our well-being beyond just academics. In the midst of the uncertainties of lockdowns and social distancing, Zoom and Draw served as a bridge that connected us digitally while we were physically apart. It became a sanctuary where students could escape the monotony of lockdown life and find solace in creative expression. Personally, I looked forward all week to this hour of peace, artistic exploration, and communal bonding.

These sessions also facilitated personal growth and artistic development for me. While I had dabbled in drawing before, the consistent practice and supportive environment brought my drawing skills to new levels. I learned different drawing techniques from my professor and peers. What began as a simple activity soon evolved into a journey of discovering and polishing my creative skills.

Beyond the realm of art, Zoom and Draw significantly impacted my academic performance and overall well-being. The connection I forged with my professor outside of the classroom provided invaluable motivation and support throughout the semester. Unlike the typical virtual classroom experience, where students submit work online to a professor they do not really know, these art sessions established a personal connection and made a profound difference. This sense of familiarity and rapport created a feeling of accountability and a genuine desire to do my best academically. This connection fostered a deeper commitment to learning and academic achievement, extending far beyond the confines of the virtual classroom. Even after the semester concluded and I was no longer enrolled in the class, I continued attending the weekly Zoom and Draw sessions, highlighting the enduring impact of this initiative.

For professors interested in implementing similar activities for their students, I would recommend starting with a genuine intention to foster connection and creativity by incorporating nonacademic, creative elements where students can interact outside of the traditional class setting. Create a relaxed and inclusive environment where students feel comfortable expressing themselves. Consider encouraging participation, perhaps by offering extra credit for those who attend while ensuring that attendance remains optional to accommodate different preferences.

### An Unofficial Drawing Club, Nicholas Bashore, Brookdale Community College

COVID-19 drastically impacted my life as it did for many others. In addition to the stress that came along with the pandemic, I was also taking an online class for the first time. I was very concerned about my future until I met Professor Sabrina Mathues.

Professor Mathues knew this was a stressful time for all of us and went above and beyond by creating an unofficial art club where we could express concerns and create interesting works of art. Drawing and painting were a great way to escape the stresses of COVID-19 and having to take online courses. When we met in this unofficial club, we would watch tutorials and use techniques from YouTube. The casual nature and flexibility of the club made it an excellent place to share ideas. Everyone mostly worked independently on drawings or projects, but we did this while in the same space. This unofficial club was a great way for us to connect with peers during a difficult and confusing time. After meeting online for two years, we had an opportunity to meet in person. It felt refreshing to connect with peers who were not just boxes on a screen.

Professor Mathues shared some of her free time to do something she loved and engage with students outside of the classroom. Some of the best academic conversations I have had happened during these club meetings. There were only a few of us in this unofficial club, and this small number of participants helped us build meaningful connections. Professor Mathues and my peers gave me helpful career advice and guidance during these informal meetings.

Small clubs and organizations outside of class like these can really help students break out of their shells and connect with others. I encourage professors to create club opportunities for students related to what they enjoy. Students who share those interests will treasure this type of opportunity to connect with them and their peers. Participating in a club like this can really make a difference for students, providing them with a way to connect with others outside of class. For an hour a week, over Zoom, you can impact the lives of students who may need guidance or some assistance in meeting others.

ഔഔഔඣඣඣ

Although it can be more challenging for online students to be given opportunities to connect with others via campus events, colleges and universities have leveraged technology tools to enable online learner participation. Roddenberry (2017) found that students participating in campus events virtually through streaming found them to be just as engaging and valuable as students who attended the event in person. Professors teaching online courses are encouraged to find ways for students to connect with them in a variety of ways to support their growth and development. Professors can also inform students of opportunities to connect with other professors virtually through clubs or organizations to expand their network and support system further.

## FACULTY REFLECTION QUESTIONS

1. How can students reach out to me for guidance and support? How can I share this information in a welcoming and encouraging way?
2. How can I help students know what to expect from me in terms of communication and email response time?
3. How can I encourage students to schedule virtual meetings with me or drop by open office hours?
4. How can I determine which students may need additional support? In what ways can I reach out to students to express concern and care?
5. How can I learn about resources that are designed to help students struggling with personal or financial challenges? How can I connect students to on- and off-campus resources?
6. What adjustments can I make for students in need of grace?
7. What microaffirmations can I give to students to encourage and motivate them to persevere despite challenges?
8. How can I help students engage in career exploration and decision-making? How can I help students build and strengthen their professional network and identity?
9. How might I create an online club for students to connect with me and their peers online? How can I encourage students to connect with other professors who are advising clubs or organizations?

# REFERENCES

Abrams, Z. (2022, October 12). Student mental health is in crisis: Campuses are rethinking their approach. *Monitor on Psychology.* https://www.apa.org/monitor/2022/10/mental-health-campus-care

Addy, T. M., Dube, D., Mitchell, K. A., & SoRelle, M. E. (2023). *What inclusive instructors do: Principles and practices for excellence in college teaching.* Routledge.

Afzal, A., Rafiq, S., & Kanwal, A. (2023). The influence of teacher-student relationships on students' academic achievement at university level. *Gomal University Journal of Research, 39*(1), 55–69. https://doi.org/10.51380/gujr-39-01-06

Akram, H., & Li, S. (2024). Understanding the role of teacher-student relationships in students' online learning engagement: Mediating role of academic motivation. *Perceptual & Motor Skills, 131*(4), 1415–1438. https://doi.org/10.1177/00315125241248709

Barnett, E. A., & Cho, S. (2023). Caring campus: Faculty leadership in student success. *Community College Research Center.* https://ccrc.tc.columbia.edu/media/k2/attachments/caring-campus-faculty-leadership-student-success.pdf

Broton, K. M., & Goldrick-Rab, S. (2018). Going without: An exploration of food and housing insecurity among undergraduates. *Educational Researcher, 47*(2), 121–133. https://files.eric.ed.gov/fulltext/EJ1171368.pdf

Cleveland Clinic (2023, August 23). Tested: College students and mental health. *Cleveland clinic health essentials.* https://health.clevelandclinic.org/mental-health-in-college-students

Darby, F., & Lang, J. M. (2019*). Small teaching online: Applying learning science in online classes.* Jossey Bass.

Demetriou, C., McNulty, C., Powell, C., & DeVita, J. (2024). "Confidence to continue": A qualitative investigation of college student experiences of microaffirmations. *Journal of Postsecondary Student Success, 3*(2), 99–123. https://doi.org/10.33009/fsop_jpss132942

Dickinson, A. R., & Kreitmair, U. W. (2021). The importance of feeling cared for: Does a student's perception of how much a professor cares about student success relate to class performance? *Journal of Political Science Education, 17*(3), 356–370. https://doi.org/10.1080/15512169.2019.1659803

EAB. (2021, July 26). 3 ways to equip faculty to support student mental health. *EAB.* https://eab.com/resources/research-report/faculty-support-student-mental-health/

Felten, P., & Lambert, L. M. (2020). *Relationship-rich education: How human connections drive success in college.* Johns Hopkins University Press.

Flaherty, C. (2024). Students' biggest career influences. *Inside Higher Education.* https://www.insidehighered.com/news/student-success/life-after-college/2024/01/12/survey-college-students-talk-career-influences

Gay, G. H. E., & Betts, K. (2020). From discussion forums to emeetings: Integrating high touch strategies to increase student engagement, academic performance, and retention in large online courses. *Online Learning, 24*(1), 92–117. https://doi.org/10.24059/olj.v24i1.1984

Gay, K., & Barth, D. (2024). Customized care: Addressing the unique mental health needs of online students. *The Online Learning Consortium.* https://eric.ed.gov/?id=ED657311

Griswold, W. G. (2024). Experience report-Meet the Professor – A large-course intervention for increasing rapport. *Proceedings of the 55th ACM technical symposium on computer science education, 1,* 415–421. https://doi.org/10.1145/3626252.3630844

Guzzardo, M. T., Khosla, N., Adams, A. L., Bussmann, J. D., Engelman, A., Ingraham, N., Gamba, R., Jones-Bey, A., Moore, M. D., Toosi, N. R., & Taylor, S. (2021). "The ones that care make all the difference": Perspectives on student-faculty relationships. *Innovative Higher Education, 46*(1), 41–58. https://doi.org/10.1007/s10755-020-09522-w

Hopkins, S., Workman, J. L., & Truby, W. (2021). The out-of-classroom engagement experiences of first-generation college students that impact persistence. *Georgia Journal of College Student Affairs, 37*(1), 36–58. https://doi.org/10.20429/gcpa.2021.370103

Jaggars, S. S., & Xu, D. (2016). How do online course design features influence student performance? *Computers & Education, 95,* 270–284. https://doi.org/10.1016/j.compedu.2016.01.014

Kember, D., Trimble, A., & Fan, S. (2023). An investigation of the forms of support needed to promote the retention and success of online students. *American Journal of Distance Education, 37*(3), 169–184. https://doi.org/10.1080/08923647.2022.2061235

Kezar, A., & Maxey, D. (2014). Faculty matter: So why doesn't everyone think so? *Thought and Action,* 29–44. https://eric.ed.gov/?id=EJ1047910

Knifsend, C. A. (2020). Intensity of activity involvement and psychosocial well-being among students. *Active Learning in Higher Education, 21*(2), 116–127. https://doi.org/10.1177/1469787418760324

Lammers, W. J., & Gillaspy, J. A. (2013). Brief measure of student-instructor rapport predicts student success in online courses. *International Journal for the Scholarship of Teaching and Learning, 7*(2), 1–15. https://digitalcommons.georgiasouthern.edu/ij-sotl/vol7/iss2/16/

LaSota, R. R., Polanin, J. R., & Perna, L. W. (2022). Effects of postsecondary grant aid on college student outcomes: Briefing of results from a systematic review and meta-analysis. *Institute of Education Services.* https://eric.ed.gov/?id=ED618409

Legay-Jones, S. (2023). Evaluating how an Ed.D. Community College Leadership program supports women of color. (Order No. 30420259). Available from ProQuest Central; ProQuest Dissertations & Theses Global. (2803671285). https://eric.ed.gov/?q=and+mentoring+in&ff1=eduTwo+Year+Colleges&ff2=dtySince_2015&id=ED633386

Martin, F., & Bolliger, D. U. (2018). Engagement matters: Student perceptions on the importance of engagement strategies in the online learning environment. *Online Learning, 22*(1), 205–222. https://doi.org/10.24059/olj.v22i1.1092

Martin, F., Budhrani, K, Kumar, S., & Ritzhaupt, A. (2019). Award-winning faculty online teaching practices: Roles and competencies. *Online Learning, 23*(1), 184–205. https://doi.org/10.24059/olj.v22i1.1092

Mowreader, A. (2023, June 13). Financial wellness impacts student success indicators, survey finds. *Inside Higher Education.* https://www.insidehighered.com/news/student-success/health-wellness/2023/06/13/survey-financial-concerns-impact-academics-student

Quality Matters. (2023). *Specific review standards from the QM higher education rubric* (7th ed.). Author. https://qualitymatters.org/qa-resources/rubric-standards/higher-ed-rubric

Roddenberry, C. (2017). The value and challenges of using web conferencing technology to integrate online students into campus activities. *Journal of Educational Multimedia and Hypermedia, 26*(4), 413–424. https://www.learntechlib.org/primary/p/178512/.

Sarraf, K. S. (2021, October 24). Beyond gatekeepers. *Inside Higher Education.* https://www.insidehighered.com/views/2021/10/25/how-professors-can-support-students-mental-health-opinion

Shane-Simpson, C., Obeid, R., & Prescher, M. (2024). Multimedia characteristics, student relationships, and teaching behaviors predict perceptions of an inclusive classroom across course delivery format. *Teaching of Psychology, 51*(3), 298–308. https://doi.org/10.1177/00986283221117621

Snijders, I., Wijnia, L., Dekker, H. J. J., Rikers, R. M. J. P., & Loyens, S. M. M. (2022). What is in a student-faculty relationship? A template analysis of students' positive and negative critical incidents with faculty and staff in higher education. *European Journal of Psychology of Education, 37*(4), 1115–1139. https://doi.org/10.1007/s10212-021-00549-x

Supiano, R. (2020, February 6). To improve persistence, this college asks professors to have a 15-minute meeting with each student. *The Chronicle of Higher Education.* https://www.chronicle.com/newsletter/teaching/2020-02-06

Wilkie, L., & Rosendale, J. A. (2021). Undergraduates' email response expectations and instructor responsiveness: Traditional versus online courses. *Distance Learning, 18*(1), 37–50. https://eric.ed.gov/?id=EJ1307641

CHAPTER 3

# Teaching Strategies

One of the most obvious ways that professors can engage students is by using effective and innovative teaching strategies. Garrison et al. (2000) noted that teaching presence is essential to creating a community of inquiry in online learning environments. Online professors can use teaching strategies such as providing direct instruction and facilitating discussions in synchronous and asynchronous courses to create a teaching presence (Garrison et al., 2000). Students shared stories highlighting the importance of attending to their mental health and well-being, using inclusive practices, engaging them in collaborative learning experiences, utilizing technology tools, and ensuring that the teaching approach is varied and creative.

## ATTENDING TO MENTAL HEALTH AND WELL-BEING

Students are more likely to stay in school and be successful when their professors display acts of kindness that convey they care (Demetriou et al., 2024). Researchers have found that feeling cared for contributes to improved academic performance for students (Dickinson & Kreitmair, 2021). Darby and Lang (2019) noted the importance of conveying care to online students. Students taking an online course believed being 'emotionally supported played a key role in their experiencing a more meaningful connection to their online learning communities' (Scheepers & Van den Berg, 2022, p. 199).

Sato et al. (2024) emphasized the importance of supporting the well-being of students by encouraging them to engage in self-care practices and to set boundaries on screen time and online activities to avoid digital fatigue. Online students, many of whom are working full-time, may spend all day staring at a

DOI: 10.4324/9781003490012-4

computer for work and educational purposes. Professors can remind students about the importance of work–life–school balance and help them develop time management practices that build in breaks from screen time (Sato et al., 2024).

Professor support, affirmations, and acts of kindness can be particularly important in online courses. A student in a study conducted by Demetriou et al. (2024) noted that receiving positive messages from the professor can be encouraging for students, especially when they are facing challenges. Small actions can help students feel a sense of community in online learning environments (Darby & Lang, 2019). For example, starting class with a brief activity focused on student well-being can engage students. In the following three student stories, Adeoluwa, Adedoyin, and Patricia explain how mindfulness and well-being activities at the start of class conveyed that their professor cared about them. They also note how a brief activity centered on emotional well-being helps set the stage for a productive class because they are more focused after participating in this type of activity.

ಀಀಀಅಅಅ

### The Mindful Minutes, Adeoluwa O. Folami, Morgan State University

When I registered for an online research course, I expected it to be staid and perhaps a bit tiresome. I was determined to bear down and do my best because it was required for my program. My professor made the course enjoyable for all of us, and it all started with how she began our synchronous meetings. At the beginning of each class, my professor set aside time for us to mentally get ready for the class. My professor called this activity the mindful minutes.

The class was held between 4:30 p.m. and 7:30 p.m., when most of us would either be just getting home or be in transit on our way home from work. My professor recognized that we had many competing priorities and that transitioning to a class mindset could be challenging. She dedicated the first five minutes of each class to this activity.

My professor used the Headspace app (https://www.headspace.com/) to guide our session. We began by setting our cameras on or off, depending on our preference. Then, the app would guide us through the process of clearing our minds and attending to our breathing. We would be encouraged to take deep breaths, hold our breath for a few seconds, and then slowly release our breath several times over. The prompts for clearing our minds were usually the same, but the breathing exercises varied.

By the end of this activity, I noticed that my breathing stabilized, and I was ready for class. These sessions at the start of each class helped me release some of the tensions from whatever I had faced during the day and transition to become present in the class. I found that I was better

TEACHING STRATEGIES

focused and ready to learn after spending just a few minutes on this activity. I liked the transition process and the fact that my professor took time to enable the class to focus on self-care before starting the class.

Professors who are interested in including mindful minutes in their classes are encouraged to do so at the start of the semester and to use this approach at the beginning of each class. Many online tools can be used for this purpose. Although it might not be beneficial to everyone, students are likely to appreciate that you care about them enough to spend a few minutes of class time on this helpful activity. Your students will also be more likely to be fully present in the class discussions after participating in this brief activity.

ಬಬಬಲಲಲ

ಬಬಬಲಲಲ

## The 15-Minute Check-In, Adedoyin Soyele, Westfield State University

My professor, who was a clinical psychologist, made a point of starting every class with a 15-minute check-in. This course was taught in a hybrid format, with some meetings in person and some online. All classes were three hours in duration. During this check-in, she acknowledged the complex lives we had as graduate students, with most of us having full-time jobs. She would briefly talk to each one of us and would acknowledge our stressors. This class was held on Mondays, so she would ask us how our previous week had gone, what was stressful about last week, and what was particularly rewarding.

Applying psychological concepts that we would learn about later in this class, she would then go on to ask us how we could better cope with the emotional and psychological stress of graduate school. For instance, she asked us to identify at least one minor change that we could commit to making that would reduce our stress levels. By taking turns unburdening ourselves briefly, we were in a better psychological state for the day's lecture. Although I cannot speak for every other student, those few minutes of talking to someone else about my stress and committing to do something to alleviate my stress were helpful.

These 15 minutes of class became even more important to me as the semester progressed and the workload became heavier. Just talking for a few minutes, whether it was about the upcoming exams or having to juggle work, family, and school was helpful, but what was even more helpful was having these weekly reminders to engage in coping strategies. When I heard about others taking a walk or listening to music for

30 minutes on the weekend to relieve their stress, this helped me prioritize my mental health, too. By the time we were formally learning about the psychological concepts related to stress management in class, we had seen enough of the practical applications that it was easier to understand the content.

For other professors who might want to implement this strategy, I would suggest learning about ways to give space for students to share both stressors and action plans for coping with their stressors. You can reach out to psychology colleagues for ideas about how to do this. If your students are like me, they will find it easier to focus in class after unburdening some of their stress.

☙☙☙❧❧❧

☙☙☙❧❧❧

### Emotional Well-Being Checks, Patricia B. Ateboh-Briggs, Morgan State University

One of the strategies that Professor Grimes uses in her teaching is emotional well-being checks. She understands that students have different needs and challenges, and she tries to create a supportive and flexible learning environment for all of us. She checks our mood at the beginning of each class and addresses any concerns we share. For example, she may ask us how we are feeling, what we are looking forward to, or what we are struggling with. During these emotional well-being checks, she often shared tips and resources to help us deal with our challenges.

She is empathetic and accommodating to students who have genuine reasons for not meeting the deadlines or attending classes. She does not penalize them for late submissions or absences. Rather, she encourages them to communicate with her and seek help when needed.

Professor Grimes listens and supports students who are going through difficulties or need guidance. She is open and accessible to students and has an ever-ready attentive listening ear. She offers to meet with us during her office hours and has online chats with students who want to talk to her about their challenges. She clearly cares about our mental health and happiness and encourages us to engage in self-care practices such as gratitude, mindfulness, meditation, and exercise. She creates a culture of compassion and kindness in her classroom, where students feel valued and respected. Because of this caring culture that she created, we feel more comfortable and confident in our learning, and this helps us perform well.

Professors who want to use this strategy in their classes should first establish a rapport and trust with their students and then provide them with various supports and resources to cope with their challenges. They should also be aware of the signs of stress and distress among their students and refer them to appropriate services when needed. Professors should also model and practice self-care and well-being for themselves. By using emotional well-being checks, professors can create a supportive and flexible learning environment for their students.

## USING INCLUSIVE TEACHING PRACTICES

Inclusive teaching practices have numerous benefits, including increasing student engagement (Addy et al., 2023; Shane-Simpson et al., 2024). Inclusive professors create safe spaces, inviting students to reflect on their lived experiences and make connections between their experiences and the course content (Addy et al., 2023). In a study conducted by Thormann and Fidalgo (2014), a student in an online course shared, 'it is necessary that everyone feels safe, comfortable, and welcomed before they will fully engage, enabling them to make personal connections and grow from each other' (p. 379).

Moreu and Brauer (2022) discussed how inclusive teaching practices can be used to combat equity achievement gaps in college. One inclusive strategy that they shared was promoting multiculturalism 'by assigning texts from authors from diverse backgrounds, inviting guest speakers from different backgrounds, simply stating how valuable perspectives from members of different social groups are, or adding a multicultural diversity statement to their syllabi' (p. 172). In the following student story, Daylan shares an experience where a professor created a safe space and encouraged dialogues around research and race. This inclusive teaching approach engaged Daylan.

### Inclusive Pedagogy with Active Cultural Humility, Daylan Moore, Regent University

During the first research course in my online Ph.D. program (Qualitative Research), I was fortunate to have a professor who ignited student excitement through his teaching strategies. First, this professor made connections with us on a personal and professional level as he prepared us for research assignments. In class, he made the concepts in qualitative research more concrete and relatable by connecting them to our research interests. Outside of class, he invited us to send him research ideas, and he was readily available to meet offline or correspond via email. This professor treated us as competent scholars who could trust his collaborative assistance to advance our diverse research interests.

Notably, this professor also often introduced culturally relevant connections and expressed humility concerning research ethics. One example was when he led the class in a lecture on mistrust and unethical practices in research, exploring historical and current issues. He emphasized how racially and ethnically marginalized groups and other vulnerable populations have experienced harm during various studies and subsequent ways to remedy and mitigate those harms in the future. Also, he left space for us to discuss additional instances where marginalized groups have been disadvantaged in the research process. I recall him acknowledging that he learned from a student who shared how a research study in the medical sciences violated the rights of a racially and ethnically marginalized individual, noting that this should not be considered research. As a White professor teaching a predominately African-American doctoral class, it was apparent that this professor's inclusive teaching strategies were guided by cultural humility and curiosity. I found this to be a safe space and felt encouraged to ask questions in class and outside of class about race, clinical care, and research.

Based on my experiences in this class, I have some suggestions for professors. First, get to know your students and then use this information to share examples that will help students find a meaningful connection to the material. Professors can use live chats to learn about their students and share meaningful examples or can offer to meet formally or informally with students outside of class. The first few minutes at the start of a synchronous class session can also be used for this purpose, with students being invited to share personal stories or updates. Professors can also look for ways to practice cultural humility while engaging with students. Drawing upon diverse voices in a particular discipline while facilitating opportunities for students to learn from each other's perspectives can foster engagement, collaboration, psychological safety, and excitement in a course.

৪০৪০৪০০৪০৪০৪

Daylan provides excellent suggestions for professors who want to create safe spaces where students can discuss important issues such as race. Addy et al. (2023) emphasized the importance of students being able to learn about diverse perspectives on course topics. Discussions, especially ones where students are challenged to think about how potential biases may negatively impact others from historically marginalized communities, can be an excellent inclusive teaching strategy.

Goering et al. (2022) noted that another inclusive teaching practice is using course materials that reflect diverse perspectives. Prevatt et al. (2021) indicated that it is important for students to see themselves reflected in the curriculum and the field. They conducted a study where students were asked to find additional readings representing diverse perspectives. Students appreciated the opportunity to learn about the contributions of psychologists beyond those traditionally discussed in the textbooks (Prevatt et al., 2021). Annabelle, in the next student story, shares how it was engaging to read about and discuss feminist perspectives in a course on French literature. This story provides a great example of how intentionality around selecting course materials and designing learning experiences can engage students.

## Weaving Feminist Perspectives into a Course, Annabelle Hicks, University of Connecticut

In this course, I was deeply immersed in the exploration of how French literature and philosophy portray love, sexuality, and transformation, particularly through the lens of women's experiences. Led by a professor who encouraged critical reflection and creativity, this course delved into the powerful themes of metamorphosis – both personal and collective – within French literature.

This course provided space for thoughtful reflection on gender and power dynamics in romantic relationships. The dual focus on love and sexuality as transformative experiences invited me to question traditional portrayals of women in literature. While I was taking this course, I was also engaged in writing poetry centered around themes of women's experiences in French literature. This creative endeavor allowed me to engage with the course materials on both personal and intellectual levels, enriching my understanding of the narratives we studied. Writing poetry based on these themes offered me a space to explore the complexities of love, transformation, and identity, helping me to connect with the literature beyond the confines of academic analysis. In this context, my project became a continuation of a broader literary conversation about women's voices, agency, and transformation in French literature.

The professor's guidance provided an academic framework for engaging with feminist theories of love and transformation. At the same time, my poetry enriched this experience by allowing me to internalize and express these themes personally. Together, this intersection between creative and analytical work helped me cultivate a nuanced understanding of French feminist literature, as well as the ways in which literature and creative expression can work in tandem to foster a deeper comprehension of identity, gender, and cultural metamorphosis.

I appreciated how my professors encouraged us to engage in personal reflection, considering our interpretations of gender, power, and transformation. This professor fostered a learning environment that fostered intellectual curiosity and creativity. I drew connections between the characters' experiences and my personal exploration of similar themes, bridging academic study and personal application. We were all encouraged to be active participants to explore themes beyond the classroom. What we learned extended into personal interests and creative endeavors. By synthesizing these elements, the course fostered both academic and creative growth.

The professor made a conscious effort to weave feminist perspectives into the course, placing women's voices at the heart of discussions around love, power, and transformation. She encouraged us to look at the material from various angles and brought in perspectives that allowed each student to connect with the content in their own way. This inclusive environment made it clear that all interpretations were welcome and that our diverse backgrounds enriched the conversation. As a result, I felt more comfortable sharing my thoughts and was confident that my personal experiences and creative expressions were valued. I hope that other professors will also help their students examine issues from different lenses and theories and validate and challenge their students when they do. These actions can have a profound impact on how students think about and approach issues.

ಹಿಹಿಹಿಲಿಲಿಲಿ

Another way to bring diverse perspectives into courses is by inviting outside guests. Online courses more easily allow guests to participate in class because virtual meetings eliminate the need for travel and can require less of their time (Harrington et al., 2021). Inviting diverse guests can enrich the learning experience by exposing students to different viewpoints and perspectives on course topics. In addition to live conversations, recorded webinars and podcasts can also be used for this purpose. Goering et al. (2022), for example, reported using podcasts featuring diverse scientists, encouraging students to reach out to these professionals to network and ask questions.

As professors aim to create inclusive learning experiences for their students, they will want to consider frameworks that can guide their work. Universal Design for Learning is a framework for promoting inclusivity in learning, especially as it relates to students with disabilities. Courses designed using this framework create equitable learning paths for diverse students who learn differently (Rogers-Shaw et al., 2018). The guiding principles of this framework, 'multiple means of representation, multiple means of action and expression, and multiple means of engagement,' are particularly important in online courses (CAST, 2024, para 6).

Applying the Universal Design for Learning framework requires professors to select course materials that represent diverse perspectives and that are accessible in various formats. For example, professors may choose text-based work available in print and audio formats and may also include video options. Course documents, such as the syllabus and assignment information, are provided in easy-to-understand formats and have been checked and edited for accessibility.

Professors using the Universal Design for Learning framework would use various teaching and assessment strategies, often providing students with choice. Fleming (2023) found that 'multiple options made students feel welcomed, included, and less anxious in the class' (p. 81). Professors are encouraged to reach out to their colleagues working in instructional design and disability services to understand better how to ensure their online course is accessible and put the Universal Design for Learning principles into practice.

Cash et al. (2021) advocated for increased professional development opportunities around inclusive practices for professors. These researchers adapted the Teaching Strategies Inventory to create a new tool designed for distance education. They explored professor attitudes and actions related to inclusive teaching practices. Based on survey data, Cash et al. (2021) found a significant relationship between professor attitudes and actions, meaning that professors who had a positive attitude about being inclusive were more likely to use inclusive teaching practices. However, in a study by Donovan et al. (2021), when professors who believed they were using inclusive practices in their graduate courses engaged in self-reflection, they discovered there was room for improvement. Professors in this study noted a need to be more intentional around inclusive teaching practices and to strengthen their knowledge about issues of equity and inclusion. Increasing awareness of the importance of inclusive practices and how to use them can lead to wider and more systematic inclusive teaching practices.

## PRIORITIZING COLLABORATIVE LEARNING OPPORTUNITIES

Engaging students in collaborative and other active learning approaches is an evidence-based teaching practice that has been associated with positive student outcomes, including higher engagement and student achievement levels (Eynon

& Iuzzini, 2020). Online students especially appreciate opportunities to collaborate with their peers. They want to develop a sense of community and believe this helps them learn (Thormann & Fidalgo, 2014). Collaborative learning opportunities can foster a sense of community and belonging in the online learning environment (DiGiacomo et al., 2023). Professors will, therefore, want to prioritize collaborative learning opportunities in their online courses. Two excellent ways to promote collaboration are discussions and group projects (Darby & Lang, 2019).

Although discussions do not take place in real-time in asynchronous courses, they still provide an opportunity for students to share their thoughts and perspectives with their class and to also hear and learn from their peers. Kember et al. (2023) noted that professor–student relationships often develop through online discussions. In a study by James et al. (2022), many students indicated an appreciation for asynchronous discussion boards. One student noted the discussion board 'gives students a way of interaction on a given topic without having to gather together in the same place and time' (James et al., 2022, p. 8).

In addition to helping students connect, discussions provide students with opportunities to connect course content to broader, real-world contexts (Howard, 2023). Discussions can promote engagement and learning; this was illustrated in a study conducted by Nestor et al. (2024). These researchers reported that when discussion questions were posed at the end of a recorded lecture, student engagement and comprehension increased (Nestor et al., 2024).

A unique feature of asynchronous online discussions is that the work product of peers is visible, so students will get to read about their classmates' perceived connections between course material and applications in the world. Students have reported appreciating hearing the perspectives of their classmates through discussion boards (Sandjdge & Schultz, 2024). Students learn from reading what their classmates post, not just from the readings or other course materials (Aloni & Harrington, 2018).

In the following student stories, Steven and Richard share examples of how online discussions increased their engagement. Steven discusses the critical role of peers in the learning process and shares how online discussions promote more critical thinking skills. Richard provides an example of how a social media platform was used to increase engagement during asynchronous discussions.

ಬಿಬಿಬಿಜಜಜ

### Online Discussions, Steven Revelian, St. Louis University

Hailing from Tanzania and upon embarking on my Ph.D. studies in the United States, I was pleasantly surprised by the innovative teaching methodologies employed by my professors. The emphasis on active student participation and engagement played a pivotal role in fostering a dynamic learning environment for me and my classmates. One such effective teaching strategy that stood out was the implementation of online discussions.

In this approach, my professor posed thought-provoking questions for us to discuss after delving into assigned readings. The beauty of this participatory strategy lies in its ability to encourage students to immerse themselves in the chapter content, leading to the formulation of insightful observations and a deeper understanding of the material. What makes this strategy particularly impactful is its potential to transcend the confines of the assigned chapter, allowing students to explore and discuss broader aspects of the topic. Discussions not only enrich the learning experience but also facilitate the exchange of diverse perspectives among students from various backgrounds.

The professor employed a pedagogical approach aimed at fostering students' reading and comprehension skills. In this method, students were tasked with perusing assigned chapters prior to class discussions. Subsequently, the professor assessed and assigned grades based on the quality of discourse and students' capacity for engagement.

This instructional strategy proves beneficial as it cultivates a habit of regular reading among students. Moreover, the requirement for students to familiarize themselves with the content before class alleviates the need for extensive lecturing by the professor. The approach transcends conventional teaching methodologies by promoting creativity and independent learning, steering clear of rote memorization and cramming.

The efficiency of this strategy lies in its collaborative nature, wherein students learn from one another. Importantly, it fosters an environment that encourages diversity, contributing to a richer learning experience. In my recent research topics course, the professor implemented this reading and discussion technique. By the semester's end, I had successfully covered all the assigned books. This method serves as a motivational tool, inspiring students to explore a multitude of books in manageable sections.

A pivotal aspect of this strategy is that it hinges on students using their own language during discussions, discouraging the use of copy-pasting. Additionally, all discussions must be substantiated with references from the assigned readings. The inclusion of citations, complete with page numbers, mandates students to delve into the chapters thoroughly, ensuring informed and contextually rich participation in discussions. Ultimately, the strategy not only facilitates comprehensive learning but also ensures that each student completes the required readings, promoting a deeper understanding of the subject matter.

ಬಬಬಞಞಞ

ಬಬಬಞಞಞ

**Yellowdig, Richard A. Hilpert, Florida State University**

It can be difficult to engage students in online classes because there are many distractions, and they are often not under your control as a professor. Yet, one of my professors managed to do a great job of engaging us in an online course. To begin with, this professor had very clear guidelines and regular homework assignments that were due every single Sunday of the semester without fail. I found this weekly structure for the course helpful.

For one of the weekly assignments, we had to use Yellowdig, a social media software. To go into a little more detail, Yellowdig has the same sort of setup as any social media platform, with the most recent and most popular post being shown at the top of your newsfeed. Posts acquire popularity (and thus publicity) via the number of comments and likes or reactions received. This meant that students were rewarded for writing content that engaged and informed others. The professor gave rewards for outstanding posts, and rewards were also given for student comments and reactions. This type of online platform was much more engaging than a traditional online discussion.

In our class, we had to acquire a certain number of points each week using Yellowdig to receive full participation credit. At the beginning of the semester, our professor informed us that the goal of our posts was to connect our personal observations and life experiences with the course content covered during the week. For example, when we were learning about herd mentalities, I connected this content to a current real-life example of the university's football team.

We could also earn some points by receiving comments. Thus, well-thought-out or interesting posts were incentivized in this environment and kept both the author and the commenters engaged. I enjoyed reading the posts of my peers as their insights really helped me solidify my understanding of the course topics. I found it engaging to interact with others who had different perspectives. These Yellowdig activities helped me stay engaged, gain a thorough understanding of our course's content, and connect with some of my classmates.

My advice for professors would be to find creative ways to have us, as students, work together to see the relevance and value of what we are learning. Furthermore, I would urge professors to create a consistent structure (pick one way for students to interact and gain a deeper understanding of the topic and stick to it) so students clearly understand what is expected of them and can focus their energy on learning the content rather than having to figure out new expectations with different assignments. On top of that, I would recommend implementing both content monitoring (to ensure discussions do not stray too far from related topics) and rewards for especially engaging conversations. Periodically join in the conversation so we see that our efforts are noticed and appreciated. It can also be helpful to provide guidance on how we should engage with each other. For example, my professor encouraged us to leave at least one thoughtful comment on one of our classmates' posts, explaining why we did or did not agree with their observations and how reading their posts helped us learn. While it is best to let these discussions take place organically, giving examples of how healthy and informative interactions can take place can be extremely helpful to your students.

ಙಙಙఔఔఔ

As Steven and Richard shared, the structure of the conversation is important. Professors play an important role in designing, structuring, and facilitating discussions. Thormann and Fidalgo (2014) found that students wanted their professors to ask thought-provoking questions and engage in online conversations, adding their expertise.

Based on a review of the literature, Foo and Quek (2019) identified three primary ways professors can illustrate teaching presence and facilitate critical thinking through online discussions.

1. **Design**. First, professors need to design discussions that set the stage for high-level thinking. Research has shown that scenario-based discussions such as debates and role plays have fostered critical thinking (Foo & Quek, 2019).
2. **Scaffolding**. Second, critical thinking was more likely when professors provided support (Foo & Quek, 2019). Types of support included providing the purpose and guidelines for the conversation, asking Socratic questions, and sharing grading rubrics. Professors are encouraged to communicate the purpose and expectations of the discussion and to set a structure for it (Aloni & Harrington, 2018). Rather than asking students to engage with two peers, professors can provide guidelines on how to do this in a way that elevates the conversation and strengthens critical thinking and writing skills. As an example, students could be first asked to respond to the initial prompt

by Wednesday. Then, students could be asked to read the contributions made by their peers and ask at least two Socratic questions designed to encourage peers to think more deeply about the content by Friday. Professors could provide examples of Socratic questions as a model. Aloni and Harrington (2018) provided a list of examples such as 'What do you mean by...?, What are the assumptions behind these statements? How are X and Y similar? and What would someone who disagrees say?' (p. 284). For the final contribution, which could be due on Sunday, students could answer questions posed by their peers.

3. **Expert Contributions.** Finally, Foo and Quek (2019) found that critical thinking was developed when the professor shared their expertise in the discussion. The amount and nature of professor involvement may vary depending on the nature and level of the course. Professors may want to be more involved in online discussions with undergraduate students who are new to online learning or the discipline to ensure student contributions are accurate and to offer corrective instruction if needed. On the other hand, professors may want to be more of an observer in discussions with graduate students or students with a strong background in the topic. Based on a research review, Aloni and Harrington (2018) suggested a moderate amount of involvement to foster teacher presence. They cautioned against over or under-involvement as some studies found that this can reduce student engagement in the conversations (Aloni & Harrington, 2018).

Some students may be less comfortable participating in online discussions. Providing clear guidance about expectations can be helpful. For example, professors may want to assign students different roles. Assigning roles such as questioner or synthesizer can contribute to increased and more thoughtful student–student interactions (Truhlar et al., 2018). Another option could be to offer anonymous participation options. Students may be more comfortable participating in online conversations when they know their responses are anonymous. Providing students with an anonymous option, Fleming (2023) found that

> the anonymous format of the online discussion responses allowed for all students – regardless of confidence, anxiety, English language proficiency, or personality type – to participate fully and equitably in class discussion. Additionally, more students felt comfortable speaking out loud in class as a result of positive feedback to their anonymous posts online.
>
> (p. 84)

The traditional asynchronous discussion is text-based, with students typically writing responses to questions posed and interacting with peers through additional written posts. Findings from a recent study indicated that only 36% of students agreed or strongly agreed that traditional online discussions that required them to post a response and interact with two peers helped them connect with their classmates (Sandidge & Schultz, 2024). Adding more interactive elements and creative structures to discussions may be needed to engage students and help them learn the course content.

Videos are one way to make discussions more interactive and personal. Bickle and Rucker (2018) found that using a technology tool that allowed students to record videos and content predicted their sense of community and ability to learn the content. Clark et al. (2015) found that students who were randomly assigned to a discussion where videos were incorporated reported significantly higher social and teacher presence than students assigned to a text-based discussion. One student commented, 'I preferred it [video] because you can hear somebody's voice…After you do a few Hangouts…you get a lot better feel for them…You know them a lot better than you do just by reading some text. There's no emotion in text' (p. 12).

Several researchers have suggested engaging students with innovative and creative asynchronous collaborative learning activities (Dailey-Hebert, 2018; Kerrigan & Aghekyan, 2022; Nestor et al., 2024). For example, professors could use an online debate or role-playing approach to asynchronous discussions where students would be required to convey their ideas not only through words but also through videos and graphics (Kerrigan & Aghekyan, 2022). Another suggestion was to use discussion boards for peer-review activities and group work (Dailey-Hebert, 2018). Lin et al. (2024) found that incorporating the use of ChatGPT into online discussions positively influenced student participation, engagement, and sense of community and also helped students develop essential critical thinking skills. In this study, students were required to ask ChatGPT questions related to the discussion and share the outputs along with their critical analysis of what Chat GPT produced.

Although widely used, the discussion board is not the only way for students to benefit from working together in an asynchronous environment. Morse (2021), for instance, compared the discussion behaviors of online graduate students using either traditional discussion threads or a Google Doc. Students in the Google Doc group made significantly more contributions to the discussion than those in the traditional online discussion thread group. Specifically, the average number of posts per student across the discussions in the course was 14.45 for the Google Doc group and 8.62 for the online threaded discussion group. In the online discussion thread group, the average number of views of posts made by classmates ranged from 1.75 to 4.08, while the total possible posts that could have been viewed ranged from 13 to 56. Morse (2021) noted that having all the posts in one document may have led to students reading other students' comments more.

In synchronous courses, professors can ask students to participate in live discussions using video conferencing tools. Synchronous discussions, as opposed to asynchronous discussions, more closely mirror the experience of a traditional in-person classroom. Online students appreciate the opportunity to have live class sessions to engage with their peers and ask their professors questions. Milovic and Dingus (2021) found that students had a strong preference for synchronous conversations over text-based asynchronous discussions. In the following student story, Madyson shares an example of how discussions via Zoom were used in engaging ways. Madyson emphasizes the importance of students being able to direct the conversation and how students can engage in collaborative problem-solving during Zoom sessions.

### Student-Directed Conversations, Madyson Poole, Brescia University

Many courses are very structured. One of my courses, field practicum, was a bit different. Professor Palmer allowed us to direct the class conversations via Zoom. In each class, he gave us all the time we needed to voice our concerns and raise any issues related to our practicum placements. He then wanted us to work through the challenges together.

Although he always had an agenda for class, he approached teaching in a flexible way, allowing us to steer the conversation in a way that we saw fit based on our practicum experience. Every class started with an opportunity to bring up issues related to our practicum experience. Being able to focus on issues related to our practicum made the class conversations engaging for all of us. I absolutely loved participating in his classes even though I was typically the quiet student who only listened. He opened up each class by asking if there were issues or challenges we would like to discuss about our placements. This opening enabled us to direct our learning.

Ultimately, someone would describe a situation that they experienced, and the conversation would go from there. The conversation took up the entire class period. The topics we talked about often related to what was on the draft agenda, but it did not feel as structured as any other class I have been in. These conversations were so meaningful and interesting. The discussions also helped us know what to do in our placements.

Instead of giving answers to the questions or challenges identified, he encouraged us to problem-solve. In situations where everyone seemed to get stumped or did not know what to say, he would ask us questions, rephrasing them if needed to help us continue the conversation and come up with solutions to the problems encountered by our classmates.

He was not the type of professor who would skip over things if we did not understand something. If we were not sure what to do in a particular scenario relating to our practicums, we would work together as a group to figure out the best action or resolution. Professor Palmer encouraged us as we shared ideas and challenged us when needed, making us think even more critically. I felt comfortable participating in this class because he made it clear my ideas were valued.

I encourage other professors to use this approach and let their students direct the conversations so that they are discussing what is meaningful to them. Do what my professor did and push your students to determine solutions instead of providing them with the answers. This will help them gain confidence and will keep them engaged. When they share their ideas, show them that they are making valuable contributions so they keep participating and learning.

In synchronous classes, live discussions can either take place with the whole class present or in small groups. DiGiacomo et al. (2023) found that students liked having opportunities for small group discussions via breakout rooms. In a study conducted by Read et al. (2022), one student stated, 'It is a safe space, without the professor and with less people than a normal classroom, so it's easier for students to engage' (p. 7). In the following student stories, Ashley and Lori share examples of how breakout room discussions via Zoom were used in engaging ways. Ashley describes how breakout rooms were used to develop critical thinking skills through case studies. Lori explains how a student can discover they are not the only ones who are confused or struggling when they get to connect with classmates during a class breakout room session.

### Virtual Verdicts: Mock Trial of Supreme Court Case Arguments via Zoom, Ashley Jaramillo, Rutgers University

Taking the Law and Public Policy course at Rutgers Camden was a memorable experience that I feel has prepared me well beyond the scope of the classroom. I enrolled during my first year of graduate school, amid the upheavals of the COVID-19 pandemic, I found myself stepping into an entirely new academic territory of online learning. I was apprehensive at the start, being new to both the field of law and the challenges of remote learning, but the experience proved to be exceptionally rewarding.

My initial concerns stemmed from the fact that I had never studied law before. The idea of tackling complex legal concepts and Supreme Court cases from behind a Zoom screen was daunting. However, the professor's expertise and teaching style quickly alleviated these worries. The class was structured to maximize engagement and facilitate learning, even in the virtual environment. One of the key elements that made the course enjoyable was the professor's approach to the readings.

The curriculum was a blend of books and scholarly articles, with the articles provided digitally. Each session began with a thoughtful discussion of the assigned readings, which lasted about 15 minutes. This segment was crucial for setting the stage for deeper dives into the material and addressing any questions or ambiguities. The professor's adept facilitation ensured that these discussions were as dynamic and interactive as one would expect in a physical classroom setting. The opportunity to share and debate ideas with classmates helped solidify my understanding of the material and made the Zoom format feel more engaging.

The course revolved around the analysis of high-profile Supreme Court cases. We examined these cases from a historical perspective and through the lens of applied theory and decision-making models. This analytical approach was designed to help us understand the complexities of legal decision-making processes and how theoretical frameworks are applied in real-life scenarios.

One of the most valuable aspects of the course was the interactive component that involved group activities. In these sessions, we were divided into small groups of 2–3 people and were given 6–7 minutes to argue either in support of or against various cases. This exercise was instrumental in applying what we had learned from the readings and discussions to practical situations. It required us to think critically, engage in structured arguments, and consider multiple perspectives, which are skills that are essential for effective policy analysis. The professor's ability to foster an environment where these group exercises were seamlessly integrated into the curriculum played a significant role in my learning experience. The discussions and debates that followed these exercises often led to deeper insights and a more nuanced understanding of the material. It also helped bridge the gap between theoretical knowledge and practical application, making the course highly relevant to real-world policy issues.

Moreover, the course also emphasized the importance of open discussion in the process of policy writing. Understanding how to write effective policy analyses was a significant learning outcome. The discussions about Supreme Court cases and the application of various decision-making models equipped us with the tools needed for crafting well-informed policy memos. This aspect of the course was particularly valuable as it provided practical skills directly applicable to my current professional settings as a legislative analyst. The dynamic nature of online learning offers a deeply engaging and interactive environment when done in a way that blends structured academic rigor with innovative, participatory elements.

My advice to professors is to ensure that reading materials and discussions are thorough and designed to spark debate and critical thinking. This is key for keeping dialogue flowing. Utilizing breakout rooms for small group discussions and creativity through mock trials encourages students to argue various positions, which can bring theoretical concepts to life. By facilitating an atmosphere where students are actively involved and encouraged to voice differing viewpoints, professors create a richer learning experience that transcends the limitations of the virtual format. This approach not only enhances comprehension but also gives students the practical skills that are crucial for their future careers. These strategies make the online classroom a vibrant and effective space for legal education.

## Breakout Rooms and Receiving Feedback, Lori Jean Bushey, Rockhurst University

The use of breakout rooms in virtual learning environments has been an important learning experience in my four-plus years as an online student. The first minute or two of a breakout room often consists of students discussing what they do or do not understand about the content or task. The first few times I participated in breakout rooms, I was concerned that discussing how we were feeling about the class and content was too off-topic. After experiencing this strategy many times, I feel strongly that this small group time is important and helps us connect with each other. When this happens, students often empathize with one another. In my experience, this frequently leads to students discussing the common experiences or needs of the breakout group members.

In an online setting, it is easy to feel as though you are the only student who does not understand the content. It also may be daunting to unmute and interrupt the teacher during class, and group chats may not be consistently checked throughout the lesson. It is so helpful to have this time to unpack and analyze the learning process in a smaller setting. Through these conversations, I also became empowered to ask the professor questions.

I want to share one particular experience that highlights the importance of breakout rooms. I was in a master's degree program that, because of COVID-19, had gone from hybrid to completely online. Unfortunately, but not unsurprisingly, the curriculum was not seamlessly translating to an online format, despite our professor's best efforts. I was very confused about basic weekly expectations and how to complete assignments. During our virtual class, I mistook everyone else's silence for understanding. I figured I would look at the new syllabus again after class before emailing the teacher for clarification. Later, during the class, we started using breakout rooms. To my surprise, everyone else in my breakout room felt just as lost as I did. One student felt very frustrated with the perceived lack of organization and communication from the professor and was very vocal with their criticism. During this rant, I realized that the professor had dropped into our breakout room and was hearing all the criticism that, while valid, was not being delivered in a constructive way. The professor received the comments with grace, apologizing to the students who felt strongly and thanking them for sharing their feedback. Within a few days, the course was reorganized, and the professor walked us through the expectations for upcoming assignments. It was a very awkward yet productive moment that I will not forget. I appreciated how receptive the professor was to the feedback and how quickly changes and clarifications were made.

For professors who want to use breakout rooms, I suggest that they allow for some unstructured time so students can get to know each other and discover shared challenges. I also recommend giving students guidance about what is expected. It is important for professors to let students know if they will be popping into the breakout rooms and give clear instructions on the task and the amount of time students will have to complete the task. Give students ample time to discuss their learning processes as well as any assigned learning task. It can be helpful to write down the expectations or tasks so that students can refer back if confused. For accountability, students could be told before the breakout room begins that the class will be discussing what was shared afterward. Tell students how they will need to report back to the whole class on their discussion. Finally, I recommend that professors seek out student feedback about their learning experience and make adjustments as needed.

৪০৪০৪০ে৪ে৪ে৪

These student stories illustrate the importance of live conversations in online classes. Ashley and Lori discussed how live small group discussions engaged them. Ashley emphasized the importance of reading assignments that can spark critical thinking in the small group discussions taking place virtually. As Lori shared, students find it helpful when professors provide clear communications about what is expected of them during the breakout room discussions.

Douglas (2023) found that professors and students had different perceptions about how clearly the expectations for breakout room tasks were communicated, with students indicating they needed more clarity. Because professors may think they are being clear, they may want to seek student feedback to find out if they found the directions clear or confusing. Ensuring students know the purpose and task of the breakout room can help students move into productive dialogue more quickly. In addition to providing clear directions around the breakout room task, Douglas (2023) recommended that professors inform students how to access help if they need further clarification on the task when they are in the breakout room.

In the next student story, RJ shares an innovative structure for live synchronous class meetings. The professor used the fishbowl technique, where students had different roles and responsibilities during the synchronous conversation. Han and Hamilton (2023) noted that although the fishbowl technique was designed for in-person classrooms, it was easily adapted to the online learning environment and supported student learning. The fishbowl technique involves assigning students to an inner or outer circle role. Students in the inner circle engage in a discussion, while those in the outer circle listen and observe the discussion. After the discussion, students debrief, with those in the outer circle sharing their observations and reflections. RJ shares why the fishbowl teaching approach was so engaging.

෭෭෭෮෮෮

### Fishbowl Technique, RJ Portella, Rutgers University

Class time over Zoom can be clunky at times, and student disengagement can easily occur. I had a great online learning experience in many classes, but one stood out to me. In this class, my professor used the Fishbowl Teaching method, and I thought it was particularly effective. The fishbowl technique works well for medium-to-large group instruction.

Here's how it works. First, the professor poses a topic for discussion and then splits the class in half. One-half of the class becomes the inner circle. Students in the inner circle will engage in a verbal discussion. Students were asked to use the raise hand feature in Zoom to speak next. Students were expected to engage in a scholarly discussion about the topic. Meanwhile, the outer circle stays muted, listening to the conversation. Students in the outer circle are expected to summarize what they heard from the inner circle members by using the chat feature. At the end of that first round, the professor then offered comments on the discussion. Then, the professor switched groups and posed another topic. The students now had the opposite roles. At the end of class, the students could save the chat so that they had multiple perspectives to draw from when completing assignments for the class.

There were about 30 students in this graduate course and lots of content to cover. Using this technique, everyone had their part to play in the class discussion, and we all knew what we had to do and when to do it. I never felt like I did not understand what was expected of me. Sometimes, just a few students can dominate a discussion, but we were all active listeners and participants in this fishbowl activity.

From conversations with classmates offline, we often found the topics we discussed were sensitive and difficult for us. These topics ranged from racial identities to gender constructs to socioeconomic class divisions. As someone who had not had a class that dealt with such sensitive issues before, I was apprehensive of how it would go. My professor did a superb job of including us all, giving us consistent notice of what was to come, and engaging us with respect and dignity.

For professors who think the Fishbowl Teaching method would be a good idea, I believe it is imperative to introduce the technique to the students first. Clear expectations helped make the class sessions run smoothly. Make sure that the students know who is in each group via email or through the class's online platform announcements. Also, the topics for discussion should be introduced, and students should be directed to literature or readings from class that they can use to familiarize themselves with the topic. This way, they will feel ready and prepared to participate. On a final note, please do what our professor did – alert us with trigger warnings about sensitive content so that we can brace ourselves and come to class ready to engage in important discussions on equity and equitable practices.

༄༅༄༅༄༅

Dedicating part of synchronous class time for student group work can also be useful. In the following story, Krista shares how a professor incorporated consistent group meeting time into Zoom classes. Krista also explains the importance of having a consistent group and sharing the rationale for group assignments.

༄༅༄༅༄༅

### Peer Debriefing Groups, Krista Quinn, Manhattanville University

In my fieldwork research remote synchronous online class, the professor put us into small groups called peer debriefing groups. The peer debriefing activity in this class involved getting peer feedback on the aspects of our dissertation. The professor grouped us based on our dissertation progress. She clearly explained this to us so that we understood why we were placed with others. I was in a group with three other students. We served as informed analysis partners. In this role, we listened to challenges encountered, talked through possible solutions, and provided valuable feedback to one another.

We stayed with our peer debriefing group for the whole semester. What I really appreciated was that the professor built in-class time for us to meet with our group each week, dedicating at least 20 minutes out of the 1 hour and a half class for this collaborative work. Finding time to connect with group members outside of class can be challenging, so this was really helpful. Having the professor available to answer questions while we engaged in the activity was also beneficial. The professor would drop into each group's breakout room to check on us and offer guidance or answer any questions we had about the class topics and activities for that week.

The professor often posed questions for us to ponder before moving us into the breakout rooms for the peer debriefing activities. These questions gave us a good starting point for our work as each student would respond to the prompt before engaging in a small group discussion. Sometimes, though, she did not provide us with a structure for the activity and encouraged us to continue the conversation from the prior week.

I found it really beneficial to stay with the same group throughout the semester. Our group formed a bond, and as a result, we provided encouragement and support to each other. We truly cared about each other and our work. In addition to supporting each other, we also became accountability partners. Because I knew I would speak to my group every week and I wanted to have progress to share with them, I worked harder each week to move forward so that I would have something to share with them. These groups helped me progress with my research in a timely way. The professor encouraged us to keep in contact outside of class time, and we did. We formed a text group, and we checked in with each other when we knew deadlines were approaching. We cheered on each other's successes.

Each week, we helped each other think through problems and come up with possible solutions. I think professors often change group membership so we can work with different people, but I found it beneficial to stay in the same group for the entire semester. Because we had 15 weeks together, we had time to bond and develop a sense of community. These relationships helped us learn from each other.

I encourage professors who are planning to use peer debriefing groups to take care in choosing group membership. I believe it is valuable to explain why the groups were formed in a certain way. Knowing the why or rationale can motivate students. For example, you could share how members having similarities or differences will be helpful to the task. In some cases, having things in common with group members might be important, but in others, having diverse perspectives and experiences might be more beneficial. Share your thinking process with students. It is also important to provide clear guidance about the task and how the groups should begin their work. Having a clear understanding of what is expected will help the groups be productive.

***

As Krista shared, professors requiring students to work in groups are faced with a choice to allow students to self-select into groups or to assign students to groups. Although choice is often an excellent way to increase student autonomy and engagement, Moreu and Brauer (2022) cautioned against having students choose their groups because students are likely to partner with other students who are similar to them, but students benefit from participating in groups where diverse perspectives are shared. Professors can use random assignment tools, often available in learning management systems, or rely on their knowledge of students to create diverse groups. As Krista pointed out, it can be helpful for students to understand the rationale behind group assignments.

## USING VARIED, CREATIVE TEACHING APPROACHES

At many colleges and universities, professors are asked to use a pre-established template for creating online course modules. Students have reported having a consistent template or structure in the learning management system helps them know where to find course materials (Scutelnicu et al., 2019). Although consistency in terms of how information is conveyed is important, variety may be more important when it comes to the teaching approach or method.

Students are more likely to have higher levels of motivation when they are asked to engage in different tasks that they find interesting. It is difficult for professors to identify one teaching method that works well for students of varied cultural backgrounds. Varying learning tasks can increase the likelihood that students from different cultures find the tasks interesting and rewarding (Rizvi et al., 2022). If learning tasks become overly repetitive and are too similar in nature, this may reduce student engagement. For example, students may not find having to complete discussion boards that have the same structure and approach week after week to be engaging. Introducing different and varied teaching and learning approaches into online classes is an excellent way to increase student engagement for diverse learners. In the following stories by Patricia and Annabelle, they share the benefits of professors using a variety of teaching strategies in an online learning environment.

ಲಿಲಿಲಿಲಿಲಿಲಿ

### Varied Teaching Strategies, Patricia B. Ateboh-Briggs, Morgan State University

Professor Grimes knows that students will be more engaged if she keeps the course content engaging and relevant for her diverse learners. What I really enjoyed about her class was the variety of teaching approaches she used. She used different methods and media to deliver the course material, and because of this, she stimulated our critical thinking and creativity.

Before class, she provided us with readings and videos on Canvas so we would be prepared for the various activities. During class, she incorporated real-world examples through case studies and scenarios that connected the course content to our lives and goals. No matter which teaching strategy was being used, she prioritized creating a safe and comfortable space for students to share their opinions and experiences during class discussions and be respectful of the diverse perspectives shared. She always encouraged students to ask questions, challenge assumptions, and express their views.

I liked how she used many different technology tools to engage us, too. She used PowerPoint slides, videos, audio clips, images, and charts to present the information clearly and effectively. She also frequently used interactive tools such as polls, quizzes, games, and simulations to engage us and check our understanding of the course material.

Professor Grimes also incorporated creative projects into the classroom experience. We had opportunities to complete a variety of assignments, such as essays, presentations, posters, or videos. As we worked on these assignments, she encouraged us to explore many different sources of information, such as journals, podcasts, and online webinars or training courses, to learn about topics in the course. During class, we demonstrated our learning and showcased our talents by sharing what we learned through these projects. I really appreciated the varied ways in which we learned in her class and how she gave us enough time to do assignments.

Professor Grimes invited us to engage in learning outside of the classroom, too. For example, Professor Grimes often encouraged us to attend online conferences and round table discussions related to the course material. She would then give us opportunities to share our key takeaways from the conference in assignments and discussions.

I would encourage professors to think about the various teaching strategies they could use to stimulate their students' critical thinking and creativity and foster a sense of community in the classroom. For example, professors could use PowerPoint slides, videos, audio clips, images, graphs, charts, polls, quizzes, games, simulations, essays, presentations, posters, podcasts, or storytelling to engage their students. They could also incorporate real-world examples, case studies, and scenarios that connect the course content to the students' lives and goals. In addition, they could consider inviting their students to attend conferences and other professional events and let them share what they learned with their classmates during class. I would also encourage professors to have their students explore a variety of sources of information, such as journals, podcasts, and online courses. Varied teaching strategies can be very effective and enjoyable for both the professor and the students.

ಬಿಬಿಬಿಜಿಜಿಜಿ

ಬಿಬಿಬಿಜಿಜಿಜಿ

**Learning about AI via Readings, Discussions, and Reflective Writing Assignments, Annabelle Hicks, University of Connecticut**

The utilization of artificial intelligence (AI) tools such as ChatGPT for proofreading and editing presents undeniable advantages. These tools streamline processes, mitigate costs associated with human editing, and democratize access to resources, thereby leveling the academic playing field. Furthermore, AI enhances clarity and communication, thereby augmenting productivity and fostering effective scholarly dialogue. However, the integration of AI in academia is not devoid of challenges and limitations. Instances where AI has generated erroneous information or produced misleading content, underscore the ethical considerations and risks inherent in reliance solely on AI-generated material.

Nevertheless, the potential benefits of AI in academia and beyond are extensive. From supporting neurodivergent individuals and non-native speakers to optimizing overall communication efficacy, AI holds the promise of positively impacting diverse academic communities. To harness these benefits while navigating potential pitfalls, it is imperative to adopt a critical stance towards AI, acknowledging both its capabilities and limitations. By positioning AI as a supplementary tool rather than a replacement for human intellect, we can harness its potential to enrich research, communication, and learning experiences.

These insights emerged from discussions within my college instruction class, a small and intimate group of eight graduate students who did not know each other beforehand. My professor created a learning environment where we explored the challenges and opportunities presented by AI in academia. Despite our class being two hours in length, the time always flew by due to the engaging nature of our discussions and the supportive environment fostered by our professor.

My professor used a variety of ways to engage us, including putting us in breakout room groups, sharing articles and thoughts in the chat, and actively contributing to a truly rich exchange of ideas. He also made sure we were prepared to engage in discussions by assigning engaging readings. For example, I recall a poignant pre-class reading assignment titled 'Boston University Denies It Would Use AI to Replace Striking Teaching Assistants.' This article served as a catalyst for our discussion, sparking questions about the role of AI in academia, particularly in situations where there are labor disputes or strikes. It also prompted discussions about the ethical considerations of using AI tools to offset the absence of teaching assistants and the broader implications for academic discourse and pedagogy. In addition to assigned readings, our professor also asked us to engage in reflective journaling outside of class. These journal assignments allowed for deeper introspection and consolidation of our learning.

As we are increasingly exposed to AI tools, we want to learn how to harness this technology ethically and effectively. I found the collaborative and sustained dialogue we had in class very helpful to me as I navigated how to use AI ethically. Because my professor decided to take on this important issue as a main topic for our class, I had the opportunity to dive deep into understanding the positives and negatives of AI. I am grateful that my professor introduced the topic through engaging readings and then adeptly guided our discussions. My professor encouraged critical thinking and fostered an environment where diverse perspectives could be shared openly.

I also appreciated the varied teaching approaches, such as breakout group discussions and reflective journaling. The breakout group discussions allowed us to delve deeper into specific aspects of AI's impact, while the reflective journaling encouraged introspection and consolidation of our learning. This hands-on and interactive approach served to deepen our understanding of the subject matter and empowered us to critically assess the role of AI in scholarly inquiry. One of the most impactful moments in our class discussion occurred when one of my peers, who disclosed her neurodivergence, openly shared how tools like

ChatGPT supported her academic writing and synthesis of readings for her graduate degree. This sharing is just one example that directly reflects the safe and inclusive environment cultivated by our professor. I encourage other professors to focus on important issues such as AI and to create varied learning opportunities such as small group discussions and independent, reflective writing to help them learn about the topics.

ಸಿಸಿಸಿಚಿಚಿಚಿ

These stories by Patricia and Annabelle illustrate how much students appreciate being exposed to different teaching approaches and technology tools. Student interest and motivation can increase when they get excited about both the content and the way in which they are being asked to interact with the content. In the next three student stories, Bridgette, Victoria, and Katie share additional examples of how professors used varied and innovative teaching approaches to engage them. Bridgette discusses how varied technology tools, especially those to facilitate peer interactions, were engaging. Victoria describes how a friendly chat competition kept students interested. Katie shares how being asked to identify and use pictures, a different and unique teaching approach, led to higher levels of engagement and learning.

ಸಿಸಿಸಿಚಿಚಿಚಿ

### Using Technology Tools to Foster a Sense of Community, Bridgette Harris, Morgan State University

Within the academic community, Professor Vanessa Dodo-Seriki was not just a professor; she was a catalyst for engagement and learning in our doctoral-level science education courses, even amidst the unprecedented challenges posed by the pandemic. As classrooms transitioned to virtual settings, Professor Dodo-Seriki's leadership and adaptability shone through, providing a sense of ease and continuity in our learning journey. Despite the physical distance imposed by the pandemic, Professor Vanessa Dodo-Seriki leveraged technology to create a seamless online learning experience.

Pear Deck and video conferencing platforms transformed traditional lectures into dynamic, interactive sessions. Pear Deck, a presentation tool, became the cornerstone of our virtual classroom. With features like polls, quizzes, and discussion prompts embedded directly into the slides, Professor Dodo-Seriki ensured active student participation and real-time engagement. These interactive elements not only captivated our attention but also facilitated deeper understanding and retention of course material. Furthermore, video conferencing platforms were utilized to foster meaningful discussions and peer interactions. Breakout rooms allowed for small group activities and discussions, promoting collaboration and peer learning despite the physical distance.

Furthermore, Professor Dodo-Seriki's commitment to peer collaboration remained unwavering, even in the virtual landscape. She facilitated online group projects, virtual brainstorming sessions, and collaborative discussions. It was clear that she wanted to ensure that the benefits of teamwork and collective learning were not lost in the transition to remote learning.

Professor Dodo-Seriki's personal touch extended beyond the confines of the classroom space. Through virtual office hours, personalized emails, and compassionate communication, she provided the support and guidance needed to help us navigate the challenges of remote learning. Her empathetic approach and genuine care for her students created a safe and nurturing online environment where everyone felt valued and supported. As we grappled with the uncertainties of the pandemic, Professor Dodo-Seriki provided a beacon of stability and reassurance.

By embracing technology, fostering collaboration, and prioritizing student well-being, she not only adapted to the new normal but also ensured we thrived in it. She left an indelible mark on our academic, professional, and personal growth. I hope that other professors can use the strategies that I found engaging in Professor Dodo-Seriki's class. When integrating technology tools into teaching, I encourage professors to prioritize platforms that enhance student engagement and interaction. Provide clear instructions and guidance on how to use these tools effectively, and be open to feedback from students so that adjustments can be made if needed for students to learn.

ಬಿಬಿಬಿಛಛಛ

ಬಿಬಿಬಿಛಛಛ

## Making Learning Fun through a Friendly Review Chat Competition, Victoria Bahary, Brookdale Community College

After graduating high school during the peak of the COVID-19 pandemic, I was quite anxious to begin the next chapter of my life: College. With so much uncertainty in the world, I genuinely did not know what to expect. Despite my trepidations, my classmates and I quickly adapted to our new way of learning. While learning on Zoom from the comfort of one's own home, it is easy to become distracted. However, I was lucky enough to have many professors who strived to make classes as engaging and fulfilling as possible.

At Brookdale Community College, I took Communication Media with Professor Sabrina Mathues. She made a long-lasting impression on me. She always taught with a smile on her face and with a positive disposition, which instantly resulted in students wanting to participate. I truly feel as though her enthusiasm could be felt through the screen. It is important to acknowledge that the tone of the class is often initially set by the professor, directly affecting students' attitudes throughout the course, which is why I had such a wonderful experience in her class.

Professor Mathues taught the class about important aspects of communication mediated by technology. In this class, students had to examine communication through a historical lens. It can be difficult to keep students entertained during a history lesson, yet Professor Mathues emphasized how fascinating history is by using relatable examples. She would frequently share her screen and present captivating videos and clips to the class to better our understanding and keep us interested.

I am especially engaged when there is an element of friendly competition, so I immediately got excited about a chat competition. Students are more inclined to focus during a lesson when a competition is involved, especially when there is a prize on the table. I am more eager to study when I know that I will be questioned on the spot in front of my classmates and professor.

The review chat game was simple. Professor Mathues would ask a question, and we would rush to be the first to type the correct answer in the chat. I looked forward to review game days and made sure to always study and be well-versed on the topic so I could earn as many points as possible. This friendly review game motivated us to study the material thoroughly in order to be prepared for our upcoming exams. I enjoyed how Professor Mathues incorporated games that tested our knowledge into this online course.

Keeping an online class focused is no easy task, yet Professor Mathues made it look effortless. Her passion and vibrant personality kept the energy of the class afloat. Including real-life examples and adding a bit of friendly competition to review concepts successfully engaged our online class during a difficult time. My advice to professors would be as follows: When you make learning fun, the class no longer feels like work.

ಙಙಙ ಚಚಚ

## The Power of a Picture, Katie Williver, Georgian Court University

In this online class, one of the topics we discussed was how, as teachers, we would have students who struggled with language. We talked about how language involves the interpretation of words, phrases, sentences, and connected text and how language learning begins with the use of facial expressions, repetition, and pictures. In elementary settings, teachers often use wordless picture books to facilitate reading and tell their students to 'write' by drawing pictures. In this class, we discovered that wordless picture books can be a beneficial way to use storytelling for learning at any age.

I vividly remember when one of my professors helped us learn how to engage students who struggle with language or have learning disabilities using pictures. During an online class, my professor showed us a picture. The picture's title was 'Figure 5 in Gold.' Many of us had never seen the picture before, but we were asked to describe how it made us feel and to tell a story about what was going on in the picture. The responses we gave varied. I recall one student saying it was a picture of an address number on a house. Our professor encouraged us to continue sharing our ideas, providing positive feedback for all ideas that were shared.

The professor then read us a poem titled 'The Great Figure' by William Carlos Williams. This poet explained the picture of the number five. The picture, without a doubt, helped us better understand the poem. It was because of this lesson that I now value the importance of putting a visual with a text. I doubt I would have been as engaged and invested in the poem if I had not been given an opportunity to see and think about a related image.

This strategy made such an impact on me that I used it several times when I was teaching. I know that my elementary school students come to my class with varied background knowledge on the subject areas we discuss. Some have very limited knowledge, while others have a wealth of knowledge. For example, my fourth-grade class just read three articles on beekeeping. Some of them had a wide range of knowledge and had seen hives, had stories about being stung, and had tasted honey. I opened the lesson by showing them a picture of a beekeeper and some tools they utilized and asked what they thought the person's job was. This visual strategy can get all students, even college students, engaged. I encourage other professors to think about what images relate to their content and how they can use these visual images to help students be engaged and learn.

These stories showcased how different online teaching approaches can engage students. Sometimes, simple actions such as asking students to respond via the chat feature in synchronous courses can make a huge difference in terms of student engagement. Students report enjoying tasks that they perceive as interesting and fun.

Katie's story illuminates the power of pictures. For years, professors have been using images in their lectures to promote learning. Extensive research has demonstrated the value of pictures in learning. Based on numerous experimental studies, Mayer (2009) reported that visual image use improved learning and recommended the use of images related to content be used in multimedia tools such as PowerPoint.

One of the reasons that pictures are so powerful is because of a phenomenon called the picture superiority effect, meaning that the memory of pictures is better than the memory of words. Defeyter et al. (2009) demonstrated the picture superiority effect across different developmental stages and found that young adults benefitted the most from having access to a picture while learning. Professors are encouraged to create slides that primarily consist of an image related to the content being discussed to help students take in and learn the course material.

Pictures do not have to be provided by the professor. In fact, research has illustrated that having students determine the images can help them process the content more deeply, which can result in increased learning. The power of identifying images was demonstrated in an experimental study conducted by Cuevas and Dawson (2018). In this study, college students were randomly assigned to one of two groups and asked to learn novel content. The experimental group was asked to form a mental image of the content, and the control group was asked to focus on pronunciation. Cuevas and Dawson (2018) found that students in the mental image experimental condition performed significantly better (M = 16.37), recalling more than twice as much content as the control group (M = 8.03). Based on these findings, professors may want to encourage students to identify images related to course content. One approach could be for professors to ask students to include pictures in their discussion posts. Another approach could be for small groups to be tasked with creating a summary document of key concepts and related images.

Videos are another tool that can be used to promote learning. Kimbrel and Gantner (2021) reported that students found videos made by their professor valuable and that it helped them connect to the content and their professor. Shane-Simpson et al. (2024) found that it can also be helpful to feature videos of other professionals in the field. They found that one of the predictors of students perceiving the online classroom to be welcoming and inclusive was the use of videos featuring experts beyond the professor. Shane-Simpson et al. (2024)

postulated that these noninstructor 'videos communicate to students that an instructor values and welcomes diverse voices (including those of students) in the classroom' (p. 306).

Despite students perceiving videos to be engaging, research has shown that many students do not watch the videos shared on online course platforms. Akçapinar et al. (2024), for instance, found that most students did not watch the entire video that the professor posted. However, Parker et al. (2024) found that videos were more likely to be watched when they were shorter, they were shared at the beginning versus the end of the semester, and when there were grades associated with watching them.

In addition to incorporating creative teaching approaches into established courses, there can be times when professors can apply creative teaching practices to individualized learning experiences. One type of individualized learning experience is the independent study. In the following example, Chelsea shares her appreciation for how a professor helped her leverage an independent study opportunity to make connections between her professional and student roles.

80808003030303

## A Creative Independent Study: Connecting Work with School, Chelsea Bock, University of Maryland, College Park

Although I had earned a graduate degree in humanities, I was working at the National Academies of Sciences, Engineering, and Medicine in Washington, D.C. I decided to pursue a second master's degree in English to sharpen my skills as an adjunct professor and potentially set myself up for a full-time faculty position. While in my program, I noticed that my coursework connected to my job at the National Academies in thrilling and surprising ways. After all, scientific research and advancements do not exist in a vacuum. They exist to better the lives of people, and for the people to understand them, they must be communicated effectively. I wondered if there was a way to make my work in science communication more tangible within my studies beyond my occasional comment in the classroom connecting the two.

Professor Scott Wible made this happen. Together, we crafted a proposal for an independent study course that would focus on professional and technical writing so that I could immediately apply what I was learning to my current career. Additionally, this independent study would give me a better understanding of visual rhetoric and science communication so that I could help my students in the classroom with similar interests.

Some of the questions for exploration that Professor Wible and I developed for the course were 'How does writing in organizational contexts advance some social goals and hinder others?' and 'What constitutes "good" writing in professional contexts, both in terms of expediency and ethics?' We identified primary texts such as Beverly Sauer's *The Rhetoric of Risk: Technical Documentation in Hazardous Environments*, which explored technical communication's relationship with policy and safety standards, and Charles Kostelnick's and Michael Hassett's *Shaping Information: The Rhetoric of Visual Conventions*, which covered the history and best practices of visual scientific communication.

That summer semester consisted of weekly meetings with Professor Wible (including a generous Skype session while I was on work travel in Paris), brief essays, an annotated bibliography, and a ton of reading. The independent study culminated in a final research paper on the visual rhetoric in my division at the National Academy of Sciences, Engineering, and Medicine. I analyzed a handful of infographics and interviewed several colleagues. Ultimately, I learned an incredible amount about visual rhetoric as a crucial part of science communication.

I remain grateful for Professor Wible's flexibility and creativity in developing this independent study experience. I was especially grateful that he recognized the value of applying professional work to academic research. I encourage other professors to create independent study experiences either through a separate course or, if that is not possible, perhaps through an alternative assignment option.

૱૱૱൱൱൱

## FACULTY REFLECTION QUESTIONS

1. How can I convey care about the mental health and well-being of my students through synchronous and asynchronous teaching methods?
2. Will the students in my course see themselves represented in the course materials? Will students learn about diverse perspectives? What inclusive teaching methods can I use in my online courses?
3. How can I structure online discussions to encourage students to learn from one another and appreciate different perspectives?
4. In what way can I allow students to take the lead on conversations, and how can I support them in this role?
5. What synchronous and asynchronous innovative group activities can I use to promote connection and learning?

6. How can I balance consistency with course format so students know what is expected with varied learning tasks to keep them interested and engaged?
7. What technology tools can I use to foster a sense of belonging, increase learning, and help students enjoy the learning process?

## REFERENCES

Addy, T. M., Dube, D., Mitchell, K. A., & SoRelle, M. E. (2023). *What inclusive instructors do: Principles and practices for excellence in college teaching.* Routledge.

Akçapinar, G., Er, E., & Bayazit, A. (2024). Decoding video logs: Unveiling student engagement patterns in lecture capture videos. *International Review of Research in Open and Distributed Learning, 25*(2), 94–113. https://doi.org/10.19173/irrodl.v25i2.7621

Aloni, M., & Harrington, C. (2018). Research based practices for improving the effectiveness of asynchronous online discussion boards. *Scholarship of Teaching and Learning in Psychology, 4*(4), 271–289. https://doi.org/10.1037/stl0000121

Bickle, M. C., & Rucker, R. (2018). Student-to-student interaction: Humanizing the online classroom using technology and group assignments. *Quarterly Review of Distance Education, 19*(1), 1–11. https://eric.ed.gov/?id=EJ1190065

Cash, C. M., Cox, T. D., & Hahs-Vaughn, D. L. (2021). Distance educators attitudes and actions towards inclusive teaching practices. *Journal of the Scholarship of Teaching and Learning, 21*(2), 15–42. https://doi.org/10.14434/josotl.v21i2.27949

CAST. (2024). Universal design for learning guidelines version 3.0. https://udlguidelines.cast.org

Clark, C., Strudler, N., & Grove, K. (2015). Comparing asynchronous and synchronous video vs. text based discussions in an online teacher education course. *Online Learning, 19*(3), 48–69. https://olj.onlinelearningconsortium.org/index.php/olj/article/view/668

Cuevas, J., & Dawson, B. L. (2018). A test of two alternative cognitive processing models: Learning styles and dual coding. *Theory and Research in Education, 16*(1), 40–64. https://doi.org/10.1177/1477878517731450

Dailey-Hebert, A. (2018). Maximizing interactivity in online learning: Moving beyond discussion boards. *Journal of Educators Online, 15*(3), 1–27. https://www.thejeo.com/archive/2018_15_3/hebert_interactivity

Darby, F., & Lang, J. M. (2019). *Small teaching online: Applying learning science in online classes.* Jossey Bass.

Defeyter, M. A., Russo, R., & McPartlin, P. L. (2009). The picture superiority effect in recognition memory: A developmental study using the response signal procedure. *Cognitive Development, 24*(3), 265–273. https://doi.org/10.1016/j.cogdev.2009.05.002

Demetriou, C., McNulty, C., Powell, C., & DeVita, J. (2024). "Confidence to continue": A qualitative investigation of college student experiences of microaffirmations. *Journal of Postsecondary Student Success, 3*(2), 99–123. https://doi.org/10.33009/fsop_jpss132942

Dickinson, A. R., & Kreitmair, U. W. (2021). The importance of feeling cared for: Does a student's perception of how much a professor cares about student success relate to class performance? *Journal of Political Science Education, 17*(3), 356–370. https://doi.org/10.1080/15512169.2019.1659803

DiGiacomo, D. K., Usher, E. L., Han, J., Abney, J. M., Cole, A. E., & Patterson, J. T. (2023). The benefits of belonging: Students' perceptions of their online learning experiences. *Distance Education, 44*(1), 24–39. https://doi.org/10.1080/01587919.2022.2155615

Donovan, L., Green, T. D., Besser, E., & Gonzalez, E. (2021). The whole is greater than the sum of the parts: A self-study of equity and inclusion in online teacher education. *Studying Teacher Education: Journal of Self-Study of Teacher Education Practices, 17*(1), 57–81. https://doi.org/10.1080/17425964.2021.1897975

Douglas, S. (2023). Achieving online dialogic learning using breakout rooms. *Research in Learning Technology, 31*, 1–16. https://doi.org/10.25304/rlt.v31.2882

Eynon, B. & Iuzzini, J. (2020). *ATD teaching and learning toolkit: A research-based guide to building a culture of teaching and learning excellence.* Silver Spring, MD: Achieving the Dream. https://achievingthedream.org/teaching-learning-toolkit/

Fleming, E. C. (2023). UDL for inclusive teaching: Offering choice to increase belonging through technology. *Journal of Teaching and Learning with Technology, 12*, 72–90. https://doi.org/10.14434/jotlt.v12i1.36327

Foo, S. Y., & Quek, C. L. (2019). Developing students' critical thinking through asynchronous online discussions: A literature review. *Malaysian Online Journal of Educational Technology, 7*(2), 37–58. https://doi.org/10.17220/mojet.2019.02.003

Garrison, D. R., Anderson, T., & Archer, W. (2000). Critical inquiry in a text-based environment: Computing conferencing in higher education. *The Internet and Higher Education, 2*(2–3), 87–105. https://doi.org/10.1016/S1096-7516(00)00016-6

Goering, A. E., Resnick, C. E., Bradford, K. D., & Othus, G. S. M. (2022). Diversity by design: Broadening participation through inclusive teaching. *New Directions for Community Colleges, 199*, 77–91. https://doi.org/10.1002/cc.20525

Han, M., & Hamilton, E. R. (2023). Promoting engagement and learning: Using the fishbowl strategy in online and hybrid college courses. *College Teaching, 71*(4), 281–289. https://doi.org/10.1080/87567555.2021.2024127

Harrington, C., Hooper, K., Hughes, A., Klein, E., Melendez, J., Saddique, F., & Wasserman, E. (2021). An approach to an online Ed.D. in community college leadership program. *Impacting Education: Journal on Transforming Professional Practice, 6*(3), 7–12. http://impactinged.pitt.edu/ojs/ImpactingEd/article/view/185

Howard, D. L. (2023). The uncertain future of class discussions. *Inside Higher Ed.* https://www.insidehighered.com/opinion/career-advice/teaching/2023/05/24/uncertain-future-class-discussions

James, A. J., Douglas, T. A., Earwaker, L. A., & Mather, C. A. (2022). Student experiences of facilitated asynchronous online discussion boards: Lessons learned and implications for teaching practice. *Journal of University Teaching and Learning Practice*, *19*(5), 1–20. https://ro.uow.edu.au/jutlp/vol19/iss5/10

Kember, D., Trimble, A., & Fan, S. (2023). An investigation of the forms of support needed to promote the retention and success of online students. *American Journal of Distance Education*, *37*(3), 169–184. https://doi.org/10.1080/08923647.2022.2061235

Kerrigan, J., & Aghekyan, R. (2022). Beyond the discussion board: Engaging students in asynchronous online activities. *International Journal of Teaching and Learning in Higher Education*, *33*(3), 488–495. https://www.isetl.org/ijtlhe/

Kimbrel, L. A., & Gantner, M. W. (2021). Student perceptions of instructor made videos with quizzes in an asynchronous online course. *International Journal of Educational Leadership Preparation*, *16*(1), 24–44. https://files.eric.ed.gov/fulltext/EJ1313136.pdf

Lin, X., Luterbach, K., Gregory, K. H., & Sconyers, S. E. (2024). A case study investigating the utilization of ChatGPT in online discussions. *Online Learning*, *28*(2), 124–149. https://doi.org/10.24059/olj.v28i2.4407

Mayer, R. E. (2009). *Multi-media learning* (2nd ed.). University Press.

Milovic, A., & Dingus, R. (2021). How to not disappear completely: Using video-based discussions to enhance student social presence in an online course. *Marketing Education Review*, *31*(4), 311–321. https://doi.org/10.1080/10528008.2021.1943447

Moreu, G., & Brauer, M. (2022). Inclusive teaching practices in post-secondary education: What instructors can do to reduce the achievement gaps at U.S. colleges. *International Journal of Teaching & Learning in Higher Education*, *34*(1), 170–182. https://doi.org/10.31234/osf.io/btkzs

Morse, M. L. (2021). Increase engaged student learning using google docs as a discussion platform. *Teaching & Learning Inquiry*, *9*(2), 1–19. https://doi.org/10.20343/teachlearninqu.9.2.20

Nestor, M., Tullis, M., & Butler, J. (2024, November 8). In defense of asynchronous learning. *Inside Higher Ed*. https://www.insidehighered.com/opinion/views/2024/11/08/defense-asynchronous-learning-opinion

Parker, M. J., Bunch, M., & Pike, A. (2024). Is anybody watching: A multi-factor motivational framework for educational video engagement. *Computers & Education*, *222*, 1–15. https://doi.org/10.1016/j.compedu.2024.105148

Prevatt, B.-S., Perkins, H., & Nance, A. (2021). Psychology today: A project to increase diversity in psychology curriculum. *Scholarship of Teaching and Learning in Psychology*, *7*(4), 288–300. https://doi.org/10.1037/stl0000284

Read, D., Barnes, S. M., Hughes, O., Ivanova, I., Sessions, A., & Wilson, P. J. (2022). Supporting student collaboration in online breakout rooms through interactive group activities. *New Directions in the Teaching of Physical Sciences*, *17*(1), 1–18. https://doi.org/10.29311/ndtps.v0i17.3946

Rizvi, S., Rienties, B., Rogaten, J., & Kizilcec, R. F. (2022). Beyond one-size-fits-all in MOOCs: Variation in learning design and persistence of learners in different cultural and socioeconomic contexts. *Computers in Human Behavior, 126,* N.PAG. https://doi.org/10.1016/j.chb.2021.106973

Rogers-Shaw, C., Carr-Chellman, D. J., & Choi, J. (2018). Universal design for learning: Guidelines for accessible online instruction. *Adult Learning, 29*(1), 20–31. https://files.eric.ed.gov/fulltext/EJ1160465.pdf

Sandidge, C. R., & Schultz, B. F. (2024). Building connections and enhancing learning: Student perspectives of traditional discussion boards in online courses. *Journal of Educators Online, 21*(4), 1–12. https://doi.org/10.9743/JEO.2024.21.4.1

Sato, S. N., Condes Moreno, E. Rubio-Zarapuz, A. Dalamitros, A. A., Yañez-Sepulveda, R., Tornero-Aguilera, J. F., & Clemente-Suárez, V. J. (2024). Navigating the new normal: Adapting online and distance learning in the post-pandemic era. *Education Sciences, 14,* 1–25. https://doi.org/10.3390

Scheepers, L., & van den Berg, G. (2022). The value of providing online students with dedicated affective support, particularly during times of crisis. *Open Praxis, 14*(3), 190–201. https://doi.org/10.55982/openpraxis.14.3.497

Scutelnicu, G., Tekula, R., Gordon, B., & Knepper, H. J. (2019). Consistency is key in online learning: Evaluating student and instructor perceptions of a collaborative online-course template. *Teaching Public Administration, 37*(3), 274–292. https://doi.org/10.1177/0144739419852759

Shane-Simpson, C., Obeid, R., & Prescher, M. (2024). Multi-media characteristics, student relationships, and teaching behaviors predict perceptions of an inclusive classroom across course delivery format. *Teaching of Psychology, 51*(3), 298–308. https://doi.org/10.1177/00986283221117621

Thormann, J., & Fidalgo, P. (2014). Guidelines for online course moderation and community building from a student's perspective. *Journal of Online Learning & Teaching, 10*(3), 374–388. https://jolt.merlot.org/vol10no3/Thorman_0914.pdf

Truhlar, A. M., Williams, K. M., & Walter, M. T. (2018). Case study: Student engagement with course content and peers in synchronous online discussions. *Online Learning, 22*(4), 289–312. https://doi.org/10.24059/olj.v22i4.1389

CHAPTER 4

# Assignments

The type and nature of assignments can be important in student engagement and learning. Aliah et al. (2024) found that students who were required to complete innovative assignments reported higher engagement (M = 4.2; SD = .05) than their peers who were required to complete traditional assignments (M = 3.4; SD =. 06) and that even after controlling for prior academic achievement and level of the course, innovative assignments in the course predicted student achievement. During interviews, students shared that innovative assignments were more applied and relevant but did acknowledge the need for more clarity related to expectations (Aliah et al., 2024).

Winfield (2024) advocated for innovative assignments, noting that many traditional assignments, such as papers and exams, can be more likely to perpetuate equity gaps. Some examples of innovative assignments include project-based group work, developing infographics, podcasts, or training manuals. Researchers have found that students respond positively to innovative assignment approaches. For example, after engaging in an assignment redesign process, Pinahs-Schultz and Beck (2016) found that students reported that completing the revised assignments increased their understanding of their awareness of resources and the role of community coalitions in public health. They also reported that the assignments challenged them to engage in more creative problem-solving to serve communities better. Almost all (98%) of students met or exceeded expectations on the assignment, with over half (60%) exceeding expectations based on rubric scores (Pinahs-Schultz & Beck, 2016). Although exams and papers continue to be commonly assigned, there has been an increase in more innovative assignments (Harrington, 2024). Professors are encouraged to consider ways to engage students through creative alternatives to traditional assignments.

Many students have shared how assignments have engaged them (Harrington, 2021; Harrington, 2025). In this chapter, students share stories about how their professors engaged them with different types of assignments. Students report that assignments that help them build their foundational knowledge and master course content and those that are personalized, relevant, and authentic engage them. Online students also value opportunities to work collaboratively with their peers on assignments and for there to be variety in the type of assignments they need to complete. Student stories illuminate the reasons why assignments can be a source of engagement and provide numerous examples of how professors have used assignments to engage students.

## DEVELOPING FOUNDATIONAL KNOWLEDGE

Assignments designed to help students learn basic or foundational information about a discipline can help them increase their academic self-efficacy or confidence (Wollschleger, 2019). Not surprisingly, students are more likely to be engaged when they believe they can successfully complete tasks. Casanova et al. (2024), for example, found a strong and positive relationship between self-efficacy and engagement in first-year students. The importance of developing foundational knowledge is emphasized in major learning taxonomies (Anderson & Krathwohl, 2001; Fink, 2013).

There are a variety of ways to support the development of foundational knowledge through assignments. Because professors assign readings to help students build and expand on their understanding of the field, assignments associated with these reading tasks can be helpful. Quizzes are one example of assignments that can help students develop and showcase their foundational knowledge. Students often appreciate low-stakes opportunities to engage with the course content. Researchers such as Cook and Babon (2017) and Tropman (2014) have found that students reported quizzes motivated them to complete the assigned readings and that doing so better prepared them to participate in discussions. Although traditional quiz approaches can be effective (Kyung-Mi, 2022), students may be more engaged when professors use gamified quizzes. To gamify quizzes, professors can add features such as points, leaderboards, or time limits. There are numerous technology tools that professors can use to gamify quizzes. Students have reported that gamified quizzes help them be more active learners (Mimouni, 2022; Wilkinson et al., 2020).

Another approach to helping students build and expand their foundational knowledge is through reading assignments. Students have reported that graded reading assignments are one of the best ways to motivate them to read (Aagaard et al., 2014). Maurer and Longfield (2015) found that the use of reading guides improved student performance on quizzes. Students in the reading guide only and the reading guide and practice quiz sections performed better than the control group that was not assigned reading guides or practice quizzes; however, students in a reading guide and graded quiz condition did not perform better than the control group (Maurer & Longfield, 2015). These findings suggest that both reading assignments and quizzes may not be needed; one of these may be sufficient to support student learning.

Reading assignments that encourage students to engage in critical thinking and note-taking can be engaging for students. Ives et al. (2020), for example, investigated the usefulness of asking students to complete double-entry notes to promote critical reading and thinking. Students were provided with a table where they had to list the reading, summarize what it said, and then share their thoughts. For the part of the assignment that required students to share their thoughts, they were asked to consider how the content related to their experiences or other sources they read. In addition, students were asked to determine if they agreed or disagreed with the points being made and if reading the content shifted their thinking. Most students reported that this approach was new to them and that it helped them analyze the readings. In addition to exploring student perceptions of the tool, Ives et al. (2020) also assessed the content of what they wrote and found evidence of applying and analyzing critical thinking skills.

In the following story, Casey gives an example of a reading guide assignment where students were provided with a partially complete outline of the text, and they had to complete the missing parts of the outline. Casey found that this assignment encouraged reading with purpose. This reading guide, combined with other effective teaching strategies such as the use of recorded videos, led to an engaging experience for Casey.

ಖಖಖ෮෮෮

## Reading Guides and More, Casey Bond, Johnson County Community College

As a father of two under six who is working full-time while attending school, I do not have much time. I have taken many online classes throughout my educational career, and most of them end up being about the same. I have had to just trudge through assignments, post in the discussion board, and respond to peers. Even though activities like discussion posts are meant to engage students and provide a more personal touch to learning online, I found them to often be tedious and viewed them as something I had to do to pass the class. I also had trouble forcing myself to read the class textbook, even though I know that in many courses, it is difficult to succeed without reading it. I would try to peruse the chapters, but this always ended up with me going glassy-eyed and feeling like I was wasting what precious free time I had left in the day.

I was attending college because I was ready for a career change. I have been with a large technology company for years, filling a support role, and I decided to try to break into the field of accounting because it is a fairly stable field and could help me provide for my family in a more consistent way. In my first accounting class, I met Professor Cole. From the beginning, I could tell that this would be a much different class than I was used to.

Professor Cole started the semester by posting a video of herself giving an overview of the class and sharing the best methods we could use to succeed. She explained the importance of completing the assignments and workbooks and how these assignments would help us develop the knowledge we would need to do well on the quizzes and exams. It was nice to see how all the assignments were connected.

Each week, she posted several useful documents, including a guide to reading the text. I had never been provided with a reading guide before. The reading guide provided us with a skeletal frame or outline that helped us know what we should be looking for when reading the text. Our assignment was to complete the reading guide by filling in the key content. I found the reading guides to be very helpful, and instead of feeling like I was wasting my time, I now had more purpose when reading.

To further support us, she also provided videos of herself giving lectures on the chapter of the week, with another printable note page to follow along with her as she taught. The recording and note-taking sheet made it feel as though I was attending the classes in person, and I felt like I got to know Professor Cole more and more with every video. I tried watching the recorded lectures before and after reading them, but I found it better to watch the lectures before reading the text. Watching the lecture first helped me to 'dip my toe in' before diving in. The lecture helped make the concepts familiar in a more palatable way before seeing the details in the text. I appreciated how she used personal anecdotes to help us learn the content. All her efforts resulted in a class where I felt engaged with the professor and the material, which is not easy to do when learning behind a computer screen.

My advice to professors would be to focus on key terms and concepts in the reading guide and not make it too complicated. Although it may not be the case in every subject, accounting has a lot of jargon and acronyms, and the reading guide helped me navigate the information. I also encourage professors to create recordings where these key concepts are visually displayed. Having the information shared via a second medium will be helpful to your students.

Casey's example illustrated the value of the reading guide assignment. Concept maps or mind maps are another type of reading assignment that can be used to engage students. Based on a meta-analysis of 42 years of research, Schroeder et al. (2018) concluded 'that constructing and studying concept maps are effective learning activities relative to a variety of other teaching and learning strategies' (p. 448). Researchers have found that student engagement and learning increased after the use of concept maps (Fatawi et al., 2020). Díaz and Garmendia (2025) emphasized how concept mapping can improve learning, especially when annotations from the readings are included in the maps.

Researchers have shown that using concept maps has been associated with increased learning across different age groups (Anastasiou et al., 2024). Though some may believe the benefits of concept mapping are greatest for new learners, such as those at the undergraduate level, Bixler et al. (2015) illustrated how concept maps improved learning for fourth-year medical students. The medical students in this study indicated that although concept mapping was beneficial, it was a time-consuming process. Engaging in deep learning does take more time. In the next student story, Mia provides an example of how mind maps were used in a graduate course.

୬୦୬୦୬୦ଓଓଓ

### Mind Maps, Mia Pepe, New Jersey City University

I was pleasantly surprised that one of my graduate professors used mind maps as a teaching tool. A mind map is a creative and fun visual diagram that we can use to break down terms and organize concepts in a way that makes sense to us. Teachers often use versions of mind maps to help elementary school children find connections between concepts and engage in deeper learning, but this is the first time I have encountered the use of mind maps at the graduate level.

Mind maps can be created on paper or with technology tools. The main advantage of creating mind maps on paper is that you can do it anywhere because it only requires paper and a pen or markers. I like to use digital programs because there is so much you can do with them. I have used different websites like Canva and apps like Procreate to organize my ideas and create mind maps, and I was thrilled to see my professor using these.

Digital mind map tools allow you to create colorful mind maps, embed pictures into your diagrams, and use a variety of interconnected lines. I like how you can rearrange the mind map without erasing pencil lines. In the class, my professor encouraged us to use mind maps when participating in discussion boards. In addition to sharing a narrative, we were also asked to create mind maps on the chapters or topics. We had the freedom to create the mind maps however we wished. After posting them, we could give compliments and constructive feedback to our fellow classmates and learn from each other. Although we were expected to create the mind maps independently, it was great to be able to see how our classmates did them. Sharing our ideas about the connections between the course content was the best part.

As graduate students, we are introduced to challenging and complex concepts. I believe mind maps can be very helpful in graduate courses. I am the daughter of a music teacher and am an artist. I, therefore, view myself as creative. I find it very beneficial to make connections between concepts visually. Mind maps allow me to use my artistic skills to support my academic learning. I found mind maps to be an engaging assignment because it required us to create something so the content became meaningful to us. Sometimes, when I am recalling information from the class, I think back to the mind map that I created. Making mind maps helped me better remember the concepts from class. Thinking about the association between concepts helped me learn and remember.

In addition to mind maps being helpful to me, I find it refreshing to take a break from the typical multiple-choice exams and the long essays and papers. I encourage other professors to use this strategy. All it takes is a piece of paper and some brief instructions to help students get started with mind maps. You can create mind maps to share with students, work on a mind map as a class, or have students create mind maps on their own. After they get the basic concept of creating mind maps, you can introduce them to computer programs and apps that can be helpful, but you do not need technology to benefit from mind mapping. Please encourage students to use this tool to help them think creatively and critically.

ಽಽಽಽಽಽಽಽ

Mia's story reminds us of the importance of helping students tap into their creativity to learn. Tools like mind maps get students cognitively engaged with the course content. Darby and Lang (2019) noted that students learn more when they make connections to the material being learned. Identifying connections between concepts and determining how these concepts are related to one another encourages students to think more deeply about the course content.

Quizzes, reading guides, and mind maps are all examples of formative assessments. Formative assessments are typically brief assignments that do not count much toward the final grade and provide the student with an opportunity for feedback during the learning process (Carney et al., 2022). Drafts or smaller assignments related to a final project, often referred to as the summative assessment, are other examples of how professors can use formative assessments to engage students and help them learn. In the following story, RJ shares why formative assessments are particularly important for online students.

☯☯☯☉☉☉

### Building Blocks toward Mastery, RJ Portella, Rutgers University

Online classes can be potentially daunting, especially when there is not an immediate response to questions about assignments. Asynchronous classes dovetail well with busy schedules for adult learners; however, there is a level of distance between the professor and the students that could add stress to completing assignments. In my master's program, I was fortunate enough to have the same stellar professor for three classes in a row who intuitively understood the value of formative assignments. In these courses, the formative assessments set the stage for a summative assignment where we demonstrated our mastery of the course content.

In each class syllabus, our professor clearly explained how formative assignments served as fundamental building blocks toward the final summative assignment. Specifically, in our College Teaching class, we learned how to construct an impactful syllabus by generating and refining the various elements. These formative assignments included crafting a warm welcome statement, sharing a teaching statement that conveyed who we were and how we planned to teach the course, learning outcomes, sharing campus services that could be helpful for students to use, grading scales, classroom policies, an outline and agenda for the semester, and more.

For each of the brief formative assessments listed above, we received valuable feedback from our peers and insightful feedback from the professor. My professor also gave us the opportunity to redo and resubmit work for even more feedback. These chances to polish our work gave me an authentic feeling of confidence. Many of us had never created a syllabus before, so having this step-by-step approach with feedback along the way helped us believe in our ability to complete the final project and do it well. The peer review part was not only helpful because of the feedback we received but also because we got to see examples of how others approached this part of the project. Seeing and reflecting on these varied approaches helped me decide what I think would or would not work well for me and my future students.

The most valuable impact for me within his process came at the end of the semester when I submitted an 18-page syllabus as the summative assignment. I never felt like I was scrambling or fumbling to assemble the capstone submission. Just as I learned how to create elements of the syllabus, I gained confidence and mastery of the content expected of me.

For professors who are constructing course content, I recommend starting at the end of the class: What do you want your students to demonstrate in full? Then, work backward and segment assignments that help students arrive at checkpoints of confidence throughout the semester. Also, make sure that at each checkpoint, there is some kind of opportunity to generate feedback. You might ask yourself if your syllabus also reflects that journey in a clear, concise way so that students understand how each small assignment contributes to the final, major semester assignment. That way, students are never left wondering why they are doing certain tasks. When the class goal is clear from the start, students understand how each assignment plays its part.

൭൭൭൫൫൫

RJ's story reminds us of the importance of creating opportunities for students to build skills in a scaffolded way. The formative assessments described in this story helped RJ and his classmates gain the confidence and skills needed to complete the more complex summative assessment. In the next story, Karuna shares how her professors enabled her to develop foundational knowledge by providing easier-to-understand and briefer resources as companions to more complex legal cases and by being available for support outside of class.

൭൭൭൫൫൫

### Building Knowledge and Skills via Case Studies, Karuna Taneja, Old Dominion University

During my first semester in a doctoral program, I faced a significant challenge with a course on Higher Education Law that was co-taught by Professors Dennis E. Gregory and Williams L. Nuckols. As an immigrant from India, I found the U.S. legal system and terminology initially unfamiliar and daunting. However, with the support of my professors, I embraced the opportunity to analyze complex precedents and present my findings to the class.

To aid our understanding, professors provided links to simplified versions of court cases on law.justia.com in addition to the links to full legal cases as we explored legal issues in higher education. Preparing for these presentations pushed me to delve deeper into related cases and precedents, enhancing my understanding. I appreciated the valuable guidance offered by my professors during office hours. For example, I recall

Professor Nuckols asking me insightful questions that directed my research for the final assignment for the course. He also helped me understand how to use APA format to cite legal cases.

What made a significant impact on my learning experience were the thought-provoking questions posed by our professors. Their questions nudged us to dig deeper into the cases and topics we were presenting, ignited our curiosity to explore different angles of a case, and encouraged us to use our analyzing skills. During the preparation of my presentation, I had to research the topic thoroughly and read more related cases and precedents to be able to answer any questions directed to me by my professors and peers during the question-and-answer portion of the class. My hard work paid off well when I could answer most of the questions asked by my professors.

Despite the initial challenges, I emerged from the course with newfound confidence in navigating higher education law. The interactive and engaging approach to learning in the online environment helped me bridge the gap between legal concepts and practical application in the field of community college leadership. This journey not only expanded my knowledge but also equipped me with valuable skills in research, critical analysis, and effective communication. Through this experience, I gained a deeper knowledge of the United States legal system, thanks to the well-designed course assignments and supportive guidance from my professors.

I am grateful for the opportunity to learn from dedicated professors at Old Dominion University who fostered a supportive and enriching learning environment, enabling me to grow professionally and academically. I encourage other professors to challenge and support their students. Providing your students with easier-to-understand resources and personalized help during office hours can help them learn the content and build their confidence. Asking them questions will encourage them to explore the content further and learn even more.

෩෩෩෪෪෪

## FOSTERING A GROWTH MINDSET

When students have a growth mindset, meaning they believe they can learn and that intelligence is malleable, they are more likely to achieve than if they think they cannot change their intelligence and learn (Dweck, 2008). Researchers have demonstrated that students can learn to develop a growth mindset and that doing so has a positive impact on learning. For example, based on a literature review, Cheng et al. (2021) illustrated that brief interventions that required college students to read articles or view videos on growth mindset resulted not only in increased growth mindset but also improved academic performance.

However, some have raised caution around growth mindset interventions. Scholars such as Luke Wood, for example, have voiced concerns about the emphasis on effort in growth mindset, noting that students of color may not get the same outcome from effort as someone from a privileged background (Hilton, 2017). Additionally, not all growth mindset interventions have been shown to be effective. After conducting a literature review on growth-minded interventions for engineering students, Campbell et al. (2021) concluded that results were mixed, with some studies showing the intervention was effective and others not illustrating effectiveness.

Many variables can impact the effectiveness of a growth mindset intervention. One variable is how the growth mindset content is shared. Campbell et al. (2021) found that growth mindset content shared via an online module was found to be most effective. Conducting a study on the use of growth mindset infographics, Cheng et al. (2021) demonstrated that infographics could also be used to help students develop a growth mindset and engage in behaviors associated with a growth mindset, such as problem-solving when a challenge is encountered. Findings from Campbell et al. (2021) also suggested that repeated exposure to growth mindset content may yield the most positive outcomes.

Although professors may want to foster a growth mindset in their students, they may be concerned about not having enough time to teach students about growth mindset given their course-specific goals. They may also not believe they have the expertise to do so. In the following student story, Megan shares how a professor helped students learn about a growth mindset in a research course by using readings on this topic to teach students about quantitative and qualitative methods. Megan explains how this approach helped her develop a productive growth mindset while learning the course content.

༄༅༄༅༄༅༃༃༃

### Learning about Growth Mindset and Course Content,
Megan Doyle, Gwynedd Mercy University

In an online Foundations for Research Methods course, one of the course outcomes was that we would be able to distinguish between the characteristics of quantitative and qualitative research. We were also expected to analyze and provide examples of various types of research. My professor helped us achieve these goals in a creative and helpful way.

My professor provided us with quantitative and qualitative studies that revolved around the topic of growth mindset in students and education. The research studies that we had to read to complete the assignments focused on how mindset impacts education, motivation, and achievement gaps. The qualitative study was a case study of one teacher's classroom practices in an elementary school and how modeling a growth mindset for younger children impacted their learning positively. The quantitative study focused on the relationship between faculty fixed mindset and racial achievement gaps. The authors of this study shared the implications of the findings for educators hoping to support the achievement of students of color. Both articles explained the concept of a growth mindset and the importance of seeing mistakes as opportunities for personal and academic growth, not as failures, and the results of both studies emphasized the importance of educators having a growth mindset and using growth-minded teaching strategies.

Understanding qualitative and quantitative research can be a challenge for many students. For students who have not had much experience with statistics, like me, learning about quantitative methods can be especially overwhelming. Having the content of these preselected articles focused on a relatable topic was helpful to me. Learning about a growth mindset while also learning about research helped me be okay with not mastering the concepts immediately because the emphasis was on learning from mistakes. While I was learning the various research principles outlined by the course outcomes, I was also reflecting on my own mindset while learning challenging material. Through this assignment, the professor did more than help us learn research principles; she also helped us build confidence in our academic skills.

I felt this was an incredibly engaging teaching practice because it allowed me to learn more about myself as a student, and it encouraged me to view challenges as opportunities. As a result, I dug deep and worked hard to understand these intellectually demanding principles. Any article could have been chosen for students to dissect to accomplish the course goals; however, I applaud my professor for how she utilized research articles on growth mindset so that I could also develop a growth mindset while learning the course content. I suggest that professors think about how they could use content in their courses and assignments that provide students with an added benefit. For example, perhaps articles or other readings can focus on building our confidence and skills as students.

## ASSIGNING RELEVANT AND MEANINGFUL LEARNING TASKS

Student engagement is higher when students perceive assignments as relevant and meaningful (Arend & Carlson, 2024). Students find assignments to be meaningful when they see how the content connects to their lives (Eodice et al., 2017). For example, interview projects and memoir assignments can help students make connections between their lived experiences and the content being learned (Mack, 2023). Priniski et al. (2018) shared the following three types of relevance:

1. **Personal association.** Priniski et al. (2018) described personal association as 'the perception that a stimulus (object, activity, topic) is connected to some other object, memory, etc., that is personally valued' (p. 2).
2. **Personal usefulness.** Personal usefulness refers to whether an individual perceives what they are learning as being useful in some way, such as supporting goal achievement (Priniski et al., 2018).
3. **Identification.** Priniski et al. (2018) argued that identification was the 'most personally meaningful type of relevance' because it involves 'the incorporation of the stimulus in the individuals' identity' (p. 2).

Researchers have explored the benefits of relevant assignments. For instance, a study conducted by Mebert et al. (2020) demonstrated increased student engagement through a real-world collaborative assignment. Professors from five disciplines and colleges partnered to develop authentic and relevant assignments on the Flint water crisis. For example, students in a statistics course used actual data on lead levels in the water rather than a fictitious data set, students in a public speaking course prepared a presentation on one aspect of the water crisis, students in a writing class wrote letters to the editor about the crisis, and students in a biology course determined what dietary modifications could help reduce the impact of lead in the water. Mebert et al. (2020) found that most students (68%) 'expressed enthusiasm for the project after having completed it' (p. 37), though approximately 11% of the students did not find the assignment engaging. Students who did find the assignments engaging commented that it was engaging because of the focus on an issue that was impacting their community, and it allowed them to apply what was being learned to real-world situations. Other researchers have also found that current event assignments, which bridge content with real-world applications, increased student engagement (Trent, 2023; Ruget & Rosero, 2014).

In the following three student stories, Kamel, Annabelle, and Chelsea share examples of assignments they perceived to be relevant, authentic, and meaningful. Kamel shares how a professor engaged students with a case study discussion and project. Kamel noted that this assignment had practical applications in the real world and helped students develop skills, such as teamwork and critical thinking, that would serve them well as professionals. Annabelle describes how reflective journals that required students to make personal connections to the course content and an interview assignment that illuminated real-world applications of course content created a sense of engagement that fostered learning. Chelsea describes how having an audience for an assignment and gathering information from people added meaning to the assignment and shares why this assignment approach was engaging.

༄༅༄༅༄༅༅༄༅༄

### Emphasizing Practical Applications: Using Case Studies and Other Collaborative Learning Activities, Kamel Johal, Athabasca University

Embarking on my academic journey at Athabasca University, I was immediately struck by the institution's commitment to inclusive, supportive, and experiential learning with practical application. Through a blend of innovative teaching strategies and personalized engagement, my professors facilitated a transformative educational experience that profoundly influenced my ethical, moral, and intellectual growth as a student, citizen, mother, and continuous learner.

One of the most impactful aspects of my learning journey was the integration of real-life applications into course materials. Rather than confining learning to theoretical frameworks, my professors consistently emphasized the practical relevance of course content to everyday situations. For instance, in a business ethics course, we delved into case studies drawn from contemporary corporate scandals, allowing us to analyze ethical dilemmas and propose actionable solutions.

We were able to work with other classmates regardless of time zones or other constraints, thanks to the flexibility afforded by asynchronous communication tools and our shared commitment to the project. Our professor provided overarching guidance and a framework for our collaboration, delineating the objectives and parameters of the assignment. Despite this guidance, our professor entrusted us with the autonomy to organize our workflow and contribute our respective expertise.

Through asynchronous collaboration, we leveraged digital platforms such as Google Drive, collaborative document editors, and communication tools like Slack or Microsoft Teams. These tools enabled us to have a real-time exchange of ideas, share documents, and give feedback. Engaging in these processes allowed us to refine our work iteratively. Our professor encouraged active participation and constructive feedback within the group, fostering a culture of collaboration and accountability.

Within this framework, each member of the team took on specific responsibilities based on their strengths and interests. Regular check-ins and progress updates ensured that we stayed aligned with the project timeline and objectives. While the professor provided periodic feedback and guidance during virtual office hours or through email correspondence, the bulk of our collaboration occurred asynchronously, allowing us to accommodate our diverse schedules and time zones.

Overall, our collaborative experience exemplified the efficacy of asynchronous communication in academic settings, demonstrating how modern technology can facilitate meaningful teamwork and knowledge exchange regardless of temporal or spatial constraints. I am thankful that my professors actively cultivated a culture of inclusivity, collaboration, and support within the online learning environment. They leveraged various digital tools and platforms to foster collaborative learning experiences, enabling meaningful interactions among students from diverse backgrounds. Discussion forums, virtual group projects, and peer review activities became integral components of my learning process. The learning environment fostered empathy, respect, and mutual understanding among classmates. Case studies served as powerful focal points, allowing us to apply theoretical concepts to real-world scenarios and engage in dynamic online discussions and virtual group projects. Each participant contributed unique perspectives and insights, enriching the discourse with diverse viewpoints. Virtual group projects were pivotal in cultivating teamwork and cooperation skills, skills we knew would help us in our careers. The professor played a guiding role, providing valuable feedback and steering discussions toward a deeper exploration of key concepts. Peer review activities further enhanced our learning experience by encouraging constructive criticism and fostering a culture of continuous improvement. Through structured feedback mechanisms, we honed our analytical skills while cultivating empathy and respect for our peers' perspectives.

This approach to collaborative learning was profoundly engaging for me. It not only facilitated a deeper understanding of the subject matter but also nurtured essential interpersonal skills vital for success in diverse professional environments. As someone who values inclusive and interactive learning experiences, I found this approach to be transformative, empowering me to learn from and alongside individuals from diverse backgrounds. My professor created a learning environment that empowered me to take ownership of my education and apply newfound knowledge in meaningful ways.

For professors seeking to engage their students using similar strategies, I offer the following advice:

1. Incorporate real-life applications and case studies into the course, encouraging students to apply knowledge learned across diverse contexts. This approach promotes critical thinking and practical skills applicable beyond academic boundaries.
2. Create opportunities for meaningful dialogue and collaborative projects, utilizing digital platforms to facilitate interaction. These collaborative projects foster a supportive learning community that values diverse perspectives and engages students.

ಉಉಉಡಡಡ

ಉಉಉಡಡಡ

## Reflective Journaling, Annabelle Hicks, University of Connecticut

Reflecting on my academic journey, the standout strategy that deeply engaged me was the implementation of weekly journal reflections in one of my graduate courses. This transformative approach, employed by my professor, required us to connect personal experiences with course content. In my opinion, these journals contributed to fostering an authentic and introspective learning environment. The weekly journal reflection strategy employed by my professor transformed the learning experience for me by weaving personal narratives into academic discussions. This strategy not only engaged me in the course material but also encouraged a deeper connection between personal experiences and academic concepts.

Our professor asked us to write weekly reflective journals. In each journal entry, we were encouraged to incorporate personal anecdotes related to the course, share insights we gained from classroom discussions, and discuss our thoughts on how course topics connected to broader societal issues. The weekly reflective journals were only shared with our professor. This created a space for candid and open expression.

What made this strategy particularly engaging to me was that it required me to merge my personal and academic experiences. Each week, I drew from my own experiences to make meaning out of the course material. In the journals, I reflected on topics such as the impact of names on rapport and inclusion in the classroom, the dangers of echo chambers created by algorithms, conventional notions of success, and the lasting impact of academic tasks and assignments.

This writing task allowed me to relate course concepts to real-life situations, making the material more relevant and memorable. This assignment also created a sense of accountability, as reflections were not merely for grades but served as a channel for authentic communication with my professor. The exclusivity of sharing reflections with the professor promoted a liberated and open environment, encouraging honest self-expression without fear of judgment.

Through these weekly assignments, I also discovered the power of storytelling. I learned so much by telling stories about the content we covered each week. The storytelling aspect made the learning experience more relatable and enjoyable, turning each reflection into a narrative that unfolded throughout the semester.

For professors looking to engage students using this strategy, my advice is to create a structured yet flexible framework for weekly reflections. Please encourage students to incorporate personal experiences, relate them to course content, and express their thoughts openly. Emphasize the exclusivity of the reflections, fostering a safe space for students to share without external pressures. Additionally, provide prompts or themes to guide reflections, ensuring a balance between personal anecdotes and academic insights. Embrace and encourage students to engage in storytelling as they complete these assignments to enhance student engagement and create a more enriching learning environment.

ಬಬಬಚಚಚ

ಬಬಬಚಚಚ

### Meaningful Assignments, Chelsea Bock, Anne Arundel Community College

My story comes from the Management Strategies in the Classroom online course that was required for a continuing education certificate in Pathways to Teaching Adults offered at my institution, Anne Arundel Community College. In this class, Professor Darian Senn-Carter engaged his students through meaningful assignments that immersed us in our learning environments.

During week one, Professor Senn-Carter asked us each to write a letter to a new professor at our school or place of employment. This exercise helped me revisit my first year of teaching over a decade earlier and determine the advice I wish I had gotten at that time. While detailing examples of best practices I had observed from my colleagues, I considered how these individual interventions fostered a broader climate of student support. I believe that writing this letter served me better than writing a typical paper because I could focus on the specific professional advice that would benefit a new hire. Having an audience for my paper gave the assignment purpose.

Another meaningful assignment was when our class conducted student interviews to determine what students expect in terms of classroom management. I interviewed a 20-year-old student at my college who was about to transfer to a four-year college. His answers reinforced a lot of my own practices and simultaneously gave me ideas for how to improve my classroom management skills. Our class then had to write related papers about improving classroom management at our college. The students' experiences and ideas were useful in pinpointing areas for potential faculty training and where resources could be allocated. Personal interviews are key sources of information that can be easily incorporated into a variety of assignments, and in this instance, conducting an interview gave me a better understanding of what our school was doing well and where further work was needed.

As an adult learner, I am more motivated when the assignments are meaningful. Assignments are meaningful to me if they are connected to past or present experiences and have a clear purpose or value. Online classes, in particular, need deliberate engagement strategies so that students feel connected to one another and the learning process. By using assignments that immersed me in my workplace, Professor Senn-Carter helped me retain more information as well as investigate how my values align with those of my institution. In fact, I referenced the assignments from this course when preparing talking points for an interview I had for a different position at my college.

If you are a professor thinking about utilizing this strategy, consider the big picture in your objectives. What will students learn and produce as a result of your assignment? How can you make sure that it is meaningful to them and others? Also, how can you use assignments like interviews and letters to incorporate a more social element into your online course? I know that talking to an undergraduate student as well as a new professor made me feel more connected with the campus. Having assignments that are designed to build a sense of community and be helpful to others is engaging.

৶৶৶৶৶৶৶৶

The examples shared by Kamel, Annabelle, and Chelsea provided excellent examples of assignments that were perceived to be relevant and meaningful to students. They appreciated how their professors made the content come alive through assignments that had real-world value. As Annabelle shared, it is important for students to see connections between the course content and their lived experiences.

Chelsea highlighted how engaging it was to use people as data sources. For many professionals, people can serve as important data sources. Using people as data sources is an excellent way to prioritize diversity in perspectives. Professors can encourage students to seek out the perspectives of individuals from varied races, ethnicities, ages, genders, sexual orientations, professions, and more to learn about course topics. Many professors instead emphasize the importance of using peer-reviewed sources. Although professionals in the field have endorsed the quality of peer-reviewed articles, there is some evidence that the articles do not represent diverse authorship. For instance, although the data is limited, Wu (2020) reported that most authors and editors of scientific journals are White males (Wu, 2020).

Graduates may not have access to library databases and peer-reviewed journals after graduation. Alumni indicated being more likely to rely on the Internet versus library databases when seeking out information needed in their professional roles (Travis, 2011). Assignments that utilize multiple types of data sources can not only engage students during the learning process but also ensure they have the information literacy skills they will need as professionals.

## PROVIDING OPPORTUNITIES FOR COLLABORATION ON PROJECTS

Collaborative projects can be particularly useful in online learning environments because they provide a way for students to connect with one another while learning the course content. DiGiacomo et al. (2023) noted that students can gain a sense of belonging through collaborative group projects. When students in an asynchronous online course were assigned group work, they reported higher levels of motivation and a sense of belonging (Carr et al., 2024). Bächtold et al. (2023) found that most first-year students viewed group work in a positive light, especially if they had experiences working in groups in high school. Elmassah et al. (2020) also found that prior experience in group work influenced students' perception of its value.

In addition to increasing student engagement, researchers have also found group work to be connected to increased learning. Gay and Betts (2020), for example, found that shifting from an essay assignment to a group assignment called eMeetings led to improved academic performance. Pass rates for the course were higher after the group assignment was introduced, and student feedback about the assignment experience was positive (Gay & Betts, 2020). One of the reasons why collaborative group projects increase learning is because students get to learn from their classmates. Malan (2021) found that 80% of the students who participated in group work in an online class strongly agreed or agreed that they learned from their peers during this process.

Some students, however, do not see the benefits of group work (Kelly et al., 2022). Only 52% of students in a study by Malan (2021) strongly agreed or agreed that the final product their group created was better than it would have been if it had been created on their own. One reason given by students was that they did not believe some of their peers had the skills necessary for groups to function well (Malan, 2021). Students may need support and guidance to gain the most from group assignments. Professors can help students working in virtual teams determine goals, engage in ongoing and respectful communication, and balance the workload among members to have a more meaningful and productive experience.

To address concerns that some students do not view group work favorably, Kelly et al. (2022) explored the benefit of an online intervention, which highlighted the benefits of group work. In this study, online students were randomly assigned to an experimental condition, where they viewed a video that showcased the academic and career benefits of participating in group work and shared strategies to increase group productivity, or a control group, where they learned details about the group project and were not provided with training on how to function well in a group. Results indicated that students in the experimental condition reported having a higher utility value for online group projects than students in the control condition (Kelly et al., 2022). However, there were no differences between the two groups in terms of intrinsic value or their group project or course grades (Kelly et al., 2022). Other researchers, however, have found that training students on the skills needed to complete group assignments has yielded positive outcomes. For example, Cranney et al. (2008) discovered that students who completed a set of online information literacy modules improved their performance on a group assignment. The students also reported the group experience was useful and worthwhile.

Agonafir (2023) found that group assignments were perceived by students as engaging and valuable when they were well-planned and executed. Elmassah et al. (2020) emphasized the importance of creating positive group experiences to counteract negative ones students may have had previously. For example, professors can give clear instructions and guidance on the assignment, ask members to determine group roles, require group members to regularly report on progress updates, and provide timely and useful feedback to set the stage for productive group work experiences (Agonafir, 2023). In Harrington (2021), Edwin shared a story about how a professor supported students in developing skills needed to function productively in a group before assigning a group project. In this example, the professor learned information about the students and used this information to form groups, required students to complete an online module about the interpersonal skills needed in groups, and asked teams to establish rules and assign group roles. When professors support students in developing group skills, students are more likely to be engaged and productive (Bächtold et al., 2023). Providing students with guidance about how to build rapport among group members, identify rules for the group, determine roles for each member, and monitor progress can help ensure students have a positive and productive group experience (Harrington, 2023).

In the following student stories, Kamel and Bridgette describe collaborative assignments that enabled them and their peers to learn from classmates and the professor. Kamel explains how listening to varied perspectives led to the development of a more robust business plan, and Bridgette shares an example of a collaborative project that required students to explore a current challenge in the STEM field and determine practical solutions to address the challenge. These examples illuminate the important role peers play in learning and how structured group assignments can lead to high levels of engagement and learning.

### A Collaborative Assignment: Developing a Business Plan, Kamel Johal, Athabasca University

As an online student, I found that the assignments were really important to me and, in some cases, even empowering. I appreciated it when we had the flexibility to lean on our personal and professional experiences as long as they directly related to the task and when assignments were connected. I liked it when each new assignment built upon the previous ones, as this created a cohesive learning journey for me. Moreover, I also liked it when the assignments accommodated our diverse learning styles, lenses, ideas, and interests. This personalized approach not only enhanced my engagement with the material but also encouraged me to explore topics from different perspectives. As a result, I gained a deeper understanding and appreciation of the subject matter.

One of my most notable academic endeavors centered on the development of my MBA business plan. For this assignment, we developed a plan for wrap-around services that was tailored to one individual. As we worked on this plan, we had to address multifaceted personal and professional challenges that could arise. We had to consider all aspects of daily life, encompassing vital tasks such as transportation, shopping, financial management, and childcare.

I related to this assignment because I have grappled with a plethora of responsibilities and could lean on my experiences to guide me. As a dedicated mother and student navigating diverse obligations, I discerned the critical need for a holistic support system characterized by skill, resourcefulness, locality, and affordability, with a primary focus on ensuring the well-being, safety, and educational enrichment of the identified individual.

To realize this vision, I collaborated with my professor and peers, pooling our collective insights and expertise to devise a viable operational framework. I was acutely aware that my perspective of what I required would be different from that of someone else, and my professor helped me recognize how I needed to move beyond my viewpoint to ensure the success and feasibility of my new business venture.

Through this collaborative endeavor, I gained not only practical wisdom but also a deeper understanding of academic principles applied in real-world contexts. The iterative refinement of my business plan underscored the transformative potential inherent in the fusion of theoretical knowledge and practical application. Moreover, the mentorship I received from my professor as I worked on this project played an instrumental role in refining my communication skills, enabling me to tailor my message to specific audiences effectively. I required this as my business would require many types of capital.

This collaborative learning experience involved engaging in online brainstorming sessions and participating in discussion forums facilitated under the guidance of our professor. To maximize the effectiveness of these sessions, we were paired with colleagues whose expertise complemented our own, fostering a synergistic exchange of ideas and refinement of key concepts. Encouragement of feedback was integral to the learning process, as it fostered a culture of mutual support and constructive critique as we moved through the program. The professor prioritized creating a safe and supportive environment where students felt empowered to share their assignment ideas and contribute to each other's growth and development.

I encourage other professors to create collaborative assignments where students can lean into their personal and professional expertise while also learning from others.

ಊಊಊಗಗಗ

ಊಊಊಗಗಗ

## Current Issues Group Project Assignment, Bridgette Harris, Morgan State University

One of the highlights of Professor Joy Barnes-Johnson's course was the immersive group project focused on real-world applications of STEM education principles. What I liked about this assignment was that it encouraged hands-on learning while also fostering collaboration and teamwork among classmates.

Each group was tasked with identifying a current issue in STEM education and developing a practical solution or project proposal. In class, we had many reading assignments focused on the importance of supporting underrepresented minorities in STEM. Much of the research emphasized that helping students build relevant skills and enhancing their ability to collaborate with peers different from themselves can help increase diversity in the workforce and maintain national economic competitiveness. Hence, my group chose to address the lack of diversity in STEM fields through targeted outreach programs and mentorship initiatives.

Working on this project was both stimulating and rewarding. Professor Barnes-Johnson provided guidance and support throughout the process, encouraging us to think critically and creatively about our approach. The collaborative nature of the assignment allowed us to leverage each other's strengths and perspectives, resulting in a comprehensive and impactful project proposal.

I have some advice for professors who wish to engage their students through group projects focused on current issues. First, when designing group projects, ensure that the tasks are meaningful and relevant to course objectives. Requiring students to address current issues can ensure that students are learning about information that is relevant to the field. Second, encourage open communication and collaboration within groups. And finally, provide opportunities for reflection and feedback to enhance the learning experience.

Both Kamel and Bridgette emphasized the benefit of learning about different perspectives when working on a group assignment. They noted that the diversity in thought challenged their thinking and resulted in a better academic product. Bächtold et al. (2023) found that sharing knowledge and learning from each other was one of the primary benefits of group assignments, according to first-year students. Students also indicated that they learned valuable collaboration skills as a result of engaging in group work (Bächtold et al., 2023).

## GIVING VARIED ASSIGNMENTS AND CHOICE

In addition to students appreciating creative and varied teaching approaches, they also want variety and innovation in assignments. Winfield (2024) noted, 'By diversifying all learning experiences, and especially assignments, instructors can create more inclusive learning environments where students feel empowered to innovate and apply their learning in creative ways' (p. 82). It can be challenging, if not impossible, to create one type of assignment that will be motivating and affirming for all the diverse students in a class.

Professors can increase student motivation and engagement by infusing varied assignments into the curriculum or by offering students a choice in which assignments they complete (George & Thompson, 2024). Tanis (2020) found that the majority of professors and alumni associated with an online program believed it was important for students to have choices in terms of assignment topics and how they demonstrate what they have learned. In Harrington (2021), Caleb shared that having a choice in the type of assignment gave students ownership over their learning experience. In the following student stories, Wesley and Patricia explain how having different kinds of assignments and having choices related to assignments engaged them as students.

ಙಙಙಚಚಚ

### Diverse Assignments, Wesley Russell, University of Oklahoma

My Creating Social Change course has been one of the best classes I have taken in my undergraduate career. The key difference between this course and the numerous others that I have taken was the diverse and creative assignments. While there were some traditional assignments, such as discussion boards and essays, we also had to do social annotations of required readings, art projects, petitions, and more. When we have to do the same task week after week, it can become monotonous. Varied assignments, however, engage and challenge us in an assortment of ways while also helping us develop and strengthen a multidisciplinary set of skills so that we can become more well-rounded professionals. Although the diversified assignment approach made the course more challenging because it pushed us outside of our comfort zones, it also made it more refreshing and less tedious.

An example of an assignment was the social annotations we did through a software called Hypothesis. Unfortunately, the free web version of this software is inaccessible to screen readers, so we utilized the version for Canvas that requires a subscription. Luckily, our institution was willing to pay the fee. Several readings were uploaded into this program, and we were required to comment on something that resonated with us, something that surprised us, and something that we found confusing. We were then required to respond to several of our peers. Our response had to include a question connected to a specific idea our peer discussed and highlight something we appreciated about their insight. In a digital learning space, this created the equivalent of an in-person roundtable discussion.

As students, we were able to challenge one another, speak from our unique experiences, and feel affirmed when other students expressed their struggles with the content. This task felt distinct from a discussion board because interacting with the content was more streamlined. Our comments on the readings were made directly in the documents, so this part of the task enabled us to have a more natural conversation. Discussion boards that require us to cite sources can seem more like assignments versus discussions. I have often been disengaged in these situations, but through the use of social annotations, I found it more natural to comment any time that the content struck a chord with me. In fact, this annotation assignment became a note-taking activity that helped me learn while completing required assignments.

Professor M. Geneva Murray was also intentional with implementing scaffolding into the structure of assignments. Professor Murray did this by having each student select a social justice topic they were passionate about at the beginning of the semester. Students were then encouraged to utilize their topic as the basis for most of their assignments. By pushing us to create work about one topic in a plethora of different ways, we were able to consider our topics from more than one perspective. For example, the Creating Social Change course had a unit covering disabilities, and students were encouraged to integrate what we had learned into our social justice module. We did this by planning a hypothetical protest on our topic that addressed accessibility for in-person and remote participation.

This task created a digital classroom environment where students were challenged to develop their critical thinking skills, something vital to progress in academia. I encourage professors to consider using diversified assignments. Regardless of the field, students will appreciate having diversity and creativity in the work they do.

ಶಿಶಿಶಿಲಿಲಿಲಿ

ಶಿಶಿಶಿಲಿಲಿಲಿ

## Choice, Creativity, and Challenge in Assignments, Patricia B. Ateboh-Briggs, Morgan State University

Professor Sean Robinson, a distinguished professor at Morgan State University, has a singular mission: To extend support and make a meaningful impact on as many lives as possible. I believe that Professor Robinson's assignments foster understanding, engagement, and creativity among students. I appreciated how he empowered us by allowing us to select assignment topics that resonated with our interests.

To help us decide on a topic, he encouraged us to review a list of themes outlined in the course. This autonomy not only enhanced my learning experience but also encouraged me to take ownership of my educational journey. The variety of options for presenting final projects was another hallmark feature of the class and Professor Robinson's teaching style. We were able to choose from formats like PowerPoint presentations or photo-journalistic essays to visually narrate the concepts, theories, and ideas discussed in class.

I also appreciated how he encouraged us to be creative when completing assignments. Instead of having to follow rigid patterns of writing, we were encouraged to explore various creative writing styles. The styles we chose had to align with the assignment's objectives but allowed our individual flair to show.

Through assignments, he pushed us to become more self-aware and also to increase our awareness and understanding of others. His teaching approach was to encourage us to craft critical responses that went beyond surface-level reactions, promoting deep reflection and thoughtful consideration. This reflective practice was not just an academic exercise but a vital skill for professional development, enabling us to critically examine and respond to the significant issues that define our existence.

One assignment example was a Scholarly Personal Narrative. To complete this assignment, we had to conduct reviews and draw comparisons between social movements, all centered around social identities. These essays challenged students to articulate their viewpoints, engage with literature, reflect on real-world practices, and consider the views of others. After we completed the assignment, we had discussions that were insightful and enjoyable. Hearing about what my classmates shared about their interests, scholarly discourse, and personal experiences enriched the conversation.

Although we had room for creativity, Professor Robinson also provided guidance. His assignments were characterized by clearly defined rubrics that provided precise criteria for evaluation, ensuring that expectations were transparent and attainable. Beyond the rubrics, he provided additional guidance where he clarified each task, offering step-by-step instructions that de-mystified the assignment process.

It was also great that Professor Robinson was flexible with due dates when needed. He was considerate of genuine circumstances, upholding a policy of non-discrimination and accommodation that reflects the diverse makeup of his classroom.

I hope that other professors will give students choices in terms of topics and the nature of the projects. Choices will help students increase their ownership of their learning while working on projects that matter to them. I also hope that professors will challenge students through assignments. Help students explore how beliefs, values, philosophies, and identities shape actions. Through this process, students will learn to apply these critical lenses to themselves and the institutions or organizations that they are part of, fostering a deeper understanding and more impactful work.

༺༺༺༻༻༻

The stories shared by Wesley and Patricia shine a light on the importance of having diverse assignments. They both appreciated having the opportunity to develop their skills and expand their knowledge through innovative and engaging assignments. Patricia emphasized the importance of choice. Assignment choice is an inclusive teaching practice (Addy et al., 2023). George and Thompson (2024) noted that 'Having a role in making decisions about learning processes, including assignments, can be motivational for all students, but especially for students who may have felt excluded or marginalized previously' (p. 89).

According to Dabrowski and Marshall (2019), there are three types of assignment choices professors can give to students. Professors can allow students to choose the topic for an assignment; this is referred to as a content choice. Content choices are the most frequently used choice option (Harrington, 2024). Professors can also allow students to have product choices, meaning they can determine how they want to demonstrate their learning. Students may opt to use a traditional format such as a paper or presentation or may choose to share their knowledge through a more creative option such as a podcast or infographic. Professors can either limit the choice options or allow students the freedom to choose any type of product. George and Thompson (2024) explained that some students might find having too many options to be overwhelming, so they suggested limiting choice options. Finally, professors can also give students process choices. Allowing students to determine due dates or if they prefer to work alone or with peers are examples of process choices. Research has shown that very few professors are offering process choices to students (Harrington, 2024).

Professors who want to engage their students through assignments are encouraged to give them different types of assignments and, when possible, offer choices. As Winfield (2024) noted, there are numerous innovative types of assignments beyond traditional ones like exams and papers. Each type of assignment can help students build different skills and enable them to build on different strengths. Arend and Carlson (2024) emphasized the importance of assisting students to see the skills that will be developed through various assignments. For example, a presentation would help a student develop public speaking skills while designing an infographic would help a student develop visual communication and marketing skills. One way to convey the skills students would learn through different assignment options would be to list skills for each assignment on the syllabus.

In addition to using innovative assignments, professors are also encouraged to find ways to offer assignment choices. When students are allowed to make decisions about their learning tasks, this gives them ownership over their educational experience. As a result, students are more likely to be more engaged (George & Thompson, 2024).

## FACULTY REFLECTION QUESTIONS

1. How can I use assignments to help students build their foundational knowledge and self-efficacy for learning content and skills in this discipline?
2. What formative assessments would provide students with valuable feedback that could be used to improve their performance on summative assessments?
3. How can I incorporate growth mindset content or lessons into assignments?
4. How can I modify assignments to have more real-world relevance?
5. How can I help students make personal and real-world connections to course content through assignments?
6. How can I structure group assignments in a way that will lead to positive experiences and outcomes? What type of support can I provide students to help them be productive group members?
7. What innovative options might be good alternatives to traditional assignments like exams and papers?
8. What types of content, product, and process assignment choices can I offer students?

## REFERENCES

Aagaard, L., Conner, T. W., II, & Skidmore, R. L. (2014). College textbook reading assignments and class time activity. *Journal of the Scholarship of Teaching and Learning, 14*(3), 132–145. https://doi.org/10.14434/josotl.v14i3.5031

Addy, T. M., Dube, D., Mitchell, K. A., & SoRelle, M. E. (2023). *What inclusive instructors do: Principles and practices for excellence in college teaching.* Routledge.

Agonafir, A. M. (2023). Using a cooperative learning strategy to increase undergraduate students' engagement and performance: Bahir Dar university Psychology graduating students in focus. *Bahir Dar Journal of Education, 23*(2), 96–112. https://doi.org/10.4314/bdje.v23i2.6

Aliah, N., Swarni, A., & Natsir, N. (2024). Evaluating the impact of innovative assignment design on student engagement and learning outcomes in higher education. *International Journal of Education Language Literature Arts Culture and Social Humanities, 2*(2), 13–20. https://doi.org/10.59024/ijellacush.v2i2.769

Anastasiou, D., Wirngo, C. N., & Bagos, P. (2024). The effectiveness of concept maps on students' achievement in science: A meta-analysis. *Educational Psychology Review, 36*(2), 1–32. https://doi.org/10.1007/s10648-024-09877-y

Anderson, L., & Krathwohl, D. A. (2001). *Taxonomy for learning, teaching, and assessing: A revision of Bloom's taxonomy of educational objectives.* Longman.

Arend, B., & Carlson, E. R. (2024). What makes assignments meaningful? In C. Harrington (Ed.), *Creating culturally affirming and meaning assignments: A practical resource for higher education faculty* (pp. 37–54). Routledge. https://doi.org/10.4324/978/003443797-4

Bächtold, M., Roca, P., & De Checchi, K. (2023). Students' beliefs and attitudes towards cooperative learning, and their relationship to motivation and approach to learning. *Studies in Higher Education, 48*(1), 100–112. https://doi.org/10.1080/03075079.2022.2112028

Bixler, G. M., Brown, A., Way, D., Ledford, C., & Mahan, J. D. (2015). Collaborative concept mapping and critical thinking in fourth-year medical students. *Clinical Pediatrics, 54*(9), 833–839. https://doi.org/10.1177/0009922815590223

Campbell, A. L., Direito, I. & Mokhithi, M. (2021) Developing growth mindsets in engineering students: A systematic literature review of interventions, *European Journal of Engineering Education, 46*(4), 503–527, https://doi.org/10.1080/03043797.2021.1903835

Carney, E. A., Zhang, X., Charsha, A., Taylor, J. N., & Hoshaw, J. P. (2022). Formative assessment helps students learn over time: Why aren't we paying more attention to it? *Intersection: A Journal at the Intersection of Assessment and Learning, 4*(1), 1–12. https://doi.org/10.61669/001c.38391

Carr, S. E., Wilson, T. E., Slone, S. A., Karanja, L. W., & Osterhage, J. L. (2024). Assigned group work is associated with increased student motivation and perceptions of belonging in an asynchronous online physiology laboratory course. *Advances in Physiology Education, 48*(3), 593–602. https://doi.org/10.1152/advan.00064.2024

Casanova, J., Sinval, J., & Almeida, L. (2024). Academic success, engagement and self-efficacy of first-year university students: Personal variables and first-semester performance. *Annals of Psychology, 40*(1), 44–53. https://doi.org/10.6018/analesps.479151

Cheng, M. W. T., Leung, M. L., & Lau, J. C.-H. (2021). A review of growth mindset intervention in higher education: The case for infographics in cultivating mindset behaviors. *Social Psychology of Education: An International Journal, 24*(5), 1335–1362. https://link.springer.com/article/10.1007%2Fs11218-021-09660-9

Cook, B. R., & Babon, A. (2017). Active learning through online quizzes: Better learning and less (busy) work. *Journal of Geography in Higher Education, 41*(1), 24–38. https://doi.org/10.1080/03098265.2016.1185772

Cranney, J., Morris, S., Spehar, B., & Scoufis, M. (2008). Helping first year students think like psychologists: Supporting information literacy and teamwork skill development. *Psychology Learning & Teaching, 7*(1), 28–36. https://doi.org/10.2304/plat.2008.7.1.28

Dabrowski, J., & Marshall, T. R. (2019). Choice and relevancy: Autonomy and personalization in assignments help motivate and engage students. *Principal, 98*(3), 10–13. https://eric.ed.gov/?id=ED593328

Darby, F., & Lang, J. M. (2019*). Small teaching online: Applying learning science in online classes.* Jossey Bass.

Díaz, O., & Garmendia, X. (2025). Bridging reading and mapping: The role of reading annotations in facilitating feedback while concept mapping. *Information Systems, 127*, 1–17. https://doi-org.proxy-ms.researchport.umd.edu/10.1016/j.is.2024.102458

Dweck, C. (2008). *Mindset: The new psychology of success.* Ballantine Books.

Elmassah, S., Mostafa Bacheer, S., & James, R. (2020). What shapes students' perceptions of group work: Personality or past experience? *International Journal of Educational Management, 34*(9), 1457–1473. https://doi.org/10.1108/IJEM-11-2019-0401

Eodice, M., Geller, A. E., & Lerner, N. (2017). *The meaningful writing project: Learning, teaching, and writing in higher education.* University Press of Colorado.

Fatawi, I., Degeng, I. N. S., Setyosari, P., Ulfa, S., & Hirashima, T. (2020). Effect of online based concept map on student engagement and learning outcome. *International Journal of Distance Education Technologies, 18*(3), 42–56. https://doi.org/10.4018/IJDET.2020070103

Fink, L. D. (2013). *Creating significant learning experiences: An integrated approach to designing college courses.* Jossey-Bass.

Gay, G. H. E., & Betts, K. (2020). From discussion forums to emeetings: Integrating high touch strategies to increase student engagement, academic performance, and retention in large online courses. *Online Learning, 24*(1), 92–117. https://doi.org/10.24059/olj.v24i1.1984

George, M. J., & Thompson, J. E. (2024). Giving choice in assignments. In C. Harrington (Ed.), *Creating culturally affirming and meaning assignments: A practical resource for higher education faculty* (pp. 87–100). Routledge. https://doi.org/10.4324/9781003443797-7

Harrington, C. (2021). *Keeping us engaged: Student perspectives (and research-based strategies) on what works and why.* Routledge.

Harrington, C. (2023). *Student success in college: Doing what works!* (4th ed.). Cengage.

Harrington, C. (2024). How much assignment choice do students have? A descriptive study of syllabi. *Currents in Teaching and Learning, 15*(2), 6–15. https://webcdn.worcester.edu/currents-in-teaching-and-learning/wp-content/uploads/sites/65/2024/03/Currents15.2-Final.pdf

Harrington, C. (2025). *Keeping us engaged: Student perspectives (and research-based strategies) on what works and why* (2nd ed.). Routledge

Ives, L., Mitchell, T. J., & Hübl, H. (2020). Promoting critical reading with double-entry notes: A pilot study. *InSight: A Journal of Scholarly Teaching, 15*, 13–32. https://digitalcommons.georgiasouthern.edu/sotlcommons/SoTL/2019/42/

Kelly, A. E., Clinton-Lisell, V., & Klein, K. A. (2022). Enhancing college students' online group work perceptions and skills using a utility-value intervention.

*Online Learning*, *26*(3), 236–258. https://olj.onlinelearningconsortium.org/index.php/olj/article/view/2807

Kyung-Mi, O. (2022). A comparative study of gamified and conventional online quizzes. *International Journal of Emerging Technologies in Learning*, *17*(3), 152–172. https://doi.org/10.3991/ijet.v17i03.26349

Mack, N. (2023). Marginalized students need to write about their lives: Meaningful assignments for analysis and affirmation. *Composition Forum*, *52*. https://eric.ed.gov/?q=Narrative+writing&pg=3&id=EJ1410228

Malan, M. (2021). The effectiveness of cooperative learning in an online learning environment through a comparison of group and individual marks. *Electronic Journal of E-Learning*, *19*(6), 1–13. http://www.ejel.org/

Maurer, T. W., & Longfield, J. (2015). Using reading guides and online quizzes to improve reading compliance and quiz scores. *International Journal for the Scholarship of Teaching and Learning*, *9*(1), 1–25. http://digitalcommons.georgiasouthern.edu/ij-sotl/vol9/iss1/6

Mebert, L., Barnes, R., Dalley, J., Gawarecki, L., Ghazi-Nezami, F., Shafer, G., Slater, J., & Yezbick, E. (2020). Fostering student engagement through a real-world, collaborative project across disciplines and institutions. *Higher Education Pedagogies*, *5*(1), 30–51. https://doi.org/10.1080/23752696.2020.1750306

Mimouni, A. (2022). Using mobile gamified quizzing for active learning: The effect of reflective class feedback on undergraduates' achievement. *Education and Information Technologies*, *27*(9), 12003–12026. https://doi.org/10.1007/s10639-022-11097-2

Pinahs-Schultz, P., & Beck, B. (2016). Development and assessment of signature assignments to increase student engagement in undergraduate public health. *Pedagogy in Health Promotion*, *2*(3), 206–213. https://doi.org/10.1177/2373379915606454

Priniski, S. J., Hecht, C. A., & Harackiewicz, J. M. (2018). Making learning personally meaningful: A new framework for relevance research. *Grantee Submission*, *86*(1), 11–29. https://doi.org/10.1080/00220973.2017.1380589

Ruget, V., & Rosero, K. H. (2014). What's new? Assessing the effectiveness of current events assignments. *Currents in Teaching and Learning*, *6*(2), 17–34. https://webcdn.worcester.edu/currents-in-teaching-and-learning/wp-content/uploads/sites/65/2022/05/Currents-Volume-06-Issue-02-Spring-2014.pdf#page=19

Schroeder, N. L., Nesbit, J. C., Anguiano, C. J., & Adesope, O. O. (2018). Studying and constructing concept maps: A meta-analysis. *Educational Psychology Review*, *30*(2), 431–455. https://link.springer.com/article/10.1007/s10648-017-9403-9

Tanis, C. J. (2020). The seven principles of online learning: Feedback from faculty and alumni on its importance for teaching and learning. *Research in Learning Technology*, *28*, 1–25. http://dx.doi.org/10.25304/rlt.v28.2319

Travis, T. (2011). From the classroom to the boardroom: The impact of information literacy instruction on workplace research skills. *Education Libraries*, *34*(2), 19–31. https://doi.org/10.26443/el.v34i2.308

Trent, C. (2023). ChatGPT and current events in the economics classroom. *Business Education Innovation Journal, 15*(1), 177–186.

Tropman, E. (2014). In defense of reading quizzes. *International Journal of Teaching and Learning in Higher Education, 26*(1), 140–146. https://files.eric.ed.gov/fulltext/EJ1043037.pdf

Wilkinson, K., Dafoulas, G., Garelick, H., & Huyck, C. (2020). Are quiz-games an effective revision tool in Anatomical Sciences for Higher Education and what do students think of them? *British Journal of Educational Technology, 51*(3), 761–777. https://doi.org/10.1111/bjet.12883

Winfield, J. K.(2024) Exploring assignment options beyond the exam. In C. Harrington (Ed.), *Creating culturally affirming and meaning assignments: A practical resource for higher education faculty* (pp. 71–86). Routledge. https://doi.org/10.4324/978/003443797-6

Wollschleger, J. (2019). Making it count: Using real-world projects for course assignments. *Teaching Sociology, 47*(4), 314–324. https://doi.org/10.1177/0092055X19864422

Wu, K. (2020, November 2). Scientific journals commit to diversity but lack the data. *New York Times.* https://www.nytimes.com/2020/10/30/science/diversity-science-journals.html

# CHAPTER 5

# Feedback

Students have shared numerous examples of how they have been encouraged and motivated by feedback provided by their professors (Harrington, 2021). Professors can use feedback to engage their students and help them learn (Faulconer et al., 2022). Pan and Shao (2020) found that student's perception of feedback 'directly influenced their learning motivation' (p. 6). Feedback can inspire students to gain a deeper understanding of the content and to think in different and creative ways (Shean, 2023). Samaranayake (2024) emphasized the especially important role feedback plays in student engagement and learning in online courses because online students may not have as much access to informal feedback processes such as smiles and nods that are frequently used in traditional classroom settings.

Feedback is most effective when framed in a positive, supportive, and encouraging manner. Through feedback, professors can recognize and reinforce student efforts and achievements. Students find the validation of their efforts, strengths, and progress to be highly engaging (Lowe & Shaw, 2019; Nicol & Macfarlane-Dick, 2006). Students especially appreciate feedback that is phrased positively and guides them on how to improve (Yildiz Durak, 2024).

Murray and Scafe (2024) recommended that professors provide strength-based feedback to students. They explained that instead of hunting for errors, professors could look for examples of what students did well, point these examples out to them, and show them how leveraging their strengths and skills can improve other parts of the project. One strength-based approach to giving feedback is the 'liked best, next time' (Hoffmann-Longtin, 2019, p. 100). Hoffmann-Longtin (2019) shared the following example, 'I like what you did in this section because it effectively synthesizes your experience with the course material. In this other area, consider applying this concept. It might more effectively articulate your argument.' (p. 100). Strength-based feedback can increase student motivation and performance. In a study by Susilana and Pribadi (2021), one student commented, 'positive comments on my works enhanced my motivation to complete this online course with better results' (p. 523).

There are numerous models and frameworks that can guide the type of feedback professors provide. One frequently cited feedback model was developed by Hattie and Timperley (2007). They described the following three types of feedback:

- **Feed-Up**. Feed-up feedback helps students attend to the goal of the assignment so that they can meet expectations.
- **Feedback**. When professors provide information about how students are progressing toward the goal, this is referred to as feedback.
- **Feed-Forward**. With feed-forward, professors give guidance and suggestions about how students can strengthen and improve their work.

Hattie and Timperley (2007) further added that feedback can be provided at different levels. For instance, professors can give task-level feedback that informs the student about how well they are accomplishing the task at hand or at the process level, which would focus on the strategies or approaches students are using to accomplish the task (Hattie & Timperley, 2007). Hattie and Timperley (2007) also suggested that self-regulatory level feedback could assist students with strengthening their ability to monitor their own progress and determine what strategies they need to employ to improve.

Brooks et al. (2019) shared a matrix tool that professors could use to determine feedback strategies targeting all types and levels of feedback proposed by Hattie and Timperley (2007). They noted that student feedback needs can change over time (Brooks et al., 2019). For example, novice learners may benefit more from task-related feedback that clarifies assignment goals. In contrast, more advanced learners may benefit more from feedback focused on developing their self-regulatory skills.

For students to get the maximum benefit of feedback, professors should aim to provide the feedback promptly. Most professors teaching in an online program (75%) and graduates from this same online program (63%) indicated that it was critical that feedback be provided within one week (Tanis, 2020). Students also shared this desire for prompt feedback in a study conducted by Zepeda et al. (2023). One of the main reasons why prompt feedback is so highly valued is that it helps students know if they are on track to be successful in the course. Susilana and Pribadi (2021) found that students appreciated getting feedback in a timely manner and noted that getting immediate feedback helped them improve their performance on upcoming tasks.

Prompt and ongoing feedback not only helps online students learn but also helps them develop a strong connection with their professors (Lee, 2022). One characteristic of effective feedback is that it encourages professor–student dialogue (Nicol & Macfarlane-Dick, 2006). These feedback-based conversations can foster positive professor–student relationships and learning. One online student commented,

> I enjoy getting feedback from instructors online. Since we do not meet in person, this helps me understand what the teacher is looking for, and it helps me get to know my teacher a little bit more. With feedback I know that my instructor is truly looking at my work, and values me as a student.
> (Chang & Farha, 2023, p. 148)

Nicol and Macfarlane-Dick (2006) noted that in addition to encouraging dialogue, effective feedback also clarifies what constitutes good performance in terms of goals and criteria, encourages students to engage in self-assessment and reflection, provides students with valuable information about their learning progress, motivates and builds self-efficacy for learning tasks, and improves performance.

Researchers have found that feedback in online courses is often more structured in nature (Pan & Shao, 2020). According to Alharbi and Alghammas (2021), students reported that written feedback provided by professors was generally clear. Professors tend to provide more feedback when doing so in an electronic format, such as in asynchronous discussions (Johnson et al., 2019). Thus, students taking online classes may benefit from more comprehensive feedback.

Providing high-quality feedback can take a substantial amount of time and energy (Ketchum et al., 2020). Professors may sometimes wonder if students are reading and learning from the feedback provided. Fortunately, research has shown that students do review and use the feedback provided. Pan and Shao (2020), for instance, found that when students were provided with structured feedback, they were motivated to take on a more active role (Pan & Shao, 2020). In a study conducted by Chang and Farha (2023), most online students reported reviewing feedback provided by their professors. Specifically, 70% of students strongly agreed, and 24% agreed with a statement about reviewing professor-provided feedback in the learning management system for all or most assignments (Chang & Farha, 2023). According to Rodriguez and Koubek (2019), students reported using feedback to improve their work.

An advantage associated with feedback in online classes is that the feedback is housed in the learning management system. Students can, therefore, go back and review the feedback they were provided when needed. Alharbi and Alghammas (2021) found that students appreciated the accessibility of written feedback.

Rawle et al. (2018) found that students found it valuable to be able to go back and review feedback given on previous assignments when working on current learning tasks. Students may opt to review positive feedback they received to boost their confidence and may refer back to and use constructive feedback provided when working on the next learning task.

## MOTIVATIONAL FEEDBACK

Brief, encouraging words can make a huge difference for students. When providing feedback, spotlighting student strengths can help them see their talents, achievements, and potential. Students have reported being encouraged by professors who have noticed their strengths and saw possible futures for them (Harrington, 2025). Feedback recognizing a student's potential can be particularly impactful for students who may be experiencing self-doubt. Encouraging words may help students gain the motivation needed to stay in school, pursue their career aspirations, or even help them see other possibilities they may not have previously considered.

Students will be more likely to persevere with current tasks and even take on new challenges when they are encouraged to do so by others. Students have shared how positive feedback and encouragement from their professors gave them the motivation to put forth more effort into learning (Harrington, 2021). In the next student story, Ashley shares an example of how encouraging words by a professor made a difference. A professor's encouragement to pursue doctoral studies played an important role in Ashley's decision to enroll in a doctoral program.

### Feedback that Encouraged Me to Pursue My Goal, Ashley McWilliams, Concordia University

When I entered my very first course while pursuing my master's degree, I was filled with excitement but was also nervous. Excitement because being in a graduate program meant that I was a step closer to achieving my goal. Nerves because despite having this goal since the age of 9, recent health complications seemed to make learning very difficult for me. I come from a family of educators, so I was always eager to learn and absorb knowledge. I perceived learning to be natural and fun. However, it felt like I could only absorb so much when my health was in decline. Throughout this decline, I was worried and discouraged. I worried that no one would know how much I loved learning. I wondered if my dream was a goal worth setting. My professor had no idea about my health challenges or my goals. In my mind, if I could just ignore my health and get through the course, everything would be fine.

Throughout this online course, I noticed that my professor was very present. She created and maintained an online classroom environment that allowed us to challenge ourselves and ask for help. She was excited to learn with us. That excitement and presence from my professor is what helped me to stay in the course. Unsure about the state of my health, I knew the best option for me was to take a break from school. I was very saddened at the thought of not being able to finish school at that time, but I was able to complete the course. Then something pretty amazing happened.

After submitting my final assignment, my professor left me a submission comment. She stated that I should seriously consider pursuing a doctoral degree after graduation. At that moment, I did not feel sick or unwell; I felt hope. A professor whom I admired told me to pursue my goal without the knowledge of my goal. I have wanted to pursue a doctoral degree since I was a child, but I never told her this. She saw something in me that I lost sight of.

I made up my mind that I would not give up on my goal. My professor did not know much about my situation, but she noticed my potential. This one comment made such a huge impact. I am proud to say that I am now pursuing a doctoral degree in education.

My advice to all professors is to be present and share your excitement to learn. Conveying excitement can be especially important in an online class. Challenge your students, look for their strengths, and unlock their potential. Help students achieve the potential they may or may not be aware they have and encourage them to be lifelong learners and pursue meaningful goals.

৩৩৩৩৩৩

Ashley's story illustrates how impactful it can be for a professor to acknowledge a student's strengths and potential. In this case, Ashley's professor provided the encouragement and affirmation needed to pursue a lifelong goal of earning a doctoral degree. Professors are encouraged to take time to share encouraging feedback because this feedback can make a significant difference in the lives of students.

Austen and Malone (2018) found that students appreciated receiving specific praise because they then knew what they should continue doing moving forward. For example, one student said, 'you need to point out what was good, rather than just going "this is wrong", you need to do this' (Austen & Malone, 2018, p. 50). In a different study, a student shared this comment on an end-of-semester evaluation:

> Thanks so much for your encouraging video feedback this week. I could see your excitement and genuineness shine through. The feedback really reinforced 'hey, you're getting this' when sometimes when you're sitting at your desk alone, you wonder if you really are getting it!
>
> (Stewart, 2023, p. 12)

In the next student story, Tabatha shares how a professor's feedback that highlighted strengths and suggested strategies for improvement provided the motivation needed to continue working on tasks that were perceived to be challenging.

🙰🙰🙰☙☙☙

### A Little Encouragement Can Go a Long Way, Tabatha Jones, McLennan Community College

I have always struggled to feel motivated at school, often procrastinating and not doing my coursework until the last minute. Sometimes, I would not even turn in an assignment at all because it felt too overwhelming. This has been a struggle for me throughout school, and it even led to me taking a break from college altogether in 2021. This past semester, I have worked hard on quitting my old habits of procrastination and staying on top of my work. This has been incredibly difficult, but one of the things that has helped me stay motivated and on top of my work is the feedback I received from my Spanish professor, Professor Amber Bracken.

Each assignment I turn in for this course is met with feedback that I find to be positive due to the constructive comments and encouragement I receive from her to continue working hard and trying my best. The emails I received congratulating me on the high grade I achieved on a test and the detailed videos in response to my discussion posts motivated me to strive for greatness in this class and improve upon my mistakes.

Some of the feedback is given through written means, but primarily, it consists of short videos detailing what I did correctly in my assignment and what I can improve upon. For example, I struggle with the gendered language in Spanish as I often forget which items are male or female. Professor Bracken is very patient with me and acknowledges that it is difficult to learn a new language with all the differing rules. With her encouragement, I am more apt to learn from my mistakes instead of viewing them as ways that I have failed.

It can be especially difficult to stay motivated when attending college online, so the little things truly matter the most. I admire Professor Bracken and the way she teaches her course. She makes it engaging, and you can tell she cares a lot about her students and making sure they succeed. It is very motivating and encouraging when you can tell a professor cares about the work you put into their class.

In addition to giving us individual feedback on assignments, Professor Bracken also consistently checks in with the class through announcement posts and emails each week, giving broader feedback to the class. These announcements also get us motivated for what is to come. I am very thankful for her encouragement. I hope I encounter more professors like her in my college career.

My advice to other professors wishing to engage students, especially in an online setting, is to check in consistently and offer detailed feedback on assignments. It is helpful to include constructive criticism. Detailed feedback can include acknowledging what a student has done correctly and offering guidance when pointing out a mistake. I think no matter how difficult a subject is for a student, they can succeed in their class with consistent encouragement, check-ins, and feedback on how they are doing. At least for me, it shows me that I really matter. I think some professors forget what it was like to learn the material for the first time and that some of us may not catch on as quickly as others. It is also nice when a professor acknowledges that a course can be difficult to learn because this makes us feel that we are not the only ones who are struggling.

ಬಿಬಿಬಿಀಀಀ

Tabatha's story illustrates how a professor provided ongoing constructive and encouraging feedback. As Tabatha shared, it can be more difficult for students to stay engaged in an online learning environment. Online professors can increase student engagement by providing positive, prompt, and encouraging feedback. In the following story, Kellye shares how important encouraging feedback is, even to 'A' students.

ಬಿಬಿಬಿಀಀಀ

### Encouraging Feedback Even When I Got an 'A', Kellye Irvin, Tarrant County College

One of my professors, Professor Craig Clark, was great at giving encouraging and supportive feedback. I appreciated how he frequently shared additional resources relating to the subject matter, but what really stood out to me was how he gave feedback. Whenever he graded a discussion, assignment, quiz, test, or project, I would find encouraging comments such as 'Good work explaining features, advantages, and benefits which are the focus of this exercise' when my assignments were returned.

Because of the specific comments he made, I knew that he read my work, and this really mattered to me. I was amazed when I realized he gave this type of feedback to all his students. Given how many classes he has and how many students per class, this was remarkable. I appreciated how he took the time to personally comment on all my submissions. It was obvious that he wanted us to learn from his feedback.

I have always felt that Professor Clark went above and beyond in every way, bringing in articles, videos, and websites to enhance each lesson and assignment. Every resource he shared was always helpful and poignant to the material. He often shared these resources to help us prepare for assignments and also when he was giving feedback. For an assignment about sales presentations, he attached an outline for visual presentations and an interesting article about presenting to customers. I have already used some of these materials in my work.

Even if I earned an A, his feedback would get me thinking about how I could improve my academic and job performance. For me, the feedback was two-fold. In one way, I was validated that I am, indeed, on the right track. Second, the additional information and resources he provided brought me an even deeper understanding. It helped solidify what I was learning, and the real-world examples he shared helped me see how valuable what we were learning was. Through this process, I realized that I could grow my skills because I had the knowledge, resources, and support needed to do so.

My advice to professors is to provide feedback that is both encouraging and helpful. Even if your students have met the criteria of the assignment, challenge them a little more. Make them think. Encourage students who are doing poor or mediocre work. Use feedback as an opportunity to explain concepts in a different and more personalized way. Offer the same encouragement to students who are doing well. Make connections between their work and what is happening in the world.

ಌಌಌಌಌಌ

The student stories shared remind professors that feedback can be used to motivate and encourage students. Yildiz Durak (2024) found that students cited personalized feedback as one of the most important factors in an online course. Using a strength-based approach to assignment feedback can engage students in all course modalities but can be an especially powerful approach in online courses.

In an interesting case study by Park and Stuehm (2024), professors started providing strength-based feedback to students in an online asynchronous course mid-way through the semester. The feedback spotlighted examples of when students demonstrated critical thinking skills. Two examples of feedback statements were 'You integrated your knowledge of the theory obtained from the course contents into case analysis' and 'You reflected on your own experience and applied ... theory learned from this course to the experience' (Park & Stuehm, 2024, p. 48). Word count trends in online discussions revealed that although there was a decline in output immediately following the strength-based feedback, word count increased two weeks after the strength-based feedback was introduced. In addition to the students engaging more in the discussions, the quality of the posts also improved, with more students identifying and citing additional sources and using theories to solve problems. According to Park and Stuehm (2024), in this online course,

Strength-based feedback played three positive roles:

1. Students who had demonstrated critical-thinking skills maintained their motivation to think critically through persistent positive feedback.
2. Positive feedback reinforced students' understanding of critical thinking.
3. Students who struggled at the beginning learned how to demonstrate critical thinking skills and were motivated to try their best (p. 51).

## FOSTERING A PRODUCTIVE MINDSET ABOUT FEEDBACK

Helping students shift their mindset about feedback can also motivate students. Unfortunately, researchers have found that most students have a fixed mindset, meaning they believe their intelligence cannot be changed, and this fixed mindset results in students often having a negative reaction to feedback and not using feedback to improve (Forsythe & Johnson, 2017). Forsythe and Johnson (2017) recommended that professors teach students about the purpose of feedback early in the semester to help them develop a more growth mindset.

According to Dweck (2008), students who have a growth mindset believe that intelligence is malleable and that they can learn. Not surprisingly, students with a growth mindset will be more likely to see the value of feedback, perceiving it to be helpful as they grow and learn. Professors can help students recognize that revisions based on feedback lead to improved work and that feedback is designed to help students strengthen their knowledge and skills.

When students have a growth mindset, they will be more likely to engage in productive actions that will help them learn. For example, Cutumisu and Lou

(2020) found that students with a growth mindset were more likely to seek out critical feedback and that these actions contributed to improved performance. In the next study story, Abaynesh explains how a professor used analogies to help students understand that learning is a process that takes time and effort. Abaynesh appreciated how this professor helped students see that feedback was meant to help students progress toward their goals.

### Using Analogies as a Motivational Feedback Technique, Abaynesh Berecha, Community College of Aurora, Colorado

At the start of the semester, Professor Munnelly asked students to come up with an analogy for writing. He gave us an example of running. He told us that writing and running are both difficult to accomplish without planning and lots of effort. We discussed many of the similarities between these tasks. For instance, writing and running both require a lot of practice, and coaches can work with the people doing these tasks to help them improve. He wanted us to identify something that we related to. I came up with two analogies for writing – one was raising children and the other was baking.

In this online class, Professor Munnelly let us review drafts of our work with him individually. He, therefore, invited us to stay after class and meet with him via Zoom. During these one-on-one meetings, which were optional but encouraged, we would go over our draft together. When the meeting started, we would share the screen so we both were looking at the same part of the essay together.

He would always start with a positive, sharing what we did well in the essay first. Then, he would point out the areas that needed improvement, sharing ideas about how to improve the essay. Before we were finished, he would remind us of the analogy we chose at the beginning of the semester. If we did not select one, he would stick with the running example he shared. For instance, he might remind us how many times a runner needs to go out and practice before entering a marathon. Using an analogy that we created, or the running one, was a good reminder for us that writing is just a skill that needs practice, and guidance from him would help us get better at it.

Through these one-on-one Zoom feedback sessions, Professor Munnelly made writing feel easier. He really got me motivated to write, which was amazing. The comments and suggestions he made helped me see writing from different angles. By the end of the semester, he made me love writing, and I noticed how much my writing skills improved.

So, for professors, it will be great to share analogies or other motivating ideas that relate to writing papers. Sharing these analogies or other motivating words can help students see that although writing a paper is a difficult task, it can be done with hard work. Be encouraging and supportive when providing feedback, and find ways for students to see your comments as motivational and helpful. Give students the option to review drafts or works in progress so they can use the feedback to improve their work. When students are more motivated, they will work harder, and this will help them build their skills.

## PERSONALIZED, SPECIFIC, AND CONSTRUCTIVE FEEDBACK

Pan and Shao (2020) found that students did not find general comments such as 'well done' to be motivating. Lipnevich and Smith (2009) also found that this type of generic feedback did not lead to students exerting more effort on upcoming tasks. Instead, students had higher engagement and motivation when their professors provided them with personalized suggestions on how to improve (Pan & Shao, 2020). One student noted that constructive feedback 'makes me understand how to do my assignments in the best way' (Pan & Shao, 2020, p. 523).

Students appreciate specific and personalized feedback that helps them know how well they are progressing toward the assignment goal. Brooks et al. (2019) noted that an effective way to provide specific feedback to students was by connecting the feedback provided to the criteria for success on the assignment. In a study on the perceptions of students in an asynchronous course, Moni (2024) found that students reported feedback that focused on how well they were doing, such as feedback linked to the criteria outlined in the rubric, was helpful.

In addition to providing guidance on how to improve, students have reported that specific and personalized feedback has helped them feel more connected to their professors. This was illustrated in a study by Stewart (2023). In this study that explored student perceptions of an online course, one of the items that had the highest rating was 'I feel that detailed feedback from my professor allows me to feel connected to my professor' (Stewart, 2023, p. 11). A related example comes from a study by Chang and Farha (2023), where an online student shared, 'Feedback helps not only in improving the quality of my work but also acts as a word of encouragement and a line of communication with the instructor' (p. 148). Relationships influence the learning process. In the following student story, Kamel makes an important point about how students are more likely to receive feedback positively when they have established a trusting relationship with their professor.

**Personalized, Detailed Feedback from a Trusted Professor, Kamel Johal, Athabasca University**

One particularly effective strategy employed by my professor was constructive feedback and guidance. Rather than merely assessing my performance, the professor offered personalized and detailed insights and suggestions for improvement. This personalized and constructive feedback encouraged me to reflect critically on my work and made me strive for continuous growth. As a first-generation Canadian, getting feedback that helped me see how to improve engaged me.

Details in the feedback were important to me because this removed the ambiguous and subjective nature of feedback. In the past, when professors did not share specific reasons for their comments, I was left to guess how to improve and earn a better grade. But in this class, this was not the case. I appreciated how the feedback often made me think outside the box and beyond my perspective. While my professor may not have mirrored my demographic characteristics, their insights fostered a nuanced reevaluation of my worldview. The comments and suggestions I received made me become a better critical thinker.

Moreover, my professor was readily accessible for one-on-one consultations, providing personalized mentorship and academic support tailored to my individual needs. My professor was always accessible and available. Transcending temporal and spatial constraints, technological tools such as email, FaceTime, Teams, Zoom, BlueJeans, and other methods made it easy for us to meet. These diverse modalities were meticulously chosen to ensure inclusivity and accommodate varied preferences and circumstances.

I encourage professors who want to provide effective feedback to their students to tailor feedback to individual student needs and be specific. Students will also appreciate it if you make yourself available via one-on-one consultation. During these meetings, you can provide mentorship, sponsorship, and guidance. Students will appreciate knowing you are there for them and want to see them succeed. Students, especially those who have been oppressed, marginalized, and alienated, will find value in developing a relationship with you. Through this relationship, you can provide guidance. This guidance and feedback will be better received when a foundation of trust is established first.

Kamel's story emphasizes the importance of a trusting relationship and receiving personalized suggestions. As Kamel shared, students appreciate constructive feedback that they can use to develop their skills (Susilana & Pribadi, 2021). Feedback that provides guidance on how to improve fuels student motivation and contributes to their success in the course (Olsen & Hunnes, 2024; Tanis, 2020). Specifically, students want to receive feedback that provides suggestions, such as how to improve the organization of their essays and the technical aspects of writing (Moni, 2024). In a study by Yildiz Durak (2024), students shared that the feedback provided helped them improve the quality of their work. When students are provided with feedback that is specific in nature, they are more likely to act on the feedback (Patchan et al., 2016).

In the following story, Chantel provides an example of how the professor and peers provided specific feedback. Peers were asked to give feedback based on criteria described in a rubric. Similar to Abaynesh's story, Chantel also emphasizes the importance of professors helping students develop productive mindsets about feedback so that they get the most benefit.

༄༅༄༅༄༅

### Ongoing Specific Feedback with Reflection Assignments, Chantel Moore, University of Arkansas at Little Rock

During a six-week online course within my master's degree program, I had the privilege of absorbing valuable insights from my professor and peers through extensive feedback on facilitation skill development. Although feedback can often trigger apprehension, I discovered that my professor's feedback was not only engaging but also characterized by specificity, achievability, measurability, and genuine assistance in achieving my objectives.

One of our tasks was to teach a trainee the seemingly simple task of tying a shoe during a fishbowl activity via Zoom. The challenge was to assume that our trainee needed to gain prior knowledge of shoes or the art of tying them. Following the activity, my professor provided constructive feedback, highlighting aspects such as the smooth execution of my instructions and the efficacy of leading by example. She emphasized the importance of conducting perception checks with the trainee to ensure comprehension. Throughout the course, the professor underscored the importance of skill development, encouraging us to monitor our progress and take pride in the growth achieved.

At the core of the course was the creation and delivery of a training project. This project was dissected into manageable components with checkpoints for ongoing feedback. This approach fostered a learning environment where I could embrace failure while learning and growing alongside my classmates.

My professor implemented a peer feedback system. Using a rubric, peers provided feedback on the clarity of our explanations based on the specified criteria. Initially, receiving such feedback induced a sense of failure, but the professor consistently reminded us that feedback was a tool for enhancement, acknowledging the importance of learning from mistakes. In this supportive environment, I learned to embrace this specific feedback, which propelled my growth.

To further support our learning, our professor required us to critically evaluate the feedback we received and assess our progress. Open-ended questions prompted us to take ownership of our learning journey, identifying areas for growth and outlining steps toward achieving our goals. The emphasis was on active engagement and control over our educational path. We needed to submit a video analysis of our training sessions, responding to questions such as 'What are your strengths as a trainer?' and 'What skills do you aim to strengthen and why?' These inquiries were followed by prompts encouraging us to outline actionable steps toward our goals.

For professors seeking to foster student engagement through effective feedback, incorporating multiple opportunities for feedback is paramount. Constructive, specific, achievable, and measurable feedback is key. Rubrics can help students understand expectations, and checkpoint assignments can provide students with timely guidance. Students can reflect on the feedback and immediately implement necessary edits on the next checkpoint assignment. Because many of us may have negative emotions around feedback, professors can emphasize the importance of embracing failures as part of the learning process. Giving students reflective assignments can help them focus on the process of learning and enable them to assess the impact of feedback on their goals. By integrating these practices, professors can cultivate a dynamic learning environment that empowers students.

☙☙☙❧❧❧

In this story, Chantel recommended that professors share rubrics to help students understand the assignment expectations. Rubrics are also a great way for professors to provide specific and constructive feedback. When students review feedback provided on a rubric, they can see which parts of the assignment they excelled at and which parts needed to be strengthened. Darby and Lang (2019) encouraged professors to use the rubric tools within learning management systems to provide specific feedback to students. Researchers have found that professors are more likely to give students specific and actionable suggestions when using a rubric and providing comments on the rubric as compared to other feedback methods (Dirkx et al., 2021). Darby and Lang (2019) also noted that rubrics can make the grading process more streamlined and manageable for professors.

Chantel also encouraged professors to use checkpoint assignments, also known as formative assessments. Students have found feedback on formative assessments to be particularly beneficial because they can immediately apply the feedback to the next task. Joshi et al. (2021) pointed out that formative assessment can help professors determine what types of additional support students might need to be successful. They noted that they felt inspired to be more innovative with their teaching methods and feedback approaches when they reviewed formative assessments that students completed.

When students learn from the feedback provided on formative assessments, they are more apt to perform well on summative assessments. Students have reported appreciating feedback on formative assessments because this type of feedback provides immediate confirmation or validation that they were on the right track and, if they were not, typically provides them with suggestions on how to improve (Rae & Abdulla, 2023). Joshi et al. (2021) found that students who received feedback on several formative assessments linked to a summative assignment performed better on the final summative assignment. Meier and Lepp (2023) and Cobbold and Wright (2021) also found that student performance on the final assignments was stronger when students received feedback on weekly assignments or drafts.

## FOSTERING CRITICAL THINKING

One of the primary goals of feedback is to help students advance their knowledge and skills. Park and Stuehm (2024) found that the critical thinking skills of online students were enhanced when professors used strength-based feedback. Heft and Scharff (2017) also demonstrated that feedback played a crucial role in the development of critical thinking skills. They found that students who were taught about critical thinking but did not have repeated opportunities to practice the skills and get feedback did not improve their critical thinking skills. However, students who engaged in practice activities and received feedback on their performance were more likely to engage in actions related to critical thinking, such as questioning claims, and their critical thinking skills improved over the course of the semester (Heft & Scharff, 2017).

Feedback is an excellent way to foster critical thinking skills in online courses, regardless of whether the modality is synchronous or asynchronous. Ahmed et al.

(2021) found that there were no significant differences between feedback provided in synchronous, asynchronous, or face-to-face courses in terms of critical thinking skills. Students in all three groups demonstrated improved critical thinking skills after feedback was provided (Ahmed et al., 2021). Thus, online professors can use a variety of approaches to developing critical thinking skills through feedback.

One powerful way to help students develop critical thinking skills is through questioning. Rather than providing students with suggested ways to improve an academic product, professors can give feedback through questioning. As Chantel explained in her story, questions can help students take more ownership of the learning process.

Guasch et al. (2019) conducted an interesting quasi-experimental study investigating how students used different types of feedback. Students who received corrective feedback where professors indicated what was incorrect and shared a correct response were less likely to engage in cognitive and meta-cognitive activities. However, students who received epistemic and suggestive feedback were more likely to engage in cognitive and meta-cognitive activities and performed better on the final assignment. Epistemic feedback was provided in the form of questions, inviting students to think about how to improve, and suggestions involved professors sharing resources or actions students could take. Guasch et al. (2019) reported that these positive results were only found when both epistemic and suggestive feedback were used, not when just one of these feedback approaches was used. In the next student story, Jennifer explains how being questioned by the professor was a productive way to receive feedback.

## The Power of Questioning, Jennifer Scully, Marymount University

It was the midway point of my doctoral journey. I was finishing up my last core courses before entering the research-based courses that ushered in the last year of the program. I had a draft of a literature review completed and research questions created, but there still seemed to be something missing. The spring term began, and I was enrolled in the Program Evaluation and Decision-Making class. The main project for this class was to create a program to be evaluated using the techniques being taught by my professor. This assignment immediately engaged me because it was creative and innovative in nature.

What was most helpful about this assignment was that Professor Jessica Marotta gave me honest feedback that did not just stroke my ego. She made me think deeply about what I was creating and the effects of implementing such a program not only at my school but at any school. Most importantly, her instructional coaching guided me to consider different perspectives and angles. Her technique of having us analyze material from a 360-degree lens piqued my interest in program creation. She helped me improve my self-awareness as a student because she asked questions in a way that helped me identify my hidden strengths, weaknesses, blind spots, and gaps in learning. Further, her skillful questions helped me understand how I work best and why it is important to evaluate my learning continually. She strengthened my critical thinking muscles and, through her feedback, showed me the proper way to conduct research to ensure that the implementation of my program would be successful.

It was this class that urged me to think differently about my dissertation research. When I turned in my final project, which was an entire professional staff training program, she said the words that changed the trajectory of my entire academic future. She said, 'You know that this could easily be the focus of your dissertation.' We spoke about what that would entail, and she gave me more ideas to consider. The rest is doctoral history. I began a new literature review and formulated new research questions, and because of Professor Marotta and her class, I was reinvigorated as a doctoral student.

I recommend that other professors emulate her techniques. Feedback is seen as a way for students to discover new ways to think about their work and to engage in problem-solving. Professor Marotta was masterful at questioning. She would ask insightful questions that required me to think critically. The questions helped us have a productive exchange of ideas and enabled us to discover our own answers. Finally, it is important for professors to make sure they are giving critical yet supportive feedback. Getting us to consider different angles or perspectives helps us think through and revise our work so that the final product is of high quality. These strategies can also help us become more confident in our skills as we continue our learning journey.

ಬಬಬಡಡಡ

## DISCUSSION-BASED FEEDBACK

One of the primary teaching methods often employed in online courses is discussion. Student participation in discussions is frequently a graded assignment. Discussions can take place in synchronous or asynchronous formats.

Online discussions in synchronous courses enable professors to provide live feedback, which can more closely mirror the traditional in-person learning experience. Synchronous discussions allow students to benefit from tone, expression, and other nonverbal cues that are not typically available in asynchronous conversations unless video or audio tools are used. Farros et al. (2022) noted that in synchronous discussions, the professor can provide immediate feedback and clarification as needed when students are responding to questions. Despite these differences, they found that students who participated in synchronous and asynchronous discussions performed similarly (Farros et al., 2022).

Many professors opt to use breakout rooms in synchronous meetings so that all students can be more engaged in discussions and activities. The challenge with using breakout rooms is that the professor cannot be in all the breakout rooms at once. It is, therefore, difficult for a professor to monitor group discussions and provide feedback. To address this challenge, Richardson (2021) used a polling strategy to monitor group progress in breakout rooms and then provided feedback and guidance via messages to groups to help them be more productive. In the following story, Sean describes how a professor moved from breakout room to breakout room to ensure students were making good progress. While in the breakout room, Sean appreciated how the professor provided feedback and made suggestions.

### Keeping Us on Track During Breakout Room Group Work, Sean Connelly, Connecticut State Community College Norwalk

I appreciated how Professor Yumi McCarthy provided feedback on group projects. We used class time to work on group projects in breakout rooms, and she would move from one group to the next to see how we were performing. Rotating from breakout room to breakout room was not only effective but also highly necessary to keep us focused on the task at hand. Professor McCarthy made it a rule that all students always had to keep their cameras on to ensure that no one was taking advantage of the online environment. Holding us accountable for being present and participating is very important for an online class because otherwise, students may turn off their cameras and microphones and spend the class time watching movies or playing games. With her constant checking of the groups and ensuring that everyone was doing their work, there was no opportunity for students to avoid their responsibilities. These group activities essentially forced us to participate in the class. Through these activities, students can discover that participation is not only an essential piece of the learning process but can also be highly enjoyable.

Learning a language, the focus of this class is difficult because errors are common in the pronunciation of words, sentence structures, and grammatical correctness. There is also room for error in the correct writing of character forms and spelling of words. If we made mistakes, she would immediately tell us there was an error but would have us figure out what the error was. After we revised the work, she would review it again and give us feedback. This feedback process during discussions was helpful because it helped us learn from our mistakes and earn a better grade overall.

When students were working together as a group, Professor McCarthy took notes on her attendance sheet. She wrote down who asked questions or responded to what others shared. By logging this information, she was able to identify which students were doing well versus those who might have been struggling. She then gave individualized help and support to the partners or groups who needed it.

Professor McCarthy would also open up the classroom half an hour early and allow students to make appointments with her during that time to go over items that they were struggling with. She would also stay after every class for hours to allow students to practice work, ask questions, seek help with their assignments, and offer whatever assistance she could. I noticed that she would ask students who often came into class late or missed classes to stay after to go over the material that they missed. These one-on-one sessions were a great aid for the students because otherwise, they could very quickly fall behind, receive a poor grade, and feel discouraged. Professor McCarthy wanted to help students get back on track.

I have found that many students avoid participation out of fear or embarrassment that they might make a mistake. However, the feedback provided by Professor McCarthy helped students feel confident in their ability to contribute. Because Professor McCarthy gave feedback to all groups, students learned that making mistakes is a part of the learning process. She told us that mistakes were okay as long we learned from them. These words greatly increased the level to which students were willing to participate, and, in turn, they helped us learn the subject matter. I encourage other professors to remind students that mistakes are learning opportunities and to provide feedback while students are working on group projects in breakout rooms.

৪০৪০৪০୯୫୯୫୯୫

The example shared by Sean illustrated how a professor provided live feedback in breakout rooms. Immediate feedback can validate students when they are on track. It is reassuring for students to know they are making good progress. If students are not progressing as expected or are struggling with a task, live feedback in synchronous sessions, including breakout rooms, can guide students and help them perform better.

Although it is not possible to provide immediate feedback in asynchronous discussions, there are advantages to how feedback can be provided in this modality. All students in an online asynchronous discussion typically receive feedback on their contributions, while time constraints in a traditional face-to-face setting often prohibit professors from providing individualized feedback to each student. Because professors do not need to respond in real time, they can provide more in-depth feedback. Professors have the opportunity to reflect on student contributions before responding with feedback.

Woods and Bliss (2016) noted that professors can support student learning via asynchronous online discussions by providing positively phrased, prompt, and detailed feedback. Professors can also provide relevant resources to help students more fully understand the issues or concepts being discussed. In the following story, Andy shares how a professor provided feedback effectively and regularly in an online asynchronous course. In this example, the professor validated contributions, stretched students through questions, corrected misunderstandings, and suggested ideas or approaches via discussion posts that were visible to the entire class.

༄༄༄༅༅༅

### Feedback via Online Discussions, Andy Sokolich, Kent State University

Qualitative Research Design is a doctoral-level introductory methodology course that provides an overview of various approaches to qualitative research, and the final course project is a research proposal. The course was offered asynchronously during the eight-week summer term, and this was uncharted territory for me with the fast pace and brand-new content. The professor relied heavily on the discussion board feature of the learning management system. I had my aversions to discussion board postings because they always felt like a formality in earning points rather than a productive use of my time. This course, however, changed my view of discussion boards entirely. In this course, we utilized two different sets of discussion boards throughout the term. During each module, we were required to post on both whole-group and small-group discussion boards.

The whole-group boards functioned as reflection activities or class discussions. The prompts for the entire class were directly related to the course content and focused on helping us develop our understanding of the research design presented in each module. For example, the first prompt was to share an idea from the readings that resonated with us and pose a question about the readings to our classmates. This questioning approach really helped the conversations to be engaging. The professor would regularly answer questions we posed to classmates, validate what we contributed, or offer thoughtful reflections on a different interpretation of the text. She was an active participant throughout, and her engagement enhanced my understanding of qualitative methodology.

As an example, I responded to the prompt that I was seeing a creative way to employ a constructivist approach through a critical lens in my research study, noting that these approaches were not usually in alignment. When she responded to my prompt, she critiqued one of the readings, noting that the author missed the point that qualitative approaches can have some overlap, and validated my contribution, stating that we can construct local meaning through a critical lens of larger social structures.

The syllabus described the small group discussions as a workshop in which students submitted assignment components for peer review. Working in groups of three students, we worked together with the shared expectation that our feedback was intended to strengthen the work of our overall research proposal. The prompts in each module deconstructed the final research proposal into manageable components: Ideas for topics, developing research purpose statements and questions, exploring which qualitative approach would work best for our topic, drafting interview questions, thinking critically about how we would recruit informants, analyzing data, and more. Throughout this peer review process, the professor would often validate constructive points that classmates provided and add some additional clarifying points to help refine our project. She also directly addressed inconsistencies in our approach to help us get back on the right track. The professor was especially effective at helping me align my research questions to my qualitative approach to my interview questions and my proposed methods of analysis. I noticed that my classmates received the same level of detailed feedback.

Because we were able to see each other's feedback in the discussion boards, we were able to learn more. For example, in one module, we were prompted to share a first draft of our purpose statements. When I posted mine, the professor replied and specifically suggested that some of my verbiage was too broad and encouraged me to use more direct language that would influence my research questions. Other group members also replied and provided some suggested language changes to refine my questions. Their collective feedback really helped me think through my questions, break free of my preconceived notions, and write more clearly so others who do not have the same depth of knowledge on the subject that I did would understand my purpose.

In closing, I recommend that professors use a combination of whole-class and small-group discussion boards in asynchronous courses and that the prompts be focused on supporting students with a major assignment. Following the model used by my professor, whole-group discussion prompts can concentrate on helping students understand the course material, and the small-group discussions can provide a way for students to engage in a peer review process to help them develop and refine ideas related to their final project. The key element, however, is active and constructive participation from the professor, who serves as a role model for how students should interact. This does not mean that a professor should reply to every single post, but I appreciate it when professors actively participate in discussions. This way, students can see the feedback being provided to all students. Seeing feedback given to peers enhances the collective learning experience.

While we learn from the texts we read, we also learn from the professor's expertise in the subject matter. My prior experience with asynchronous online courses was one where I needed to learn independently and in isolation, but it does not have to be this way. Through this effective use of discussion boards and receiving public feedback, I felt as though I was part of a learning community in which we strengthened our shared understanding of qualitative research. Comments that validated the ideas of students created a sense of reassurance that we were understanding the material and were on the right track with our assignments. Comments and questions that redirect our thinking help us think more critically about our assignments. The active engagement of the professor during the whole-class and small-group discussions demonstrates a sense of care for us and how much we are learning throughout the process. Strategic structure and consistent feedback made this an exceptional educational experience for the students taking this course.

৪০৪০৪০৫৩৫৩৫৩

As Andy shared, receiving regular feedback from the professor enables students to know if they are on the right track. Andy also found it helpful to receive peer feedback. Peer feedback can provide students with additional ideas about how to improve. However, students do not always view peer feedback positively (Achen, 2018). Students may give generic feedback, which, although it may be encouraging, does not always provide the guidance students need to improve their work.

Training peers on how to give feedback and giving them specific guidelines about how to engage in this process can be helpful (Facey, 2011). In a study conducted by Mirick (2020), students were informed of the benefits of peer review and provided with instructional resources, including a 20-minute overview of the peer review process and guidelines on how to give meaningful written feedback to peers. Students found engaging in this peer review process to be helpful, with students indicating that receiving peer reviews strengthened their writing (Mirick, 2020). Filius et al. (2019) also found that giving and receiving peer feedback led to deep learning. In this study, students were provided with video and text explanations about how to give feedback to promote learning. They then had to provide either audio or video-based feedback to their online peers (Filius et al., 2019).

## USING VIDEO AND AUDIO TOOLS

Most feedback is shared with students in writing, especially in online courses. Although there are advantages to written feedback, such as it being clearer (Alharbi & Alghammas, 2021) and students being more easily able and likely to review it (Máñez et al., 2024), there are limitations associated with written feedback. Darby and Lang (2019), for instance, pointed out that even when professors carefully choose their words, students may miss out on cues that convey empathy or encouragement when feedback is shared in a written format.

Professors are encouraged to use video tools when providing feedback (Darby & Lang, 2019). Students have reported a preference for receiving feedback via video (Marshall et al., 2020). Students have also expressed that they appreciate the efforts of their professors to create video feedback. They perceive it to be more personal, and they found more detailed information and guidance to be shared in video feedback (Pryke et al., 2024). Based on a review of the research, Mahoney et al. (2019) discovered the following characteristics of video feedback:

- More positive and conversational in nature.
- More detailed, with approximately double the words than written feedback and increased elaboration on points made.
- More substance versus technical focused, with more comments about skills such as argument, analysis, and synthesis versus the mechanics of writing.
- More constructive in nature, with several suggestions provided. Love and Marshall (2022) found that using videos was a way to increase the professor's social presence in online courses. For example, one student commented:

A lot of my professors in the past would take a pen and write on my paper or just put a grade on my paper or attach a rubric to it and circle where I fell on the rubric. But this was different because I could see her face...I think it was as if I was sitting down in front of her in person and she was going through my paper with me, which was incredibly helpful.

(Love & Marshall, p. 50)

Students also shared that the emotional expression conveyed through their tone and nonverbal communication when providing video-based feedback helped humanize the learning experience. The videos helped them feel connected to their professor (Love & Marshall, 2022). One student commented that they did not even know what many of their online professors looked like. However, in a course with weekly videos, they developed a relationship with their professor (Love & Marshall, 2022). In a quasi-experimental study, Máñez et al. (2024) found that students who received video feedback outperformed students who received written feedback and noted that students who were less academically engaged could gain the most benefit from video feedback.

Professors have noted that it can take more time to provide feedback using video but that the time investment is perceived to be worthwhile (Ketchum et al., 2020). Love and Marshall (2022) reported that it took professors approximately 20–25 minutes per student to provide video feedback. Mahoney et al. (2019) indicated that professors are becoming more comfortable with sharing imperfect videos, recognizing that errors can humanize the professor. Some researchers have found that the time needed for video versus written feedback is similar (Mahoney et al., 2019). Using imperfect video versions can reduce the time necessary for professors to provide feedback in this way. To further reduce professor workload and increase the effectiveness of feedback, Lowenthal et al. (2022) recommended keeping video feedback short, less than five minutes. Pryke et al. (2024) indicated that one minute of video feedback equates to 125–150 words.

Although there are a number of benefits associated with video feedback, there are some limitations. Students have reported that it is not convenient to access and review video feedback (Pryke et al., 2024). Students have perceived written feedback as being more efficient because they can more easily refer back to written comments when revising work (Ari & Arslan-Ari, 2022). Students in the study conducted by Ari and Arslan-Ari (2022) made the following recommendations:

- Share feedback in writing and via video.
- Provide a summary of the comments shared in the video.
- Caption videos so there is a written record to refer to.

- Create several shorter videos focusing on different points or sections to make it easier to go back and relisten to comments relevant to the part they are revising.

Researchers have found that online students who were provided both video and written feedback performed better on academic tasks than their peers who only received written feedback (Yiğit and Seferoğlu, 2023). Pryke et al. (2024) recommended providing brief written summaries with video feedback. In the following student story, Charlenne shares how class-level feedback on assignments shared via video, in addition to other uses of video, was engaging.

ೞೞೞ಄಄಄

### Using Videos to Share Class-Level Feedback and Create a Sense of Community in an Asynchronous Class, Charlenne Medina, Rockhurst University

One of the best professors I have had was Professor Lauren Hernandez, who taught the Diversity, Equity, Access, and Belonging class. I was raised in a very conservative and close-minded household, so I did not necessarily anticipate being so engaged with this course. Professor Hernandez's strategies, however, made me feel a real connection to her, my classmates, and the course content. This course was an asynchronous online class that was a requirement for the DEI certificate program. She used videos to help us connect in this online course.

Professor Hernandez recorded video lectures weekly for our class. I really appreciated how she recorded these specifically for our class rather than recycling video lecture content from previous classes or using generic videos from YouTube. During these 30- to 60-minute video lectures, she would give us feedback about our assignments as a group, go over reading material from the previous week, and share new content for the week ahead. This class-level feedback was in addition to the specific feedback she gave us individually through Canvas grades. I felt more connected to the class than I usually would for an online class where it may seem I am the only person submitting work and feedback is only for my assignments rather than for the whole class. Because she shared class-level feedback on the videos, I was able to learn not only from my mistakes but also from those made by my classmates.

My professor also encouraged us to use videos too. She would ask us to record a video and post it rather than submitting a typed response to the discussion boards. We could also respond to the discussion posts shared by our peers in video form. The use of videos kept me engaged. I liked being able to put a face to the names of my classmates because it made the conversations feel more personal and more similar to face-to-face encounters.

She also engaged me by sharing personal examples related to the diversity and equity issues we were discussing in class. I benefitted from learning about how she dealt with various situations. These disclosures made me see my professor as a human who experiences the world in a similar way that we, the students, do.

I recommend that professors use videos as a way to help students feel more connected to their professor and their classmates in an asynchronous class. In the videos, share examples and give class-level feedback on assignments. Also, please encourage students to use video submissions for their assignments. The video element can really help your class develop a sense of community.

༄༅༄༅༄༅

Although providing video feedback may be ideal for students, it can sometimes pose a challenge for professors. When professors are grading assignments, they may not be camera-ready (Mahoney et al., 2019). For example, professors may be grading assignments early in the morning or late at night and may not be comfortable using their cameras to provide feedback.

Fortunately, researchers have demonstrated that audio feedback is also effective. For example, Rawle et al. (2018) and Hoffmann-Longtin (2019) found students reported that it was helpful to receive audio feedback. Voelkel and Mello (2014) discovered that students were better able to understand feedback provided via audio versus in a written format. Hoffmann-Longtin (2019) reported that student performance, especially in terms of vocabulary, clarity, and research evidence, improved after audio feedback was provided.

Screencasts are another excellent strategy, especially when providing feedback on a writing assignment (Pryke et al., 2024). 92% of students reported watching screencast video feedback given by their professors, and approximately 80% expressed satisfaction with this type of feedback (Lowenthal et al., 2022). Most students (85%) indicated they used feedback provided in the screencast videos to improve their work (Lowenthal et al., 2022).

## FACULTY REFLECTION QUESTIONS

1. How can I encourage students through the feedback I provide?
2. How do I draw attention to student's strengths when providing feedback?
3. In what ways can I help students develop a productive, growth mindset about feedback?

4. How can I build more opportunities for students to benefit from feedback on formative assessments?
5. How can I provide feedback that is more personalized, specific, and constructive?
6. How can I emphasize substance over technical feedback?
7. How can I use questions rather than suggestions to help students have more autonomy over their learning and develop critical thinking skills?
8. How can I incorporate more structured feedback into synchronous and asynchronous discussions?
9. What type of training and guidance can I provide to students before asking them to engage in peer review processes?
10. How can I use video or audio tools to make feedback more conversational, motivational, and helpful?

## REFERENCES

Achen, R. M. (2018). Addressing the "my students cannot write" dilemma: Investigating methods for improving graduate student writing. *Journal of the Scholarship of Teaching and Learning*, *18*(4), 71–85. https://doi.org/10.14434/josotl.v18i4.23040

Ahmed, M. M. H., McGahan, P. S., Indurkhya, B., Kaneko, K., & Nakagawa, M. (2021). Effects of synchronized and asynchronized e-feedback interactions on academic writing, achievement motivation and critical thinking. *Knowledge Management & E-Learning*, *13*(3), 290–315. https://www.kmel-journal.org/ojs/index.php/online-publication/article/view/481/477

Alharbi, M. A., & Alghammas, A. (2021). Teacher written vs. audio feedback on undergraduates' written assignments. *Theory & Practice in Language Studies (TPLS)*, *11*(12), 1562–1570. https://doi.org/10.17507/tpls.1112.08

Ari, F., & Arslan-Ari, I. (2022). Examining nontraditional graduate students' experiences with video feedback in a fully online course. *The Internet and Higher Education*, *55*, 1–11. https://doi.org/10.1016/j.iheduc.2022.100858

Austen, L., & Malone, C. (2018) What students' want in written feedback: Praise, clarity and precise individual commentary. *Practitioner Research in Higher Education*, *11*(1), 47–58. http://insight.cumbria.ac.uk/id/eprint/3841/

Brooks, C., Carroll, A., Gillies, R. M., & Hattie, J. (2019). A matrix of feedback for learning. *Australian Journal of Teacher Education*, *44*(4), 14–32. https://doi.org/10.14221/ajte.2018v44n4.2

Chang, C. W., & Farha, N. (2023). Student's perspectives vis-à-vis instructor-provided feedback on Blackboard in an online course. *International Journal of Technology in Teaching and Learning*, *19*(2), 141–152. https://files.eric.ed.gov/fulltext/EJ1446317.pdf

Cobbold, C., & Wright, L. (2021). Use of formative feedback to enhance summative performance. *Anatolian Journal of Education*, *6*(1), 109–116. https://doi.org/10.29333/aje.2021.619a

Cutumisu, M., & Lou, N. M. (2020). The moderating effect of mindset on the relationship between university students' critical feedback-seeking and learning. *Computers in Human Behavior, 112.* https://doi.org/10.1016/j.chb.2020.106445

Darby, F., & Lang, J. M. (2019). *Small teaching online: Applying learning science in online classes.* Jossey Bass.

Dirkx, K., Joosten-ten Brinke, D., Arts, J., & van Diggelen, M. (2021). In-text and rubric referenced feedback: Differences in focus, level, and function. *Active Learning in Higher Education, 22*(3), 189–201. https://doi.org/10.1177/1469787419855208

Dweck, C. (2008). *Mindset: The new psychology of success.* Ballantine Books.

Facey, J. (2011). "A is for assessment"… strategies for A-level marking to motivate and enable students of all abilities to progress. *Teaching History, 144,* 36–43. https://eric.ed.gov/?id=EJ944283

Farros, J. N., Shawler, L. A., Gatzunis, K. S., & Weiss, M. J. (2022). The effect of synchronous discussion sessions in an asynchronous course. *Journal of Behavioral Education, 31*(4), 718–730. https://link.springer.com/article/10.1007/s10864-020-09421-2

Faulconer, E., Griffith, J., & Gruss, A. (2022). The impact of positive feedback on student outcomes and perceptions. *Assessment & Evaluation in Higher Education, 47*(2), 259–268. https://doi.org/10.1080/02602938.2021.1910140

Filius, R. M., Kleijn, R. A. M., Uijl, S. G., Prins, F. J., Rijen, H. V. M., & Grobbee, D. E. (2019). Audio peer feedback to promote deep learning in online education. *Journal of Computer Assisted Learning, 35*(5), 607–619. https://doi.org/10.1111/jcal.12363

Forsythe, A., & Johnson, S. (2017). Thanks, but no-thanks for the feedback. *Assessment & Evaluation in Higher Education, 42*(6), 850–859. https://doi.org/10.1080/02602938.2016.1202190

Guasch, T., Espasa, A., & Martinez-Melo, M. (2019). The art of questioning in online learning environments: The potentialities of feedback in writing. *Assessment & Evaluation in Higher Education, 44*(1), 111–123. https://doi.org/10.1080/02602938.2018.1479373

Harrington, C. (2021). *Keeping us engaged: Student perspectives (and research-based strategies) on what works and why.* Routledge.

Harrington, C. (2025). *Keeping us engaged: Student perspectives (and research-based strategies) on what works and why.* 2nd ed. Routledge.

Hattie, J., & Timperley, H. (2007). The power of feedback. *Review of Educational Research, 77*(1), 81–112. https://doi.org/10.3102/003465430298487

Heft, I. E., & Scharff, L. F. V. (2017). Aligning best practices to develop targeted critical thinking skills and habits. *Journal of the Scholarship of Teaching and Learning, 17*(3), 48–67. https://doi.org/10.14434/v17i3.2260000

Hoffmann-Longtin, K. (2019). Hearing is believing: Using audio feedback in the online interpersonal communication course. *Journal of Communication Pedagogy, 2,* 96–102. https://scholarworks-wmich-edu.proxy-ms.researchport.umd.edu/jcp/vol2/iss1/17/

Johnson, W. F., Stellmack, M. A., & Barthel, A. L. (2019). Format of instructor feedback on student writing assignments affects feedback quality and student performance. *Teaching of Psychology, 46*(1), 16–21. https://doi.org/10.1177/0098628318816131

Joshi, R., Ghosh, S., Simileysky, A., & Bhanot, M. (2021). Structuring formative feedback in an online graphics design course in BME. *Biomedical Engineering Education, 1*(2), 325–333. https://link-springer-com.proxy-ms.researchport.umd.edu/article/10.1007/s43683-021-00046-z

Ketchum, C., LaFave, D. S., Yeats, C., Phompheng, E., & Hardy, J. H. (2020). Video-based feedback on student work: An investigation into the instructor experience, workload, and student evaluations. *Online Learning, 24*(3), 85–105. https://doi.org/10.24059/olj.v24i3.2194

Lee, S. (2022). Factors affecting the quality of online learning in a task-based college course. *Foreign Language Annals, 55*(1), 116–134. https://doi.org/10.1111/flan.12572

Lipnevich, A., & Smith, J. (2009). "I really need feedback to learn:" Students' perspectives on the effectiveness of the differential feedback messages. *Educational Assessment, Evaluation & Accountability, 21*(4), 347–367. https://doi.org/10.1007/s11092-009-9082-2

Love, S., & Marshall, D. (2022). Video feedback and instructor social presence in an asynchronous online course. *Journal of Effective Teaching in Higher Education, 5*(2), 43–58. https://doi.org/10.36021/jethe.v5i2.324

Lowe, T., & Shaw, C. (2019). Student perceptions of the "best" feedback practices: An evaluation of student-led teaching award nominations at a higher education institution. *Teaching & Learning Inquiry, 7*(2), 121–135. https://doi.org/10.20343/teachlearninqu.7.2.8

Lowenthal, P. R., Fiock, H. S., Shreaves, D. L., & Belt, E. S. (2022). Investigating students' perceptions of screencasting style of video feedback in online courses. *TechTrends: Linking Research & Practice to Improve Learning, 66*(2), 265–275. https://doi.org/10.1080/01587919.2022.2088479

Mahoney, P., Macfarlane, S., & Ajjawi, R. (2019). A qualitative synthesis of video feedback in higher education. *Teaching in Higher Education, 24*(2), 157–179. https://doi.org/10.1080/13562517.2018.1471457

Máñez, I., Skrobiszewska, N., Descals, A., Cantero, M. J., Cerdán, R., García, O. F., & García Ros, R. (2024). Channeling feedback through audiovisual presentations: Do higher education students perceive, use and benefit from video feedback compared to written feedback? *Journal of Computer Assisted Learning, 40*(4), 1886–1897. https://doi.org/10.1111/jcal.12993

Marshall, D. T., Love, S. M., & Scott, L. (2020). "It's not like he was being a robot:" student perceptions of video-based writing feedback in online graduate coursework. *International Journal for the Scholarship of Teaching and Learning, 14*(1), 1–10. https://doi.org/10.20429/ijsotl.2020.140110

Meier, H., & Lepp, M. (2023). Effectiveness of feedback based on log file analysis in introductory programming courses. *Journal of Educational Computing Research, 61*(3), 696–719. https://doi.org/10.1177/07356331221132651

Mirick, R. G. (2020). Teaching note—online peer review: Students' experiences in a writing intensive BSW course. *Journal of Social Work Education*, 56(2), 394–400. https://doi.org/10.1080/10437797.2019.1656582

Moni, A. (2024). Learner perceptions of the feedback process in the online component of a blended course. *Online Learning*, 28(2), (359–384). https://doi.org/10.24059/olj.v28i2.3967

Murray, M. G., and Scafe, R. (2024). Providing assignment support and feedback. In C. Harrington (Ed.), *Creating culturally affirming and meaning assignments: A practical resource for higher education faculty* (pp. 114–132). Routledge. https://doi.org/10.4324/978/003443797-9

Nicol, D. J., & Macfarlane-Dick, D. (2006). Formative assessment and self-regulated learning: A model and seven principles of good feedback practice. *Studies in Higher Education*, 31(2), 199–218. https://doi.org/10.1080/03075070600572090

Olsen, T., & Hunnes, J. (2024). Improving students' learning-the role of formative feedback: Experiences from a crash course for business students in academic writing. *Assessment & Evaluation in Higher Education*, 49(2), 129–141. https://doi.org/10.1080/02602938.2023.2187744

Pan, X., & Shao, H. (2020). Teacher online feedback and learning motivation: Learning engagement as a mediator. *Social Behavior & Personality: An International Journal*, 48(6), 1–10. https://doi.org/10.2224/sbp.9118

Park, T. K., & Stuehm, N. (2024). A simple but powerful way to enhance critical thinking skills among undergraduate social work students in online class: Strength-based feedback. *Journal of Open, Flexible, and Distance Learning*, 28(1), 41–58. https://doi.org/10.61468/jofdl.v28i1.625

Patchan, M. M., Schunn, C. D., & Correnti, R. J. (2016). The nature of feedback: How peer feedback features affect students' implementation rate and quality of revisions. *Journal of Educational Psychology*, 108 (8), 1098–1120. https://doi.org/10.1037/edu0000103

Pryke, S., Rees, M., & Witton, G. (2024). "It makes you feel like they've actually put effort into it." Students' perceptions of screen-capture video feedback on assignments on a social science course. *Interactive Learning Environments*, 32(7), 3125–3135. https://doi.org/10.1080/10494820.2023.2167839

Rae, M. G., & Abdulla, M. H. (2023). An investigation of preclinical medical students' preference for summative or formative assessment for physiology learning. *Advances in Physiology Education*, 47(3), 383–392. https://doi.org/10.1152/advan.00013.2023

Rawle, F., Thuna, M., Zhao, T., & Kaler, M. (2018). Audio feedback: Student and teaching assistant perspectives on an alternative mode of feedback for written assignments. *Canadian Journal for the Scholarship of Teaching and Learning*, 9(2), 1–21. https://doi.org/10.5206/cjsotl-rcacea.2018.2.2

Richardson, J. (2021). Asynchronous polling: An innovative approach to improving effectiveness of virtual small group sessions. *FASEB Journal*, 35, N.PAG. https://doi.org/10.1096/fasebj.2021.35.S1.01568

Rodriguez, R. J., & Koubek, E. (2019). Unpacking high-impact instructional practices and student engagement in a teacher preparation program. *International Journal for the Scholarship of Teaching & Learning, 13* (3), 1–9. https://doi.org/10.20429/ijsotl.2019.130311

Samaranayake, N. (2024). Online learning and instructor feedback. *Journal of Online Learning Research, 10*(1), 75–89. https://files.eric.ed.gov/fulltext/EJ1427929.pdf

Shean, A. (2023, December 20). Guiding growth: Crafting feedback that empowers learners. *Inside Higher Ed.* https://www.insidehighered.com/opinion/views/2023/12/20/providing-equitable-student-feedback-coursework-opinion#

Stewart, O. G. (2023). Understanding what works in humanizing higher education online courses: Connecting through videos, feedback, multimodal assignments, and social media. *Issues and Trends in Learning Technologies, 11*(2), 2–26. https://doi.org/10.2458/itlt.5566

Susilana, R., & Pribadi, B. A. (2021). Constructive online feedback to enhance learning achievement of open and distance students. *World Journal on Educational Technology: Current Issues, 13*(3), 514–528. https://doi.org/10.18844/wjet.v13i3.5959

Tanis, C. J. (2020). The seven principles of online learning: Feedback from faculty and alumni on its importance for teaching and learning. *Research in Learning Technology, 28.* https://doi.org/10.25304/rlt.v28.2319

Voelkel, S. , & Mello, L. V. (2014). Audio feedback—better feedback? *Bioscience Education Electronic Journal, 22*(1), 16–30. https://doi.org/10.11120/beej.2014.00022

Woods, K., & Bliss, K. (2016). Facilitating Successful Online Discussions. *Journal of Effective Teaching, 16*(2), 76–92. https://files.eric.ed.gov/fulltext/EJ1117812.pdf

Yiğit, M. F., & Seferoğlu, S. S. (2023). Effect of video feedback on students' feedback use in the online learning environment. *Innovations in Education & Teaching International, 60*(1), 15–25. https://doi.org/10.1080/14703297.2021.1966489

Yildiz Durak, H. (2024). What makes an effective online course experience?: Student perceptions and needs for online course design elements in the context of feedback and collaborative learning. *Technology, knowledge and learning: Learning mathematics, science and the arts in the context of digital technologies.* http://dx.doi.org/10.1007/s10758-024-09748-z

Zepeda, C. D., Ortegren, F. R., & Butler, A. C. (2023). Learning from feedback in college courses: Student beliefs, practices, and preferences. *Applied Cognitive Psychology, 37*(6), 1238–1257. https://doi.org/10.1002/acp.4118

# About the Author

**Christine Harrington** is a national teaching, learning, and student success expert. Harrington earned her BA in psychology and MA in counseling and personnel services from The College of New Jersey and her PhD in counseling psychology from Lehigh University. She has worked in higher education for 25 years. She is a professor in the Department of Advanced Studies, Leadership, and Policy at Morgan State University. She also teaches part-time in the Learning and Teaching Department at the Graduate School of Education at Rutgers University. Previously, she worked at Middlesex College for 18 years in various roles, including professor of psychology and student success, director for the Center for the Enrichment of Learning and Teaching, first-year seminar course coordinator, counselor, and disability services provider. Harrington also served a two-year appointment as the executive director for the Center for Student Success at the New Jersey Council of County Colleges and was a professor and coordinator of a community college leadership doctoral program at New Jersey City University.

Harrington is the author and editor of numerous books and articles related to teaching and learning. She edited *Creating culturally affirming and meaningful assignments: A practical resource for higher education faculty*, published by Routledge in 2024, and authored the first and second editions of *Keeping us engaged: Student perspectives (and research-based strategies) on what works and why* with 50 students (Routledge, 2021, 2025). She was the lead author of *Dynamic lecturing: Research-based strategies to enhance lecture effectiveness* with Todd Zakrajsek (Routledge, 2017), *Designing a motivational syllabus: Creating a learning path for student engagement* with Melissa Thomas (Routledge, 2018), and *Why the first-year seminar matters: Helping students choose a career path* with Theresa Orosz (Rowman and Littlefield, 2018). She authored

*Engaging faculty in guided pathways: A practical resource for college leaders* (Rowman and Littlefield and the American Association of Community Colleges, 2020) and *Ensuring learning: Supporting faculty to improve student success* (Rowman and Littlefield and the American Association of Community Colleges, 2020). She also authored a research-based first-year seminar textbook titled *Students success in college: Doing what works! 4th edition* (Cengage, 2023). She has been the recipient of several awards including the Rutgers University 2025 Excellence in Online Teaching award, the 2016 Excellence in Teaching First-Year Seminar award that was presented at the Annual Conference of First-Year Students and Students in Transition, and the 2016 Middlesex College Faculty Excellence in Teaching award. She is frequently invited to give plenary presentations at national and local conferences as well as at colleges and universities across the nation. She has also consulted for colleges, universities, and national organizations. Harrington is an associate editor for *Innovative Higher Education* journal and an editorial board member and reviewer for several other journals.

# Index

academic achievement 6
academic performance 18, 44, 73, 120, 128
accessible 23, 44–46
accessibility 81, 144
announcement 18, 30
anonymous 86
anxiety 26, 66, 86
asynchronous 2–4, 18, 25, 44, 52–53, 82, 87–88, 128, 144, 150, 152, 156–161
audio feedback 167
authentic 18, 112, 122
autonomy 96

belonging 7, 10, 14, 19, 43, 52, 66, 82, 128
breakout room 89, 91–93, 159, 161

career 10, 59–63, 129
ChatGPT 87, 100
chat feature 104
choice 81, 96, 132–136
club 66, 69
cognitive engagement 6
cognitive presence 7
collaboration 82, 128–132
comfort zone 7, 64
community college 14, 25–26, 43, 53
community of inquiry 6, 73

confidence 46, 66, 86, 112, 118, 145
constructive 145, 148, 152, 154–155, 164
corrective feedback 157
counseling 60
course design 8
creativity 116
critical thinking 7, 82, 85–89, 92, 113, 123, 150, 156–157
culture 96
curriculum 133

data source 128
debate 85, 87
digital fatigue 73
direct instruction 4, 8, 73
disabilities 81
discussion board 82, 87
distance education 2–4
diversity 77, 128, 132

effort 120, 145, 152
email 10, 14, 18, 32, 44–46
emotional expression 165
enthusiasm 14, 122
epistemic feedback 157
errors 142, 165
examples 25, 86
exams 111

expectations 8, 18, 25–26, 28–29, 85, 111, 155
expert contributions 86

federal regulations 3–4
feedback model 143
financial burden 51
financial challenges 52
financial support 58
first day of class 19, 34–35
first-generation 14, 18, 26, 43, 66
fishbowl technique 93
flexible late policies 33–34
formative assessment 34, 116–118, 156
foundational knowledge 112, 118

gamification 2, 5
general comments 152
Google document 34, 87
group project 129
growth mindset 119, 150–151
guests 80

icebreakers 19
images 103–104
inclusive teaching 77, 79, 81, 136
independent study 105
informal feedback 142
innovative assignments 111
interests 19, 66
introductions 18, 35

late work policies 33–34

mental health 52, 55, 73
mentor 60–66
microaffirmation 57
mind map 115–116
mindfulness 74

names 19
network 58, 63, 69, 80
nonverbal communication 5, 7, 25
novice learner 143

office hours 23–24, 65
online discussions 82, 85–88, 150, 159, 161

peer feedback 164
peer review 164
photo 15
picture superiority effect 104
podcast 136
polling 159
praise 146
professional identity 60, 63, 66
professional network 63
professor involvement 86

questioning 157
quiz 112–113, 116

rapport 130
rationale 96
reading assignment 112–115
regular interaction 52
reflection 144
relevance 122
research skills 63
roles 86, 93, 129–130
role-play 87
rubrics 85, 155–156

scaffolding 85
screencast 167
self-efficacy 112, 144
sense of belonging 7, 14, 19, 66, 128
social presence 6–7, 164
Socratic question 85–86
start here module 28, 35
strength-based feedback 142–143, 149–150
substantive interaction 3–4
suggestions 143, 152, 154, 156
summative assessments 117–118, 156
surveys 19
syllabus 26, 28, 33
synchronous 1, 3, 15, 34, 88–89, 94, 159

teaching presence 7–8, 73, 85
technology tools 2, 19, 69, 73, 87, 100, 112
textbook 79
tone 32, 159, 165
transparency 25–26

trust 7, 77, 153–154

universal design 81

varied teaching 10, 97, 132

videos 15, 18, 25, 35, 87, 105, 113, 165–166

well-being 23, 34, 52, 73–77

written feedback 144, 164–166

For Product Safety Concerns and Information please contact our EU
representative  GPSR@taylorandfrancis.com
Taylor & Francis Verlag GmbH, Kaufingerstraße 24, 80331 München, Germany

www.ingramcontent.com/pod-product-compliance
Lightning Source LLC
Chambersburg PA
CBHW061715300426
44115CB00014B/2703